Humility of the Brain

In defence of humanity

Prince Ezem Ihenacho

III Clink Street

London | New York

Published by Clink Street Publishing 2014

Copyright © Prince Ezem Ihenacho 2014

First edition.

ISBN: 978-1-909477-53-7
Ebook: 978-1-909477-54-4

Dedication

To my late mother, Mrs Christiana Nnenna Ihenacho. A teacher and mother of eight children who, was a victim of a fairy tale climate riddled with a superstitious belief system. She paid the ultimate price having been coerced to believe that an illness which required hospital treatment was 'a spiritual attack that needed spiritual intervention.'

The pain that she endured through her illness; the sadness surrounding her death and funeral in 2005 formed part of the catalyst behind the chapter below captioned 'World's Most Uninhabitable Place.' May her gentle soul continue to rest in peace until we 'hopefully' meet again, to part no more!

Beneficiaries

This book contains self-help materials and short stories focused on human emotional development. Having worked in the Mental Health field for over a decade and worked with many depressed and suicidal patients without recording any untoward incidents, I wish to encourage everyone, especially those who are prone to depression and/or suicidal thoughts to read, '**Hope on The Horizon**', '**A Mother Who Left Before Her Hope Arrived**', '**Suicidal, Let's Talk**', & '**A Man Without Shoes.**' It is my take that, with the right kind of information and messages of hope, suicide will be kept at the barest minimum, if not completely eradicated. Therefore, I urge people to develop some philosophical mechanisms to help them cope and deal with the strains and stresses of life none is imune to.

Being that all the carnage in our world routes from the families of this world, from whence all human beings make their entry into this planet and, in recognition of the fact that families are usually a by-product of cohabitation; those wishing to cohabit and/or marry are encouraged to read '**Cohabiting.**' The message here is; once the base or foundation is right, the structure and entire building will be firm and stronger. However, the structure will continue to crack and remain problematic once the foundation is faulty. Our world has struggled and will continue to struggle because human beings have continued to build on a faulty foundation whilst papering over the cracks.

For those who feel they cannot gain or learn anything from the least our world has to offer or from certain nations, communities or individuals, I invite them to read **'The Majestic Toilet Seat.'** Here, it is hoped that one can learn something from the encounter between the world's most powerful figure (Dike) and the only thing he struggled to conquer (the toilet seat).

Finally, I wish to donate two percent each of the proceeds from the sale of this book to the following; a charity or organization of choice supporting the education of girls and women, Owerri Motherless Babies Home in Imo State, Nigeria, Oh! MOTHER, mothers led organisation campaigning against youth killings and Youth Against Crime not Crime Against You (YACnCAY). Which is a youth led charity fighting against youth stabbings and shootings

Acknowledgements

I wish to once again express my profound gratitude to members of my household whose names I have mentioned in my previous books. Moreover, it is with great joy and thanks to the Almighty that, we welcomed our newest arrival to the household after an eleven year-break, King-david, Uchechi, Sochima, Ezenwa Ihenacho. Though much of my writing takes place when they are asleep, they have had to put up with all my running around, mini discussions about the book, lectures, and, as they put it at times, 'preaching'. They have sacrificed a lot so that others can get to hear my message in the spirit of sharing and love. They have come to realise that, in this world of sharing and love, I am not theirs alone but also a father to their friends and other children whose health and safety is as important as theirs. No one is ever safe in their brand new Rolls Royce if other vehicles on the road have no brakes.

To all my colleagues in the eight local councils I have worked in, particularly in Haringey Council, Surrey County Council and London Borough of Barking & Dagenham who shared in this, my latest adventure, and were previewers to the story behind this book. I have a fond memory of some colleagues who even wrote in my leaving card: 'enjoyed the preaching' and one who wrote 'something about the anus and brain', in reference to this book. It has been great fun and testament to the fact that success can never be achieved alone, as such, there is no such thing as 'a self made person'.

My warm appreciation and thanks go to all the staff at BBC Radio 5 (909 medium wave) for being the 'invisible' inspiration behind my writing, Ben Television for 'Bridging the Gap' and Nigerian Watch Newspaper for supporting my writing. Greetings also to Middlesex University Alumni Association, All the Staff & Students of Havering College in Romford, Archdeacon Dennis Junior Seminary Old Boys Association, Topaz Gentlemen Club (United Kingdom & Northern Ireland), Ogwa Community Association (United Kingdom & Northern Ireland), Mbaitoli Association (United Kingdom & Northern Ireland), Imo State Union (United Kingdom & Northern Ireland) and the entire Ihenacho Ogbuehi Dynasty of Amaegbu, Ekwerazu, Ogwa in Mbaitoli Local Government Area, Imo State, Nigeria. I would never have become who I am today without you being part of my heritage.

I want to thank HRH Eze Dr George Ihenacho, Most Rev. Dr. Emmanuel O. Chukwuma Archbishop of Enugu, Dr Sir Lazz & Canon Lady Dr Addy Onyenobi, Chief Ngozi Evelyn Nwandu, Toyin Idowu PhD, Mr Alistair Soyode, Dr Gilbert & Mrs Bernadette Igboaka, Charles Okpalanwankwo PhD Researcher, James Porter, Captain Henry & Mrs Chinna Okoroafor, Mrs Alicia Ada Meniru (Nee Ihenacho), Jon Hughes, Chief Kate Anolue, Susan Jumoke Fajana- Thaomas, Prince Ephraim & Lady Elizabeth Ihenacho, Prince Martin & Princess Comfort Edoro Nwamuo (Nee Ihenacho), Captain Ryan & Mrs Lucy Claussen, Chief Dr Ejikeme Uzoalor, Chief Bimbo Roberts Folayan, Princess Ifem Enwerem, HRH Theodora (Nollywood) Ibekwe-Oyebade, Councillor Anna Mbachu, Jenny

Chika Okafor, Jacqueline Wabara, Hon. Justice Goddy & Lady Nancy Goddy Anunihu, Ms Ogechi Anita Mbadiwe, Mr Henry Mbadiwe, Mr Chijioke & Mrs Susan Ojji, Mr Joseph Klass & Mrs Sonia Adam, Mrs Victoria Enyobi, Nikki Plastiras, Prince & Lady ChiomaEddy Ihenacho, Ms Ruffina Adimora, Princess Oma Abel-Unokan, Prince Chukwukere & Lady Florence Ihenacho, Benjamin & Reine Achogbuo, Dr Godwin & Lady Chidiebere Duru, Miss Kristy Duru, Ify P. (Dj Ify) & Vivian I. O'Nwere, Adanma Carol Okoro, Dr Philip & Mrs Irene Onyii Nwachukwu, Olumide Kolade, Councillor Nneka Keazor, Dilibe & Nkiru Chinweze, Tochi Brown, Dr Mike & Mrs Virginia Adilih, Chijioke Adilih, His Worshipful Councillor Adedamola Aminu, Barr. Aloy & Mrs Nnenna Onyerindu, Dr Austin & Mrs Tina Okolie, Hon. Kingsley & Lolo Chinasa Dimaku, Sharon Tamale, Nze Onyeka Uzoukwu, Mrs Victoria Akudike, Rev. Nnamdi & Mrs Chinwendu Obioma Maduka, Mr Tony & Mrs Michaela Anaka and His Grace, Anthony J.V. Obinna, The Catholic Archbishop of Owerri for their suggestions, advice and insightful contributions to this book. In particular, I want to give special thanks to Harjit Bansal for her powerful and moving story ('I was born in Kenya', below). I want to thank all participants, men, women and children who took part in the survey. I want to make it known to all of you that I am the anus and you are the brain. We needed one another in order to make this book a reality. Therefore without you, there would be no me. I remain most grateful.

Finally, I want to give profound and special thanks to my big cousin and mentor Professor

H.N.C & Mrs Beryl Ihenacho, for their unwavering support and encouragement throughout the production of this book.

Contents

Dedication...v

Beneficiaries... vi

Acknowledgements.. viii

The Little Bird And The Body...1

The Majestic Toilet Seat...36

The Two Metaphorical Buildings Existing In Human
 Life... 42

One World, One Entity.. 67

World's Most Inhabitable Place..................................104

Best Practice Hepworth Ward in Focus.......................107

World's Most Uninhabitable Place..............................110

Men Are The Problem, Women Are The Solution......145

Cohabiting...186

Human Excesses And Limitations...............................212

Hope on The Horizon..244

A Mother Who Left Before Her Hope Arrived...........249

Suicidal? Let's Talk!... 251

The Man Without Shoes...258

Yet Another Baby... 263

Abiding Legacy Of the Man.......................................265

The Cost of Inaction...271

About the Author... 281

The Little Bird
And The Body

It came to pass that, various parts of the human body went into war of words in the quest for supremacy, survival and honour. This was because the body would face an imminent death, but only the most useful and important part of it would survive, live forever and be accorded with an honour never seen bestowed on any living creature by the Grand Master of the universe, according to the little bird. However, for this to happen, the most useful part of the body must convince the rest and the rest of the body parts (that are less useful, destined to perish) must agree. How did this come about? Now judge for yourselves. Which part of the body gave the most compelling case, deserving of the crown from the Grand Master of the Universe? What factor(s) swayed it in their favour? What do you think happened to the body and what happened to the little bird that brought the message? How did the humility of the brain save the day (or did it)? And what are the morals of this story? Let's find out, shall we?

It all started when a little bird that was destined to live forever suddenly had an awful dream. A little bird that knew of its immortality, with freedom to fly anywhere, perch on any tree and do as it pleased, had suddenly been made aware of its mortality. In the dream, it was revealed that the only person living within the little bird's vicinity was going to kill and eat it soon. In the same dream, the little bird was told that the secret of how it could avoid this imminent death and continue to live forever was with a tortoise that lived about five thousand miles away. The little bird woke up full of fear and anxiety. It had only one thing on its mind. 'How and where can I find this tortoise?' the little bird muttered as it paced around.

The little bird flew off in search of the tortoise. It flew north, south, east and west but there was no clue in sight. As it returned to its nest pacing around and pondering how to locate the tortoise, it felt a gentle touch on its shoulder; in panic, it turned round and there was a guardian angel. The guardian angel said, 'Little bird! Worry no more; I have come to take you to the tortoise.' The little bird became excited and gave the guardian angel a big hug. The guardian angel then said to the little bird 'I will tell you just a few things you need to know, the rest I keep to myself and you are not to ask any questions. The great tortoise and I are connected to you in ways you don't and would never know. We are here to protect and take care of your concerns whenever they arise. You have not seen or heard from us since because your mind had been at rest throughout, until now. We both are aware of your troubled mind now, hence I have been despatched to assist you. However, I have one rule that must be strictly followed. It is not for me to tell you what will happen if you fail to follow this rule. Now, when I take you on this journey, I escort you because of the importance and significance of it. Primarily, you would never have located the tortoise on your own. As a result, I am not here to play, chat or be too friendly with you in spite of all I have already told you. I am not here to answer any of the questions you may have or discuss any burning issues that you may have from your dream. If you have any questions originating from what I have told you or relating to your dream, you may ask the tortoise. Everyone has their role to play and my specific role is to take you to your destination and nothing else! So, as we set off on this journey, you must not utter a word no matter how pressured you feel. The only clue you will have of our arrival to the destination is when you cannot see me anymore. When that happens, you must stop and listen. Did you understand?' asked the guardian angel.

'Yes Ma,' said the little bird.

'Now follow me!' instructed the guardian angel. The little bird became very anxious but at the same time, excited that it had allies it never knew existed. The bird was particularly excited as it was finally en route to meeting this tortoise that is the custodian of its everlasting life.

The journey of five thousand miles began with the guardian angel leading the way. The journey was so long that they had to have a couple of stops to rest and feed with no one uttering any word. Eventually the guardian angel disappeared. As instructed, the little bird stopped and listened. As it listened, a voice suddenly emerged and said, 'Hello little bird, what brings you to this corner of the universe, risking everything to get here?'

In total shock, the little bird turned round and there was the tortoise! 'Oh well,' said little bird, 'I am so pleased to see you Mr Tortoise, I had an awful...'

Before the bird could complete the sentence, the tortoise interrupted, 'Don't worry, I just asked to see how you would respond. I already know why you are here. If I get you to say why you are here, how then would you trust me and the instruction I would give you?' The little bird was astonished and became more curious in anticipation. The tortoise asked in a gentle tone, 'Do you now want me to tell you why you are here?'

'Oh…with all pleasure sir! I have been so worried,' said the little bird as it shivered. 'Okay!' said the tortoise, 'it is about the dream you had, is it not?'

'Oh yes, how did you know that?' asked the little bird.

'Don't you worry,' said the tortoise, 'that's what I am here for and that's why you travelled over five thousand miles to be here. You would not have been directed to me, if I am here for nothing or here to do guesswork. If I may ask, how did you get to know where to find me and what I would do for you?'

'I was told in the dream and a mystery angel guided me to you, sir,' said the little bird.

'That's all right,' said the tortoise, 'I knew all that as well, I only wanted to hold a bit of a conversation with my little guest. I must say, I had gone a few days without visitors and I began to wonder whether I had run out of business. I benefit from crisis and if there is none, then my usefulness and livelihood is threatened. I share a common place with my friends who make and sell coffins. They don't pray for anything to go wrong with anyone but their businesses are adversely threatened when they are not making sales and they don't find it funny. In fact, they become frustrated and unhappy when no one dies, to put it mildly.'

'Oh Mr Tortoise, are you mentioning death because I am going to be die?' asked the little bird.

'Well, quite the opposite if all goes well, you have come because your promise of everlasting life has been threatened, hasn't it?' asked the tortoise.

'Well, in this beautiful world, with freedom to fly anywhere I want, whenever and anyhow I want and to perch on any tree of my choice, who wouldn't want to live forever?' asked the little bird.

'Anyway,' said the tortoise, 'I am sure the guardian

angel told you the link between the three of us. You had not been aware of us because your mind had not been troubled until now. I am aware you have some burning questions to ask but unfortunately I can only take two due to certain rules I have to observe. Therefore think carefully and choose your two most important questions.'

'Okay, okay, okay...' said the little bird. 'My first question is, was the dream I had real?'

'Well,' the tortoise replied, 'you must consider it as real because I do. Having said that, all I am privy to is what is happening to you and all the other creatures I am connected with. I have no connection with human beings especially the person that lives within your vicinity. From that perspective, I am not really sure whether he intends to kill and eat you. But it is best to deal with the threat and not worry whether it is genuine or not.'

'You are with me indeed, you are a true friend, for a friend in need is a friend indeed,' said the little bird. 'You are so reassuring. Now, I want to know why this person wants to kill and eat me. I am only very little and I don't understand.'

'Oh well,' said the tortoise, 'as I told you earlier, I can't account for the thoughts of human beings but my only guess would be that the person may have run out of protein and may have become desperate, that's all I can say. My job today is to give you a possible solution, nothing else! Now you have asked your two questions, you have to excuse me for a while,' said the tortoise, as it withdrew its head into the shell.

The little bird began to wonder and became very tense in anticipation. It was not sure what to expect but was full of hope for a solution to the problem confronting it. The little bird was still reeling with shock that the tortoise was able to say what its mission was about. It was still in meditation mode when the tortoise's head emerged from the shell and began to laugh.

'What is funny, Mr Tortoise?' asked the little bird.

'Nothing,' replied Mr Tortoise, 'I had to laugh because I have an idea of the solution by which you, my little bird, can continue to live forever. The threat to kill you seems a possibility. However, there was no confirmation whether the intention to kill you is real. Like I said earlier, there is no point thinking about that. But you must act as though everything in your dream is real. Your frame of mind should be that the only person that lives in your area is the obstacle... the obstacle between you and everlasting life. He plans to kill you soon and eat you for dinner. In a very short time he will begin the plan to kill you. Just assume that he had observed you a few times and because there is great shortage of protein, if nothing is done to stop him, you would be dead. With these thoughts, you have to act and act quickly. There is a little problem though.'

'Oh... what is it?' asked the little bird.

'Well,' said the tortoise, 'it is unfortunate that because of limited time, I would have to send you home with the task of developing the plan, because all I can give you is an idea of what to do. There isn't enough time for me to assist you in developing the plan. The forces in control of this area would not tolerate your presence for too long here. You must be on your way very soon! I know it would take you some time to get back. But whatever happens you will have at the very least two months to come up with a perfect plan based on the idea I will give you now. However, you must act quickly in developing the plan.'

'Oh please,' said the little bird, 'I cannot wait.'

'Now,' said Mr Tortoise, 'you must come up with a plan that can instigate a fight, a war amongst the differ-ent parts of that person's body. The various parts of that person's body need to fight against themselves. Once the fight starts, and if it is a good plan, it is very likely that the body would die as fast as you never expected and you can continue with your "everlasting life, uninterrupted". However, the consequences of not getting the right plan, I cannot tell you because I know you are aware of the possibilities. Even though neither of us is definite about this, we cannot take chances. For in the animal kingdom, the person who dares wins! You must be on your way now!'

'Thank you sir, thank you sir, thank you sir,' said the little bird. 'What can I offer you sir, for saving me? What do I owe for your kindness?'

'Oh no, don't worry,' replied Mr Tortoise, 'this is my job, I get my reward in so many other ways. When "prophecy" and/or "healing" are genuine there is no compulsion or any set condition. Freely I have received and freely I am charged to give. Those who request items or collect gifts as pre-requisite for prophecy or healing are at best gamblers and at worst thieves. You have to go now; when you have succeeded, when you have achieved your desired outcome, you can make another trip to say your thank you, if you so wish. You need to be on your way now due to the factors I told you about earlier.'

'Thank you sir, goodbye and I hope to see you again in the near future.' With these words the little bird departed and flew off.

On its way back, thoughts of how to set war among the different parts of the person's body filled the bird's mind. 'Wish I had more time to devise a perfect plan with the awesome Mr Tortoise. I know Mr Tortoise is a wizard and he would have given me a perfect solution to my problem. I really do not want to get it wrong. I am so scared! I have such a perfect life. I can go wherever I want, perch on any tree. I was free to fly to anywhere and enjoy the scenery. I have always been assured an everlasting life, until this terrible nightmare. I don't want to give up this beautiful life easily. I had always believed I owned this place, indeed the entire universe, what a nightmare! I can't get this wrong, as this is a matter of life and death,' muttered the little bird.

'A-ha,' said the bird, 'I have an idea. I have a plan! I have to give them something big, with huge benefit, something the parts of the body cannot resist. Something they can fight and die for. Yes! I think I have got it right! The various parts of the body would have to compete for supremacy, honour and everlasting life. Any part that can prove to the rest that they do the greatest job for the body, and their role is the most important to the body, would be promised to become the King or Queen of the body. That "most important" part would not only become the king or queen but would also live forever whilst the rest of the body parts die. Above all, the coronation of the special, most important part of the body would be the most significant and awesome event ever held anywhere in the entire universe, with all the dynasties represented, the Great Tortoise and the Grand Master of the universe in attendance. This would surely offer the parts of the body the incentive to fight and compete for supremacy. This would put them in disarray and cause the body to die,' proclaimed the little bird as it hailed the Great Tortoise and its 'wisdom'. 'Now I understand what the Great Tortoise meant when it said, I might succeed if I can instigate a war between the various parts of this person's body. This will surely get them going... this will get all of them to die and guarantee my enjoyment galore!'

The little bird flew straight to this giant of a person in excitement and addressed the mouth, hands, legs, eyes, ears, anus and the brain. The little bird informed them that it had come with both good and bad news from the 'Great Tortoise'. The bad news was that the body would face a certain death, and the good news was that one part of the body would survive, live forever and be crowned the king or queen of the body. The part that would survive and live forever would have to prove that it did the most work for the body and be acknowledged by the rest as the most vital part of the body. That part of the body would not only survive but would be crowned the king or queen of the body. The little bird proclaimed 'The Great Tortoise, the dynasties and the Grand Master of the universe would descend on this planet (for the first and only time) to crown the most useful part of the body King or Queen of the body. That part would reign over all things. The ceremony would be the most memorable and remarkable event of our time, never to be the equal of anything we have seen or yet to see!'

The quest for honour and survival then led the body parts into a bitter war of words, with each proclaiming how vital they were and insisting that without them, the rest of the body would at best malfunction or at worst die. Each from their own perspective was convinced that they did the most for the body.

The mouth undoubtedly started the war of words, as it was so vocal. 'Yes! It's got to be me; this is not up for debate and there is no competition to be had here. I have always known it and I will be shocked if you all do not know it already that, I am the most important part of the body. This is indisputable and not up for a contest. You all know how important I am to you. I am the most useful, I house the most venomous part of the body (the tongue), I also house the teeth, but most importantly, I am the source of nutrition and nourishment. Without me, bringing in food and drink you will all starve to death. I speak for you all and often assist the not-so-useful nose in bringing in and letting out air. I also assist the most useless part of the body (the anus) in getting rid of unwanted waste. If I shut down access, you will all die; I deserve a special place in all of you because I am the special one. You see, none of you should use the words "special one" lightly because I am the real special one. You all need to respect and appreciate what I do for all of you. I, more than deserve your honour and hope you all understand. If I go on strike, you will all be in trouble and surely die...'

Before the mouth could finish talking, the hand had begun to gesture at the mouth. 'Yap, yap, yap that's all you know. Shut up! I say shut up, you talk too much! What do you know? Now hear me and hear me good. I am the most important part of the body. I am key to everything that happens to you lot, especially you, the mouth! I am responsible for planting, tending, harvesting, preparing, cooking and putting food into you (the mouth) in order to feed the rest of you. I am responsible for fetching water and bringing liquid into you. If I go on strike, you all will be in trouble and you will definitely die.' The hand went on, 'I want to remind you of what happened yesterday. I know you have a very short memory or even none at all. But I still have to tell and remind you. Yesterday, when I put food through you, you had particles of the food all over you which would have attracted germs and destroyed you but I washed you, as I do to the rest of you lot, dried you up and kept you clean. I bathe all of you, put cream on you and not only make and prepare your clothing, but also clothe you all as well. When you get injured, I treat and dress your wounds. When any part of you is unhealthy, I medicate and nurse you. I assist all of you when you are in trouble, scratch you all when and wherever you itch. What on earth don't I do for you lot?' asked the hand, as it became emotional. 'I am a mother figure to you all and at times I feel over burdened by you all. Moreover, I am the one that defends and protects you all from harm. When dangerous objects come near you, I block them from reaching you, taking the pain and injury on your behalf. When dangerous objects are in your way, I remove them from your path. I am active all the time working for you all. How dare you, or any one of you, claim to be the most important? Think of what would happen to all of you if I decide to do nothing. I am the one to be respected and honoured, for I am truly the special one.'

The leg quickly became angry with the hand and shouted, 'Hey! Mr Hand, clap for yourself! I say clap for yourself, for your short-sightedness and stupidity! What a self-indulging brat, full of self-praise and adulation! I could easily have been fooled just like any other who may not know what they represent or understand the service they render. So, suddenly you have become a "mother figure", eh? I cannot believe how short-sighted and lacking in insight you are. Well, if you think you are the "mother figure", then I am here to show and prove to you all that I am not just the father figure but the father to all of you. You might as well clap for the mouth too. But let me remind you two, and the rest of you who might be planning a challenge against me, that you will be living in dreamland if any of you thinks they can win this contest in my presence. You would live in that dreamland until you realise how important I am to you all. I am happy you all know I don't talk too much, because I am not the mouth and I believe in action. I am the "doer", the conveyor and the transporter. I am the foundation upon which all of you are built. I am the base and the one that carry all of you. Without me, you cannot go anywhere. If I don't move, everything stops and there will be no function for any of you braggers. I help you all before you pay back, without my help you can't afford to pay back! I come first, and then you lot come second! I am the creditor and all of you are debtors. For the hand to plant crops, harvest them, go to the shop, cook food or fetch water, I have to convey it to these various assignments. The hand feeds the mouth and through the mouth the entire body gets its nourishment. However, the hand and mouth can only perform their respective duties if I take the hand to the shop, kitchen or restaurant. For the hand to use water, I have to take it where it would fetch the water. When natural disasters come, when wars break out, when the whole body is threatened by external factors, I take all of you to safety. Have you asked yourselves what would happen to all of you if I decide to take you into a deep sea or raging fire? Though I might die with you but you lot would have perished. Without my functions your health and safety would be highly compromised and you all would surely die. I am not just the father figure, I am THE FATHER! I am not only the most important but the only important part of the body. I deserve your respect and I deserve to be crowned King. Can any of you stop me? It is so glaring, we don't need a magnifying glass to view it, need I say more?'

'Oh Mr Leg, you make me laugh! I hear you,' said the hand, 'but you are forgetting a few things though! The other day you got injured, I treated you. I also removed the obstacle in your way a few days ago. You would have suffered significant damage if not for my intervention.'

'You see,' said the leg, 'whatever you think you do, I make it possible. You would not have anything to treat my injury with or any ability to remove an obstacle if I hadn't taken you to a position where you can do these, can't you understand? The more you seek to highlight your "achievements", the more you reinforce my contribution and magnify the depth of your ignorance.'

The nose, having heard the mouth try to belittle it by saying 'not-so-useful nose', was very angry and accused the mouth of being very ignorant, but said, 'I am happy you are only a helper, you are indeed my assistant. That means I am your boss. Can a helper, a mere assistant, be more important than the boss? Let me make it clear to all of you, but you (the mouth) in particular, if I do not filter the air that comes into the body, if I do not act as the air conditioning unit to generate healthy air for the lungs and if I fail to smell what is coming into the mouth, you will all be in trouble and the likelihood is you will all perish. I haven't got time to make noise. I quietly go about my business but I know, as you all know that if I pack up, you all must pack up as well. I deserve your respect, acknowledgement and honour. Without the air, without oxygen all of you would perish.'

The eye began to look around and blinked three times, then winked before addressing the rest. 'Even the Scriptures recognise and acknowledge my importance. On that bit alone, I have won the contest! Matthew 6:22 tells all of us that I am the lamp of the body and if I am good, all of you would be full of light. The reverse is that, if I am not good you will all be in darkness and die. This alone shows that I am the most important part of the body. How I wished all of you had sense. If you had sense, you would all know that if I shut down my services, the body would die. If I ask the leg to find the farm where the crops are planted or the kitchen where the food is prepared without my assistance, it would never find it. In fact, it is more likely to run into trouble than find these places. If I don't see danger and see where it is coming from, the legs could even run into the danger and all of you would perish. The hand can feed the mouth but it is me that assesses what the hand puts in the mouth. If I fail to do so, the hand can feed the mouth with poison and all of you could die. For any of you to function, it requires my clearance and all it takes is for me to shut down for all of you to pack up. If I haven't seen something, there is nothing for any of you to know or do but if you insist on knowing or doing without me, you automatically run into crisis, crisis that can destroy you. I kept quiet thinking you knew what I represent for all of you and waiting for one of you to nominate me and the rest of you to support me unopposed, as the undisputed, most important and useful part of the body. I didn't know you were all too short-sighted, consumed in your little world, wallowing in ignorance and bereft of knowledge, wisdom and understanding. You all claim to know but in the actual sense, you are all wallowing in severe ignorance. I hope now that you have been reminded and called to order, you all can now acknowledge me as the most important part of the body before I declare or pronounce myself King and await my coronation because, it is undisputed that I am the one and only! Think about it, you all would remain afraid of the darkness and remain in darkness until I bring the light. I am the light that lifts your darkness.'

The ear very quickly snapped at the eye, 'Eh, Mr Eye! I can hear you alright and I must say yours is pretty impressive. If I didn't know much about you and your limitations, I would have voted for you. Anyone else listening to you would believe you totally and I can understand why but, Mr Eye, if you are so sure you are the most important part of the body, don't you think you would lose that position, if it can be proven that another part of the body controls you?'

'I agree but no one can prove that; I am the one in control of all of you,' said the eye.

The ear then asked, 'Can we agree that anyone who controls you will be the one to be crowned?'

'Why not, I agree,' replied the eye.

'Okay,' said the ear, 'I am here to prove just that. Can I now ask, how do you know where the danger is coming from, if I haven't heard it, how do you know where to look?'

'Oh, is it that one?' asked the eye. 'But at times I don't need direction before I can see danger. I see by just looking,' explained the eye.

'Oh well, you will be looking like a zombie forward in the hope you notice danger, when danger is right behind you. I am the one who hears and directs you to where the danger is coming from. You only can see what is in front of you; you always would need me to draw your attention to look elsewhere. Otherwise you will put us all at risk,' affirmed the ear.

'Okay,' said the eye, 'after hearing and drawing my attention, what else do you or can you do?'

'No,' replied the ears, 'it is not for you to be asking me any further questions. The deal is done! You have already agreed that anyone who proves they can control you will be the one to be crowned.'

'No way,' said the eye, 'you are not that important, you can only do one thing! The rest of the body would survive without you.'

The ear became angry. 'You are being unreasonable now; how can you be crowned king if you cannot be trusted? You are now claiming that I can only do one thing but let it be known by you and the rest that even if it is only one thing I can do, that one thing is very essential, and the consequences of me not doing that one thing would be dire to all of you. It is not about quantity but quality of the work one does! Think! If I haven't informed the eye to look, the entire body can easily be run over by all sorts of things. I am the one to be crowned quite simply. I am the one to be crowned because if I stop working all of you would perish.'

'Right!' says the anus in a gentle tone, 'I have sat here all day long listening to you lot and all I can hear is how you all can do this, that and the other. I already know what all of you are thinking about me anyway. I know because I have heard some of you gossiping about me, in the past. I agree I may be useless as some of you think. I have heard how important you all are and I have no objections. **However, I am here not only to show, but prove that: in this life, it is not much about what any or all of you think about me but all about what I think about myself.** I know I am useless but even if I am useful, there is no way I can win this contest. That one is for sure because I cannot vote for myself in this one, let alone any of you vote for me. Though I have no ear, I am deafened by hearing how much you all are contributing to the functions of this body. I may look stupid but I am not stupid enough to know that there is no way I can match any of you, because the list of what each of you does is far too long. I simply cannot compete. I cannot begin to assume what I am not. Therefore, I couldn't claim to be the most important, let alone the special one. Now I know I will be condemned with the less useful parts of the body; now I know I am facing an imminent death, now I know my fate; now I know I cannot do anything about it; now I know I have nothing to lose. However, the little I can do, I will do and do right away! The little power I have, the little control left for me now, I will and must exercise. On this note, I make it known to all of you that, henceforth! I have decided to shut down the two areas by which I contribute to the functions of the body.

'From today there will be no wind coming through here and no waste passing through here. I have had and suffered enough. My sufferings have never been appreciated by any of you. You all have to find alternative means to dispose of your wastes and wind! That's it! I have had enough and I quit!'

Hearing this, the mouth couldn't resist and interjected, 'Hey Mr Anus! I can even do part of your job. When I burp, I let out wind and the vomit when you lot become sick also comes through me, disposing of some wastes. This reinforces my usefulness, my special place and goes a long way to confirm that I am not only the most useful but the most important part of the body. Before you quit though, why not vote for me and I promise even if you die, when I become King, I will resurrect you.'

The hand very quickly said to the mouth, 'You haven't been listening, I have told you to shut up and you keep yapping along! Without me you will take nothing in and you will let nothing out, period! Therefore I am the "one" and "only", because I look after all of you.'

The leg then reminded the hand, 'Earlier, Mrs Hand, I asked you to clap for yourself for your short-sightedness and stupidity. I don't know why you need to be reminded that if I haven't conveyed you, there would be nothing from you to anybody and you cannot prepare anything, let alone feed the mouth. My role is pivotal and the most important. You are wasting your time arguing blindly instead of looking at the facts. I don't need to repeat myself but if I stop my functions, you all would perish, quite simply! In fact I am getting tired now, I don't know whether my tiredness is to do with what the anus has done. But in order to prove to everyone and make it clear that I am the most important, I am now withdrawing my services to the body too. Hopefully when you all come

17

to your senses and realise my importance then I would decide what I do next. I am tired and cannot take you lot anywhere again. You better hope nothing dangerous meets all of you here because you would be up for grabs as I would not move anywhere.'

The brain, representing all the internal organs, interjected when it became obvious that this struggle for supremacy was putting the entire body at risk. The brain had planned to wait for every part to have their turn before coming in with a bang! It had assumed that its role was the most important, being the one that activates most of the parts into action. However, having heard from the other parts and taking into consideration the action of the anus which was followed by the leg, the brain panicked, as it felt the impact of those threats.

Within a few days, everything got congested as there was no exit. The brain sensed the imminent death of the entire body. It knew if every part kept fighting for superiority, they are all going to suffer the consequences. It knew that the best and only chance for survival was to come in with humility and therefore it cried out, 'Oh! My dear good friends, I am sorry to have thought that I was the most useless part of the body. Sorry for inflicting my lousy self on the rest of you and I thank all of you for putting up with me. I realised that although I am responsible for triggering some of you to act, I depended mostly on the eye to capture something before I react. But now, having heard from the ear, I now know that it is not only the eye but me also that relies on the ear. I also now appreciate how heavily I depend on the nose to smell something before I can prompt one of you to react. And if any of you fails to pass on information, gives wrong information or I misread any information given, I send out the wrong message and the entire body (which includes me) suffers. By the same token, I have also suddenly realised that though I prompt most of you to act, if you don't act or could not act for whatever reason, I would suffer with you. If the ear, eye and nose do not give me information, I could not do anything or play my own part. The actions of the anus have suddenly made me realise how limited and vulnerable I am, indeed all of us are. It has also made me realise how important the anus is. The action of the anus is now threatening all of us and if we allow this to carry on, all of us most definitely would perish. I could not see how any of us would live to be crowned anything. Look at the state of us now, nothing is going out. I am getting too tired and am about to give up as I speak. Look at the awful state of the stomach now nothing has gone out of it for a whole week. This is what could happen when there is a threat hanging over one of us, when any of us is made to feel empty and worthless and when one is pushed to a level where they feel condemned, with nothing to lose and nothing to live for. The mouth now has nothing to live for. The leg has become weak and also withdrawn its services to the body. Inside here the heart is almost unable to pump and circulate the blood. The liver, kidney, lungs and various organs are all packing up. Everywhere is congested.

'All your contributions have also made me realise that though we are all individually extremely useful and important in our own right, we cannot survive on our own and our usefulness can only work when complemented by the rest. It has now occurred to me that I did not choose to be the brain, neither did any of you choose to become what you are. We never chose where we were planted or located. It was just sheer luck what positions we found ourselves in and thank goodness all of us have an important role to play. I have also realised that when one of us is in pain, struggling or incapacitated, all of us suffer too. But most importantly, I have realised that you need to function in order for me to function well. I have now had to question myself and found that, if all of you were me, the body would not exist, if all of us were the eye, the body would not exist either and the same goes for all of us. I am the brain because you are all different, how would I have known I am the brain if we were all the same? The same applies to all of you, for example, how would the eye know it is the eye, if all of us were the eye? Would we even have a name? Whatever value I have is because of you and vice versa, because I need you in order to be me, I cannot be and don't want to be the special one. If I lose the rest of you, I would lose myself too, if I lose any of you I will suffer with the rest of you. I have no meaning without you all. I exist because of you and you exist because of me. Therefore I have become aware that the death of you would amount to the death of me. If the mouth wants to eat everything on its own and the rest of us die, where would the mouth live?

'I have been here thinking and now recalling each time we have suffered or struggled, it is usually because one of us had run into difficulty, not functioning as well as it should, made a wrong decision or been incapacitated by natural forces. I note with shame the number of times I have contributed in causing pain to the entire body by either judging things wrongly, acting based on inaccurate assumptions or a bad call from the eye, ear or the nose. I have often presumed, based on information from the eye that the legs can jump higher and based on that, pushed the leg to go beyond the call of duty. In the end the leg got into trouble which ended up affecting all of us. How many times have I agreed with the eye, leg, hand and mouth to bring into the body unhealthy or dangerous food that ended up causing the entire body problems? Though we have in most cases made the right call and acted well for the benefit of the body, I am humbled to know that I have contributed to certain problems we have all had. This is the time for all of us to think deeply and begin to understand and appreciate, not only how unique we are but also how useless we can be working independently on our own. Furthermore, we must understand that whenever we, as individual parts of the body, get it wrong, the entire body suffers as a result. Sometimes the suffering is immediate and other times it is delayed and comes when we least expect. In fact, there are times I have made certain decisions for my personal interest which served me momentarily, but the consequences became so costly to the entire body in ways I never anticipated in the long run. My weaknesses or limitations are your strength and your limitations, my strength.

'None of us has it all to give, but by sharing we complement ourselves and the body is healthier. I have learnt that if I use my strength to oppress (and thereby make any part of the body weak) for momentary pleasure, I will partake in the suffering when the adverse impact of that weakened part is felt by the entire body. None of us can be great on our own, we can only be great together. None of us can suffer alone, when one suffers the rest of us feel the pain too and over-compensate. No matter how big or healthy a branch is, it cannot survive on its own without being part of a tree. Any branch that separates itself from the tree, in the weird thought that it can stand on its own, will surely die.'

The brain then spoke directly to the mouth. 'Mr Mouth, I respect and admire you greatly for the services you render to all of us. You are a great servant to the body and everything you said about your contributions and functions to the body is true but... it is easy to say you talk too much, yet we have to all understand that that it is your job at times to talk too much, especially when others are hard of hearing or continue to repeat the same mistakes because wrong things are easy to do and easily replicated.

'This is why there is no college specifically designed to teach wrong things, as they are easy to pick up without teaching. In the same way, farmers do not plant weeds but weeds very quickly outnumber the planted crops and threaten their growth. However, it is important we all remember that whatever our roles, however important we see our role, we are called to serve and be served by others. As such, we must not oppress, intimidate or brag to others because others have peculiar roles to play too. We must not demean what others bring to the table because no particular part of the body can do or go it alone. Just think for a moment, no matter what gift we have, our ability to render them is based on many conditions out of our control. Have you considered that if you were unhealthy, Mr Mouth, you would either struggle or be unable to render your services? You would depend on another part of the body to provide care and treatment and that other part would have to provide care and treatment because it has a vested interest in you getting better, a vested interest all of us have.

'If the other parts of the body you render your services to do not exist, your value would disappear and if the other parts of the body you depend on, for example the hand, fail or refuse to function, your role would cease. Furthermore, you never chose yourself for the role you play. Therefore, I take exception to the way you tried to demean the important and peculiar services the nose and the anus render by claiming that you perform some of their roles and implying they are not that useful.

'You seem to suggest that we can survive or exist without them. Let me make this fact known to you right now:

Every part of this body has its own expertise. If we were to let you play a role you are not suitably qualified to play, because of anything other than your content and ability, then we have sold ourselves short and we will all suffer the consequences, as we are suffering now. If we allow you to play such a role because you are very outspoken, you happen to be our neighbour here, or we like how you look or the things you say, we may be momentarily happy but we would have done ourselves a total disservice in the long run. Any time we belittle any part of the body, render it useless or get it to a state where it feels worthless with nothing to live for, then we have threatened ourselves and weakened the entire body. We may feel momentarily happy and live with short-term pleasure for subduing or making another part of the body weak but the long-term adverse effect would be felt by the entire body. We should all be humbled by the gifts we are given and use them to serve, to the best of our ability.

'We must not use our gifts to oppress or intimidate others for without others we cannot exist. None of us can be tall and short at the same time. We need the short and we need the tall for different purposes. I often, in my dreams, see some of us preferring to be the head and rejecting the tail. It is rather unfortunate because without the tail, there will be no head or the head will suffer so much because the head can never do the job of the tail. The tail has its job and the head has its job as well and both are, if not equally important, very important in their own right.

'Now the leg has joined the anus and both have withdrawn their services to the body. This means further crisis for all. Both the anus and leg are not exempt from this crisis because they are suffering too. The biggest lesson here for me and hopefully all of us is that we, as individual parts of the body, are what we are without our making, we never chose what we are or where we are located. It is not by our design, but we are what we are and located where we are for a reason. We have been given different roles which must be complementary otherwise it becomes destructive and damaging to the body if any of us acts on our own. Every second, every minute and every day that passes without us understanding what is upon us and continuing to argue amongst ourselves, fighting for supremacy and honour, we threaten our very existence as we wallow in severe ignorance. We are responsible for ourselves and we have shared responsibility for one another. The situation we are in now proves that when one of us fails or becomes unable to render its service for any particular reason, all of us suffer the consequences.

'I want you all to know that I can preach for as long as it takes but if you all refuse, and continue to fight this war, we will all die and no one would be the "special one" let alone be crowned anything. The question I want all of us to again consider is if, for example, the mouth is voted as the "special one" and the leg and anus continue not to function and all the other parts including me die, how would the mouth survive and where would it live?'

The brain paused for a few moments and then said, 'Before I tell you what I think about this little bird and what I suggest we do, I want to know what the mouth, hand, eye and ear in particular think. Quite simply, I want to know whether those I mentioned want us to have a chance to survive or prefer to die. But before you do, let me make it absolutely clear, we are all dying already! I am becoming weaker and weaker as I speak.'

'Oh,' said the mouth, 'I am getting tired as well, for some time now no food or drink has come through here. The hand is no longer bringing in anything. I am so dry and even struggling to perform my main duty which is to talk all day. Please, I want to live. I don't want to be the special one. What can we do now? I am so tired; I feel I am dying already.'

'I am in the same boat as the mouth,' said the hand. 'I feel I am dying, I am even struggling to lift myself up, let alone clap. Since the leg went on strike and stopped taking me to the farm, shop and kitchen, I have not been able to bring food or drink to the mouth. Please Ms Brain, I want to live, how can I be the special one when I am weak, tired or dead? Please, do something quick! My usual hobby, which is to clap with excitement, I can no longer perform.'

'Ah! I cannot open properly anymore,' says the eye. 'I feel like shutting down even though I desire to stay open and awake. Something has gone terribly wrong with me and I can't find what it is. I suspect it is to do with the actions of the anus and the leg. Please Ms Brain, all I want to do is stay alive. To hell with being the special one! How can I be the special one in this state I am in right now? Please, please, please Ms Brain do something, do something right now! This is very painful and uncomfortable. I just want to be my usual self.'

'Ms Brain,' said the ear, 'I have listened to you very attentively. I simply want to live, thank you! For the humility you have shown, I feel so humbled that you even mentioned me as a source of information. I am in the same boat as all of you, struggling to take in information and at times, feeling as though I am giving up. Please tell me what you think I can do for things to go back to what it used to be. I am all ears.'

'Now,' said the brain, 'it is in humility I thank all of you for appreciating what I have been saying. My words would have meant nothing if they fell on deaf ears. The wise are not only the ones who speaketh wise words but the ones who hear, accept and act wisely. The speaker and doer are important but the doer is more effective, because action is more effective than words. My contributions would count for nothing if you all do not agree because no matter how big, a tree can never be seen or addressed as a forest. Thank you all for giving me the courage to carry on. Though I am feeling tired, your responses have energised me. I want to stress once again that I am nothing without you all. No matter what I achieve as a part of the body, together we achieve more. Just like a broom, singularly we are easily broken but as a bunch, difficult to break.

'Now, before I suggest a plan, I think we need to do a few important things within ourselves individually, and then with each other, in order to be sure there is a bit of life left in us first. This is critical because if one takes care of their thought process, their behaviour would look after itself. No building is ever built without a foundation, for no one can build in thin air. No one runs before they can walk, no tree ever grows without the root, no branch of a tree can survive detached from the tree and of course, there is no plan if we do not have life. Therefore everything we do now, both as individual parts of the body and collectively, will be geared towards our survival first before I suggest my plan.' Furthermore, the brain emphasised:

'Most importantly, we must all be aware that we are now in pursuit of success which is always out there, one must reach and stretch out to stand a chance of getting it; but failure is within, one does not need to do anything or go anywhere to get or keep it. In view of all this, we must act now, we must reach out and eat some humble pie in order to stand a chance of staying alive because success requires a minimum of one hundred

percent effort but failure demands nothing of any of us. This simply means we must positively change course and commit all our effort towards mending fences with each other. This is a minimum requirement in order to stand a chance of survival because, even with the best will in this universe, success is impossible to achieve alone, only failure can one happily achieve alone simply by continuing to do the wrong thing or doing nothing at all.

'On this note,' said the brain, 'I want you all to know that I am not a saint and I am not perfect. I am glad I'm neither because saints and perfect beings neither sin nor make mistakes. And I wonder how I would have learnt any lesson or had any understanding of what is at play here, if I had no shortcomings myself. The issue really is not the mistakes one makes, because we must all make mistakes, but the lessons one learns from their mistakes. By the same token, I hope that none of us, as parts of this body, is perfect or a saint, lest I waste my breath, as stones do not drink water and oranges do not grow from an apple tree.

'In view of all these, may I start by rendering an apology to all of you? You see, all along I foolishly thought that my role was the most important one. In fact, I grandiosely thought I owned the entire body. I apologise unreservedly and profusely to the anus in particular because I was one of those that thought it served little purpose. What is happening to us now is so bad but some good, I hope, will come from it. Though I am not sure how it will all end, I have learnt so much and I hope you all have too. The biggest lesson I have learnt is the fact that I did not choose to be the brain, I happened to be the brain and this applies to all of us. I did not choose my location. I happened to find myself where I found myself and the same goes with the rest of us.

'As important as I thought I was, I suddenly realised how useless I am if the eye, nose and ear fail to supply me with information or give wrong information. As important as I may have thought I was, I am only as good as the weakest link amongst us. Hence, in mathematical terms, one billion multiplied by zero equals zero. I have realised how vulnerable I become when the anus or any one of us stops functioning. I now understand why it takes many to build but only one is enough to destroy. I now also understand how easy it is to start a conflict but the route to peace is so long. This is because no skill is required in order to start conflict and anyone can start a conflict but in order to make peace, a lot of negotiation, compromise and delicate balancing is required and not everyone can do this. No wonder it takes only one bad egg to ruin the rest. No wonder, however many make a choir, it takes only one out of tune chorister to spoil the song. The awesome power of the bad egg! No wonder none of us can be as good as our strongest link but no matter how good our strongest link, it can only be as good as our weakest link. And no wonder the few bad ones always spoil it for the rest because most rules made that end up inconveniencing everyone are usually driven by the few rule breakers.

'In here I notice the heart, lung and kidney for example, have remained silent but I have suddenly realised what great servants each of these various parts are to the body. I am humbled by this experience and therefore apologise profusely. I would like a situation where we all see this as an opportunity to learn and grow. Therefore, no one should really be blamed because we have all gone by what was laid before us. But we all have a great opportunity to be stronger now we understand how important we are to one another. I take my share of responsibility and shame for my ignorance in spite of all I thought I knew. I now know have an idea how my behaviour may have shattered Mr Anus's confidence and damaged its morale.

'My learning came through listening to all of you, but it was Mr Anus's statement, decision and action that taught me the greatest lesson. It made me realise how important each of our roles is and how important these roles are to our shared body, proving that we are all in this and out of this together! That singular act of Mr Anus has held all of us to ransom, showing that the body requires all the parts to function well to be healthy but, in order to be unhealthy, all the body requires is for one part to malfunction. How ironic? No wonder, it is easier to do the wrong thing than do good!

'Doesn't it surprise you all that, for the body to be healthy, all the parts need to function well, but for the same body to be unhealthy all it requires is for only one part to malfunction or stop functioning! I guess we wouldn't be suffering what we are suffering now if the reverse were the case, and all the body needed is for one part to function, to be healthy and malfunction only when all the parts become faulty. As it is, we have to do whatever it takes and leave no stone unturned to get all the parts functioning again, or else from what I can see, we are all doomed. I want to thank you all for showing through the statements some of you made, and silent agreement by others, by not objecting to anything I said that, we are all ready to work toward survival. I can now clearly appreciate that when one presumes superiority over others on any grounds, they only reveal the depth of their profound ignorance, short-sightedness and inept thought process. One cannot be taller and shorter than the other at the same time.

'I will tell you a story about something that happened in a place called China' said the brain. 'Once in a place called China, there was an old man who was about to die. He went to a wise man wanting to know what heaven and hell looked like before he departed. The wise man took the old man to two places. In both places there was plenty of delicious food but no one could reach the food or feed without the use of a very long spoon. The old man initially thought there was no difference between the two places after all. However when the old man took a closer look at the residents of both places he found that in the first place, people were in agony, very skinny and suffering the pain of starvation and malnutrition. They were very sad and frustrated because each person was trying so hard to feed themselves with the long spoon without success. The wise

30

**man told the old man that this is what hell looks
like, and on the other side, everyone was healthy,
well-nourished and happy, because people were
feeding one another with the long spoon. The
wise man told the old man, this is what heaven
looks like. We are in hell now suffering, because
we focused on our individual selves. Now we have
to focus on looking after one another so each of
us can be healthy and hopefully we can all be in
heaven together.'**

'Now,' said the brain, 'I think it is time we all start to
mend fences with each other.' The brain got all the war-
ring factions to apologise to each other and start working
together again. However, the body had become so weak
as a result of the congestion in the stomach. The process was very slow and sluggish when the anus agreed to
commence its work.

The brain then said, 'This little bird is surely the subject matter here. I salute all of you for your courage in
accepting your responsibilities and magnanimity in your
apologies to one another. I remain humbled by this experience. Therefore whatever I say, think or do henceforth,
I pledge to do as a servant to all of you for I did not
elect myself to this position. I am delighted that this is a
common and shared commitment of all of us, judging
from what most of us have said. As you all were talking,
I was listening as well as thinking about this little bird.
Whilst thinking about the little bird, I suddenly realised
that action before thinking is such a bad thing. I feel that
the most important lesson in all of this is not to act hastily in a time of adversity. It is always likely for us to at
times upset one another because none of us is perfect
and we are different. It is okay for us to get angry when
we are offended. However, when such a time arises, we

must exercise patience in order to act correctly. The key is to stop first, think before we act. We must also remember that deciding not to act in anger is also a very positive action in itself. Each time we offend each other, we must learn to stop and think first because it is at such times we are offered an opportunity to learn, share and grow. Acting hastily is what comes naturally and any of us can do it. Therefore, it is not an achievement to do what anyone can do and we end up destroying ourselves in the process.'

'Now,' said the brain, 'This little bird is surely the subject matter here. I know it must be after something. It must be an enemy of ours, seeking to destroy us. It must have realised that we would die by fighting amongst ourselves. For it to have sent us on a wild goose chase is a clear intention to harm us. I have a plan! I know the little bird is after something and surely would come back to check whether we have died. I have a plan!'

'Oh!' said the eye, 'I can see the little bird, it has perched on the tree right in front of us.'

'Okay,' says the Brain, 'as I thought, it has come to see if we have died. I tell you this, if not for Mr Anus agreeing to let off some waste this little bird would have succeeded. Now we must act quickly. As we lie here tired, I want the eye and hand to perform a great duty now in service to all of us. I would like this bird caught so we interrogate it to find out about the game plan. We want to know more because it might not be acting alone. We will go step by step until we deal with it and any other who is involved in this terrible act. Knowing that the leg is still too weak to move about, we will lie here pretending to be dead but it is the bird that will die. I want the eye to pretend it has shut down completely and the hand to be ready to catch the little bird. I want all the other parts to stay still. The little bird is likely to descend and come close to us, to verify if we are dead indeed.'

As the brain spoke, the little bird descended from the tree and hovered around the body. The entire body became and remained motionless as the eye kept watch over the little bird. And suddenly the bird rested on the body and began to walk around the body in the belief that it was dead. The hand managed to catch the little bird by its leg but was still very weak to hold firm. The little bird, as a result, managed to escape. 'Oh no!' exclaimed the hand, 'I couldn't hold firm and it has escaped! Oh no, I am very disappointed!'

'Don't worry,' said the brain, 'It is not your fault. This is how weak we can become when there is a problem with any part of us. You see, what is happening to us now reminds me of a tale from China where a desperate old man who was about to die went to a wise man wanting to know what heaven and hell looked like before he departed. The wise man took the old man to two places. In both places there was plenty of delicious food but no one could reach the food or feed without the use of a very long spoon. The old man initially thought there was no difference between the two places after all. However when the old man took a closer look at the residents of both places he found that in the first place, people were in agony, very skinny and suffering the pain of starvation and malnutrition. They were very sad and frustrated because each person was trying so hard to feed themselves with the long spoon without success. The wise man told the old man that this is what hell looks like, and on the other side, everyone was healthy, well-nourished and happy, because people were feeding one another with the long spoon. The wise man told the old man, this is what heaven looks like. We are in hell now suffering, because we focused on our individual selves. Now we have to focus on looking after one another so each of us can be healthy and hopefully we can all be in heaven together. Let's continue to work on full recovery and when and if we succeed, we can then set a proper agenda to deal with this bird and whosoever is involved in this mission to set us up on a wild goose chase that would have surely killed us.

'I hope we did not do too much damage to ourselves when we were fighting each other, lest the bird succeeds? The greatest achievement here for us is that we have understood that we are all here to serve each other and one another!'

As the bird flew off it feared the worst. It was shocked and thought, 'Oh my word! I chose the wrong plan. I am in big trouble now and this means I am going to die.' It flew back to its nest and it was gripped by fear. It came out of its nest and began to pace around the tree, worried that death was imminent.

As it paced around thinking about going back to the tortoise, the guardian angel appeared again and said, 'I am here once again to help you but I must tell you I don't go on more than two missions. Therefore this is my final one! I was alerted once you began to worry, but I had to come because the great tortoise is not going to be in the same place we found it before, and we cannot afford you having a wasted journey. From the way things stand right now, this may be your last chance. We must get going so you can have enough time to do what you need to do this time and get things right, otherwise your biggest fear might be realised.

'Don't forget, once the journey begins, there will be no discussions, is that all right?' asked the guardian angel.

'Yes, I am just glad to have you here and I cannot wait for us to get going,' replied the little bird.

As the little bird was on its way to find answers from the great tortoise, the brain continued its lecture to the various parts of the body. 'This little bird had only come to bring confusion and plunge us into disarray. However, on a positive note, it has also led us to self-evaluate, helping us to realise our value and limitations. Helping us to understand how unique we are individually and how unique others are. But most importantly, how we cannot exist without each other doing what they do best.

'This has illustrated the fact that the body represents the root and we individually are the branches belonging to the same tree. We all feed from the root and if anything goes wrong with any part of the tree, all the parts of the tree are affected. This little bird has helped us realise that, as important as we are individually, others are if not equally as important more important than our individual selves. We cannot learn much from our individual selves but in others lie things we don't know... things we need to learn in aid of our development. Without one another, we are incomplete and cannot survive. Let's work and wait for our full recovery, unless we have done too much damage to ourselves already. If so, we are all facing an imminent death which would mean that the bird has succeeded. If we recover fully then we will wait for the return of the bird and surely, we will deal with it in one way, shape or form.'

The battle is set; will the bird get what it is looking for from the great tortoise and destroy the body? Will the tortoise tell the bird that it has missed the one and single opportunity? Did the body survive or did the bird die? For debate's sake, which of the body parts gave the most compelling argument as the one that did the most for the body?

The Majestic Toilet Seat

The majestic toilet seat; one of life's reminders of how vulnerable, similar and afflicted all human beings are irrespective of stature, status and differences.

One day, the greatest of all mankind, a man who conquered all the dynasties and empires of this world and triumphed over all the odds to merit the accolade 'The Greatest of all Mankind' named Dike, became very upset about the one thing he had failed to conquer - the toilet seat. Dike was so upset about not only having to answer the call of 'this little thing' called toilet seat but also stooping low before it.

Dike decided to summon the toilet seat before him. He ordered his henchmen to bring the toilet seat to the apex of his mighty building so that it can behold the glory of his majesty, power and authority. Before the arrival of his henchmen and the toilet seat, Dike in his wisdom thought, 'I must not have these henchmen around when I talk to this little thing because I am not sure what gives it the authority to control me and I don't want it to cause me an embarrassment before my henchmen who adore me. I will make it a private matter but try and intimidate that little thing the same way I have dealt with all my enemies. Firstly, I will take it around and show it all the battles I have fought and won. Secondly, I will get it to look outside from this lofty height and behold my kingdom and glory. I am sure this would frighten it but, in case it does not see or understand, I will see if I can negotiate and reach a compromise with it.' He said to himself, 'my late mother warned me to be careful when she said that, if I saw a little bird on the road dancing, I must not disturb it because there must be something supplying the beat to which it is dancing from the bush. My mother also said that, I must consider running if a chicken starts to pursue me in the morning as I am not sure if it grew some teeth overnight. However, regardless of these warnings from my mother, I am hoping that at the end of my meeting with that little thing, it will understand how important I am and, at the very least, agree to stop calling me the way it does.'

Dike went on, 'I feel very upset because no one and nothing else does this to me. Just the other day, as I was having an important meeting, and at the most critical point, that little thing summoned me and I had to excuse myself from such an important meeting before all the dignitaries and guests. What an embarrassment! This must end today and, if the stupid thing disagrees, then I will summon all my advisers and wise people to come up with the strategy to sort it out once and for all!'

When the henchmen brought the toilet seat, Dike did as he planned; dispatched his henchmen and went into negotiation having taken the toilet seat around and used all his tactics to frighten it; he made the toilet seat aware of what it did and the embarrassment it caused him before his very important guests 'the other day' as he explained it. Dike then presented the toilet seat with an opportunity to address the issues he had raised. The toilet seat responded, 'I am aware of your importance, sir. You see, you are a very strong man and full of wisdom and I respect you a lot for all that. I thank you, sir, for bringing the little me before you and making me aware of the discomfort I have inflicted on you, I am ever so sorry. I feel I should go and ask 'my *Oga* at the top' (my master at the top) before I can respond to you, sir. But knowing my *Oga* at the top, he would only agree to one compromise, which I will offer you now.'

'Oh... my dear, wait!' said Dike who was full of delight when he heard the word 'compromise' from the toilet seat, 'I... forgot to offer you something when you arrived. Please, before you say what the compromise would be, let me call my servants to get you whatever takes your fancy... I mean whatever takes your fancy. There is nothing beyond me, so please; you name it and consider it done.'

'No sir,' said the toilet seat, 'I am never in need of anything because everyone including you feeds me on a daily basis and you all feed me with the only thing that takes my fancy, so please sir, you must not worry.'

'Okay,' said Dike, 'Let me then hear the compromise you are offering.'

'Thank you sir,' said the toilet seat, 'I want you to know, sir, that I am at your service and I have this role to offer to everyone irrespective of their status, gender, creed or race; but being that you are 'the greatest' of them all, as you have shown me today, I offer you myself as I am. You can turn me into gold, silver, bronze, you can also turn me into a bucket, road or bush. I wouldn't mind. However, there are certain things I would not allow you to do. I want to spell those out to you right now. At your peril would you not answer my call or fail to bare all and stoop low when I engage you! If you fail to answer, refuse to undress and stoop low, I will generate the ultimate embarrassment and humiliation to you, I am sorry to say.'

The toilet seat went on, 'other things you must be aware of include: when I engage you just like anyone else, I expect to engage you alone. I will reduce and nullify your ability to issue orders or control anyone until I have finished with you. I expect you to attend on your own but, if you come with someone else, I would understand that to mean that you may be unable to help yourself and in need of someone to assist you. The only thing is, if you are conscious, you may suffer some embarrassment due to the presence of a third party in a two party business. You see, I am very jealous. You cannot come to me as the 'greatest' or an 'important' person. You must come to me as an individual with some vulnerability. You must come as you are because I will not only make you bare all, but I will also bring you down from whatever lofty height you have placed yourself or people have placed you. Lest I forget, talking about guests, for your information everyone is my guest: the young, old, high, low, powerful and the mighty. Being an important person, you only have important guests but as you value your important guests so I value all my guests, irrespective of their background. I want you to know that I like all my guests to be treated with respect. Therefore, after answering my call, I want you to look back and wait in readiness to ensure that you leave me the way you would like to find me when next I call you. This is something you need to do as a sign of respect for yourself, my other guests and for me. I expect all my guests, young and old, to do the same. If you fail to do so and leave without checking and making sure that you haven't left something behind, it will show that you have no respect for yourself, my guests and my humble self. Therefore you may, at some point, suffer some form of embarrassment for such dirty behaviour.

'Finally,' the toilet seat continued, 'I don't want you to take this personally because I don't discriminate on any grounds. I am called the Majestic Toilet Seat because I am the true Greatest, for your information. My dear good friends, the grave and crematorium share something in common with me. However, in my last meeting with them, I convinced them and they now acknowledge me as simply the GREATEST! You see, everyone (including you) account to one of them but no one can go to both of them at the same time. They only engage each individual once and only at the exit door. Their engagement is when people are unconscious and literary dead. Therefore they cannot embarrass anyone. Furthermore, not everyone can come to them because some people's dead bodies may not be found, some may be eaten by wild animals and whoever goes to one will not go to the other. But with me, everyone comes to me. I operate in between entry and exit points and everyone is subject to my call and there is nothing you can do about it. I deal with everyone when they are conscious and I don't intervene just once in someone's life like my dear good friends, the grave and crematorium. I constantly engage with everyone throughout their lifetime and I don't discriminate. I have no fear and I don't favour anyone. I am a servant; I serve as a reminder to everyone of their vulnerability and mortality.'

The toilet seat continued, 'The most important thing is that everyone alive must attend and answer my call. I am the Greatest of all levellers, there is none beside me. Nevertheless, I value and appreciate the work my dear good friends do too, which I am not able to do. It is only with humility I was able to appreciate that, though I am extremely useful, my friends are also useful because they do things I am unable to do. I am not sure if you under-stand what humility means? Perhaps, I need to advise you to ensure that you value, even the least in your midst because, that is the beginning of wisdom. The beginning of the downfall of an individual, community or nation stems from when one can only see themselves and no one else. When one sees themselves as all important and believes that they can learn nothing from the least in their midst, they lose out and display their immense limitation and stupidity. If you cannot see a bit of you in someone else, you are as good as deluded, I must tell you, sir'

Dike was outraged and disappointed at hearing all this from 'the little toilet seat' and ordered his henchmen to remove it from his presence. He very quickly summoned all the wise men and women under his jurisdiction and commanded them to come up with a plan as to how to deal with the toilet seat. He made them a promise that he would give any of them who comes up with a solution whatever they requested of him. He also warned them that failure to come up with a plan will result in dire consequences for all of them. The wise people requested of Dike to grant them a fortnight to think through his request and come up with a plan. Their request was granted and they dispersed. Is it not obvious here that Dike has no clue what humility means? It will be interesting to see what happens next when his wise people return in a 'fortnight' with or without a plan.

The Two Metaphorical Buildings Existing In Human Life

It will virtually be impossible for the 'brain' to come in with humility without its appreciation of these buildings. Everything that has gone wrong in our world stems from the interplay between these two metaphoric buildings. In order to conquer one must stoop low.

In our world and in human life, two figurative houses exist. These houses need to be properly analysed, appreciated and understood. When this is done, human beings will discover that serious work needs to be carried out on both houses but particularly the second building in order to get a bit of a balance. This balance would help find a solution to all the elements that have consigned our world to the perpetual fight for supremacy, honour and everlasting life; sold to them by the 'little bird' with its own hidden, ambitious and unrealistic agenda. The analysis needs to be done for our world to notice some real progress (for the first time) since time immemorial.

Everyone is encouraged to examine these metaphorical buildings as described by someone who was brought up in one of the world's largest families, where one man had 32 wives (which must never be encouraged in today's world), someone who grew up with at least 60 other children growing up at any given time. Someone who had lived and seen the two ends of the spectrum, having lived in the most deprived and affluent parts of the world. Someone who knows that squirrels may look like squirrels everywhere in the world but, in one part of the world squirrels hide from human beings while in another part, they are not afraid to play in front of human beings. Someone who is a failed seminarian, as he aborted priesthood because he did not feel he had the calling. Someone who has seen that even in the same judicial system two different rules can apply to the same subject matter (as at August 2013, in Surrey County Council, warrants under Section 135 of the Mental Health Act 1983 (as amended by the 2007 Mental Health Act) can be obtainable free of charge but in London, one pays £18 for the same warrant), someone who has worked in the social care industry (across many client groups), in different Local Authorities for over two decades and someone who remains a student at the University of Life with no possibility of graduation, to mention but a few.

It is worth noting, though, that in the game of life, **wisdom is not synonymous with, or a commodity of, any age, gender, race, creed or culture. Yours could be the invention, mine could be to better the invention and others might be to perfect the work. Those who invented football many, many years ago are not today's football world champions. Therefore sharing and learning from one another should be the desire of all mankind because similarities may only bring mutual understanding but differences are key to the mix required for human learning, sharing and growth. Nothing can ever be called food as a singular ingredient but through a mixture of more than one ingredient, food is served. Therefore no**

one should restrict themselves by focussing solely on what they are familiar with. Exploration, understanding and celebration of differences are key to the real advancement in human emotional development. No one should lock themselves up with the devil they know in fear of the unknown angel begging to come in.

First Building

The first house is where human ingenuity in terms of science and technology resides. This house is well developed and has been turned into a skyscraper. In this house, human beings have seen the transforming achievements from gliders to supersonic jets, animal propelled wheels (horses pulling carts) to unmanned automobile vehicles, telegrams and gramophones to highly sophisticated mobile phones capable of detonating bombs, analogue to digital sets, manually controlled to remote controlled and laser-guided bombs, typewriters to voice controlled and touchscreen high-powered computer/internet systems containing all sorts of information (including how to make a bomb), and the ability to interact with anyone across the globe with relative ease and privacy guaranteed with individualised passwords.

This house contains all the latest gadgets, mobile phones, laptops, tablets, chemical and biological weapons, illicit substances, alcohol, knives, guns and bombs of all kinds. These and more are placed at our fingertips, giving human beings quick access to generate both good and bad. This house has turned the world into a global village and connected human beings like never before. It has also exposed human beings to a world that would, at the very least, be unrecognisable to our ancestors, were they to return. The achievement made in this particular building was as a result of bold decisions made by human beings at various levels to uproot some old foundations, once there was the realisation that they were faulty. Human beings, in the main, were and are still committed to uprooting anything that hinders progress in this building once identified, for example, fictions and shadow-chasing such as voodoo, witchcraft or anything that could not be objectively evidenced had to be put to one side and replaced by scientific evidence-based structures which helped in producing this skyscraper we are seeing now. Time and effort spent on chasing shadows were then spent on evidence-based functional systems geared towards improving life and infrastructures. Emotion and sentiments have limited roles to play in this building; the head is primarily in charge, not the heart.

Human beings are more open minded and willing to offer, receive and share information and ideas in this house. For example, when one is ill and in need of treatment, there is no hesitation in accepting treatment believed to provide cure, irrespective of who is providing or delivering it. If someone, irrespective of status, creed, race or gender were to invent an absolute cure for cancer, the entire human race would delight, accept and welcome it with open arms and everyone would want to associate themselves with it and even try to claim to have contributed to the achievement. There would be no rejection, ignoring or demeaning of the achievement based on the inventor's background. The same applies if one was to invent a gigantic parachute capable of holding an out-of-control aircraft, ensuring a gentle landing instead of a massive crash, everyone is likely to welcome and celebrate the achievement without questioning where the inventor came from. Everyone would most likely want to associate themselves with the inventor and people across the world would then not only install the parachute in their aircrafts, but would seek to learn the intricacies of the technology surrounding it, with a view to improving and making it better for safety and commercial purposes.

However in this house, there is an intense competition going on which is at times unhealthy and engenders trade war between individuals, communities and nations. Many seek to steal other peoples' technology and then develop, mass produce and even sell them at a cheaper rate. No matter the bad seeds sown or picked up, as human beings develop from childhood based on differences; these differences are usually ignored when one is in trouble or needing to be rescued in this building. At that point all the individual is likely to know is the relief and a rescuer. Any hatred based on differences will disappear for that moment.

In this house adventure is encourage, because it does not only bolster people's image, it also boosts their bank balance. As a result, all manner of things that attract the eyes, body and soul are not only being produced but also regularly upgraded in this house. The name of the game in this house is 'What is the latest?' Hardly would six months pass without the hint of or an actual upgrade to one gadget or the other. This is where **money and materialism live!** All the achievements in this house had come about through sheer hard work in the knowledge propelled by nurture.

Nature's role here is very minor, but very critical especially as it relates to 'top dog', just like in the animal kingdom. This has driven human beings to extreme level of competition, acquisition and 'winner takes all' syndrome. This has now become the biggest threat to our very existence, in view of what is on offer in the second house described below. The relentless quest to 'win' and 'take all' has led humanity to, at times, compete without reservation and in most cases with only one notion in mind: the weight of the bank balance. There is no genuine thought given to how the content of the product produced could impact on a child negatively. Apart from this selfish drive, nature cannot afford to make any of the things available in this particular building, as nature cannot afford to brush the teeth let alone, make a toothbrush.

This building is scary to behold because enterprise, adventure and working together in partnership with a persistent urge to produce the ultimate is encouraged. The brain is consistently doing its work from both negative and positive perspectives. The biggest danger when one looks at this building as a vehicle (in a metaphoric sense) is that; it does not seem to have a break or reverse gear. Therefore serious crisis could be looming. The products available in this building include chemicals and biological weapons for mass destruction. This should lead us to the question: are these weapons for mass destruction of trees, plants or items? Can we ponder even further: who and what controls this building and where is this building heading to? Let us find out, shall we?

Second Building

This second building is where human beings' deep-seated emotions, in terms of feelings and social interactions, reside. Emotion is known to be often very irrational and extremely sensitive and sentimental. It often has no rhyme or rhythm. It is simply based on feelings. Though emotion in itself is not a bad thing and can be useful in terms of human beings being able to relate to one another in an empathetic way in good and bad situations, emotion can also be excessive, overbearing, immature and dangerously passionate.

Therefore emotion needs to be regulated and controlled due to the dangers it can often pose and extreme damage it can cause and generate. In this house, facts and objectivity rarely feature, in other words, emotion can be extremely subjective and childlike with huge emphasis on the 'here and now' immediate gratification against planned, delayed and sustained satisfaction. The little picture determines the bigger one in this building. Raw emotion in this building has led human beings to subscribe to the notion that it can only be right, proper and wise if I or we are doing or saying it, but wrong and unwise when you or they are doing or saying the same or similar thing.

Here, looking at the world in a metaphorical sense, as a football team, people have preconceived ideas as to the player(s) they would pass the ball to, and receive the ball from; irrespective of the adverse impact it would have on the team.

Imagine giving the ball to a midfielder far away behind you when it is easier to pass the football to a striker in a good position to score. The reason for not passing to the striker being that he or she is not one of those you prefer to give and receive the football from.

In this building, the little bird is in action instigating individuals, families, communities and nations that are supposed to be working and bringing their differences together for the good of the world to instead, fight for supremacy, everlasting life and honour. The predominant ethos and culture here revolve around the 'me, myself and I', 'me versus you' and 'us versus them' with cliques, 'old boy and old girl', 'closing of ranks', 'holier than thou' and mob rule mentality serving as king. The greed, selfishness and mistrust which engender the desire to cheat, steal and hoard; the negative stereotype perception of differences which creates the agenda of hate and propels the motive to extinguish what is different; the intense ignorance linked to mankind's shared similarities, which prevents harmony and denies human beings the experience of a healthy world; the insatiable appetite for power, control, dominance which propel the negative craft in human beings; the overwhelming desire for division and separation; these have never left human beings. The idea that it can only be allowed if 'I or we' should have it, not 'you or they', because 'I or we' are the special and good ones and 'you or they' are the inferior and bad ones. Human beings have continuously looked in the wrong places for genuine answers to their common issues; ascribing success which should be shared to self and failure which is individually owned to others.

In this building, human beings are quick to brush aside anything that does not look, think or speak like them, forgetting that one cannot gain much from themselves or people who think, reason and speak like them. People fail to appreciate that no matter how hopeless someone may seem, there is something different in that person that offers an opportunity for learning and growth. Even the wisest learns how not to be stupid from the foolish. This is because one cannot be taller and shorter than another all at the same time and the part of the jigsaw one is looking for may be located in someone totally different and unknown.

In this building people are often afraid of what others may be up to or are planning to do. The intense fear stems from one's awareness of one's own negative capabilities, which forces people not to trust themselves or their own friends, let alone their perceived enemies.

The personal, community and national interest agenda located in this house, has caused this immature emotion to act like the little bird seeking at all times to instigate wars, crisis and confusion in the hope for the benefit of 'everlasting' life, freedom and comfort. This emotional game has overshadowed good sense of judgement as human beings justify the slaughter of fellow human beings, women, babies and believe the overall 'gain' outweighs the loss of lives, 'the body' and the world we all share. The world that was here before our arrival and is likely to remain after our departure.

This game has remained so because across the world, human beings have struggled to tackle the faulty foundation laid by their ancestors and propelled by natural animalistic instincts, 'survival of the fittest, winner takes all, I or we are the top dog, you and they are the underdog, he who dares wins.' All the jungle justice theories are in operation in this building.

All human beings have done in this building is, at best, paper over the cracks with minor adjustment, and, at worst, advanced the tactics so that much damage can occur without trace in this 'hide and seek' immature emotional game, whilst continuing to build on faulty foundation.

Hence today, in spite of outlawing slavery many years ago, human beings are still engaged in 'modern day slavery'. And across the world, wars and conflicts are raging and brewing on. Human beings have continuously promulgated propaganda, used coveted craft and 'national interest' ideologies to pursue selfish agendas detrimental to others within the same body (our world). This is likened to the mouth depriving the rest of the body in order to eat alone, in its weird hope that it can survive independent of the rest of the body parts.

Human beings have continuously papered over the cracks in this building which suggests that, there is unconscious or conscious awareness that the foundation of this second building is shaky, but everyone seems to be afraid to tackle it, in fear that it might collapse completely. The positive aspects obtainable in the skyscraper are severely lacking in this building. Raw and undeveloped emotions have made things so bad in this building that many individuals, families, communities and some nations believe that the only way to get what they want at the expense of others is by creating or inducing conflict.

They forget that creating conflict is not an achievement. Momentary 'gain' out of the suffering of others does not translate into permanent gain and any 'benefit' gained through conflict just generates more and more conflict. Furthermore, scattering and destroying in order to gain are only gifts of nature; anyone can do it and in metaphorical terms, it is like a thief who decides to start a fire in an electronic shop to engender confusion and chaos so that they can steal the items they couldn't afford.

The thief's primary and sole interest is what they would obtain; very little or no thought is given to the possible permanent damage to the property, loss of lives and human suffering. The fact that they may be caught is usually secondary. The thief forgets that starting a fire is the easy part but knowing how far the fire would spread and the extent of damage it would cause is the difficult part. Raw and negative emotions present in this building prevent such a thief from thinking of a positive way to earn the item which would have a long-term benefit to them and the owners of the shop instead of the quick, here and now, grab and go short-term unsustainable 'gain' and destruction.

In the first building people are more open-minded, whereas in this second building, people's minds are often locked up with preconceived ideas propelled by nature. Just like other animals, here human beings are very territorial and at times not even willing to take advice on what could ultimately save their lives (so long as they feel physically well) because they have, already, stereotypically summed up the individual giving the advice.

As a result, the second building continues to fall apart. In this building people are quick to run to conclusions without looking at details of the message, as they narrow their minds down to how 'academically educated', or query the gender, creed or ethnicity of the bearer of the message.

Suggesting that they have to be of 'a kind' in order to possess what is required but how can one know the length of a string if they have not seen, held and measured the string? By assumptions human beings have missed out on a lot that would have improved this building because, as parts of a jigsaw puzzle, human beings are struggling to pull together and function properly as a unit.

The problem and irony is, although this building has not gone far beyond the foundation level, and is disintegrating, it is more powerful than the first 'skyscraper'. What happens in this undeveloped house decides and controls what happens in the skyscraper. The real problem lies with the fact that, this building has degenerated and its foundations have at best remained the same.

However, human beings have equipped and continue to equip the skyscraper with more dangerous gadgets which are more readily available for use. Technology has brought the world closer, making it easier to destroy. This, coupled with the fact that human emotions have remained at an infant level, can be likened to placing a fully loaded machine gun in the hands of a five year old. This, consequently, lends credence to the suggestion that human beings are never going to be overrun by dangerous animals, natural disaster or aliens from Mars but are very likely to implode, unless the brain comes in quickly with humility to save the day. Anyone who thoroughly analyses the interplay between these two houses would draw, if not that exact opinion, similar conclusions.

If the ancestors of this world were to return today, it would be very unlikely for them to recognise the first building but they are likely to be overwhelmed with shock at the fact that the foundation of the second building is decaying. They are likely to be overwhelmed with shock at the disaster going on within it. They are likely to be more afraid when they consider what may lie ahead in view of how this immature, undeveloped building controls every-thing going on in the skyscraper. The fact is the skyscraper now contains many dangerous gadgets and items, capable of kick-starting mayhem anywhere around the world in an instant, due to the speed at which information spreads, and with an ability to detonate bombs with mobile phones which almost everyone obtains plus so much more.

In this house, the various parts of the body have been, are still and would remain at war with each other, fighting for supremacy, honour and everlasting existence, which are far-fetched in real terms. The competition, the jos-tling for position, the fight to acquire the latest from the skyscraper (wants continuing to outstrip needs) has almost become a 'do or die' affair. There is immense contest and wide divisions between the haves and have-nots, the need to have more, the need to 'catch up or overtake' and the need to survive plus deferring religious factions, cultural and ethnicity crisis, 'I, mine or ours is the best' and 'you, yours or theirs are the worst'. All these driven by raw emotion, are putting the skyscraper with all the explosives and lethal gadgets in it at risk of crashing and wiping out everyone in this undeveloped emotional building where all human beings reside.

In this building, raw emotions have led and continue to lead some individuals and groups to go into a 'pact' with

'God' and based on this, subjectively 'justify' brainwashing, launching attacks and eliminating their fellow human
beings. Some nations have formulated laws and ideologies
driven by emotions, sentiments and fear to 'justify' and
launch attacks on fellow human beings.

In families, communities and nations of this world,
raw emotions have at times led human beings to tolerate or turn a blind eye from within to what they cannot
tolerate from outside. In this building, individuals, communities and nations have at times tolerated or turned a
'blind eye' to bad deeds carried out by those perceived as
'our own', on similar issues they cannot condone or tolerate from others 'your own.' For example, some husbands
ignore what they cannot tolerate from their wives when
they witness the same actions in their mothers, daughters
or sisters. Some wives cannot tolerate from their husbands
what they ignore when the same is done by their fathers,
sons and brothers. Some countries cannot tolerate what
another country is doing which they themselves are doing.
The collective parts of the human family, 'the body' that
ought to be working together, maximising their individual
and peculiar strengths and pulling together in one accord
for the health of the world, have continued to work against
each other and themselves, producing a very unstable and
dangerous world. The brain at various levels, in individuals, families, communities and nations, very quickly needs
to get into gear and devise a means of getting to the root
cause of our world's problem.

In this building, subjectivity, fiction and fantasy are king,
hence parents are at times the last to appreciate how bad
their children have become. It is also the reason human
beings, in the main, delight in not just revenge but revenge
in an unequal measure. At times the raw emotions of
human beings lead them to revenge in the 'third person',

as a man whose wife nags all the time is likely to agree and offers support for another man who claims on the grounds of stereotype that his wife always nags, even though there is evidence to the contrary. As a result, human beings revere the few who are able to forgive, the few who forsake revenge in pursuit of peace. Nelson Mandela is an example. He was not revered around the world primarily because of his suffering, fighting for justice and freedom or because he was made to waste 27 years of his life in prison. He was revered primarily because in spite of all he went through, when he was presented with the opportunity to seek and pursue revenge, he chose to go the other way and chose the path of peace, reconciliation and unity of mankind. This is not synonymous with human emotion.

The same can be said of Lee Rigby's family, who quelled the brewing storm as natural feelings of revenge filled the air when Lee was brutally murdered on the 'peaceful' streets of London having survived the raging war in Afghanistan. Lee's family were quick to release a statement: 'We would like to emphasise that Lee would not want people to use his name as an excuse to carry out attacks against others. We would not wish any other families to go through this harrowing experience and appeal to everyone to keep calm and show their respect in a peaceful manner.' In the main, these are not natural, normal human reactions to pain inflicted by another person, so when anyone rises above the pain and takes the moral high ground, human beings acknowledge it with a degree of appreciation and respect. This is a moral high ground not offered by nature but by thought, through a nurtured sound upbringing. It is hoped that everyone involved in Jack's (Lee's son) life contributes in planting the seeds of love and uproot those of hate which naturally would germinate when he has full appreciation of the facts surrounding his father's death.

Imagine what would happen if victims sat in judgement in terms of prescribing punishment for those who offend them? Life imprisonment or even a death sentence could be prescribed as a punishment for a slap. This is how irrational emotion can be.

In this building, one discovers how human beings relate to one another. Their interpersonal, intertribal, interracial, intergender, interreligious and international relationships reside in this house. Nature is the overriding factor in this house and nurture hasn't had a real look in since time immemorial. The heart is primarily in charge here, not the head. Though certain progress has been made in this building it is not only slow in coming, it is also superficial in nature.

Leaving a place physically does not mean departing from the place if, emotionally, one is still linked to that place. In fact, depending on how one views this house, it seems to have degenerated because human emotions have remained the same, coupled with the fact that in the first building a lot of equipment has been devised helping human beings to facilitate their hatred in a covert way by use of 'acceptable' language, masking of identities and availability of faster ways to circulate information and execute dangerous plans. All these have empowered human beings to generate mayhem in a more sophisticated, discreet and devastating way with greater impact than ever.

In this house there are so many bubbles and exclusion zones which can be likened to various parts of the body cutting themselves off from the rest of the body, constantly in battle for supremacy with each other, or withholding their particular services to the body like the anus. In this house, oppressors and the oppressed have always featured. Hatred and attacks on anything different are the order of the day. Human beings have sought to promulgate the agenda of unification of ideology, especially in religious terms, without understanding and appreciating that the values each denomination or persuasion has is based on the differences on show. The manipulators and manipulated have always been visibly present (acting like the little bird) in this building and working against the body (our world) itself.

In order to observe raw emotion at its best in this building, simply arrange a conference or gathering of different ethnicities, cultures and creeds, then observe human beings at work naturally, as individuals divide along family, gender, creed and racial lines even though their best deals may lie with the one on the opposite side. How are they to know this, if they are fixated on the devil they know?

The quest to obtain some of the things in the skyscraper has led to emotion running riot in this building, to the extent that many have even killed their closest and dearest. How many times have we seen or heard about someone killing or hiring assassins to kill their partner in order to claim their insurance money? Remembering the words of the Vicar at All Saints, Edmonton in London, Reverend Stuart Owen, in one of his sermons: 'In my work as a priest, I have had the privilege and opportunity to preside over many funerals. I can stand as a witness in confirming that, in some cases, the saying "Where there is a will, there is a way" has been turned into "Where there is a will, there is a war!" as families that are supposed to come together and support one another at the most difficult time of losing a loved one go into war with one another over a will.'

Things have become so bad in this building that, in a

particular part of our world described below as 'world's most uninhabitable place', human beings have managed to rise above the serenity of death, to view the death of their fellow human beings as an 'opportunity' to commit heinous crime against the bereaved. The attractions in the first building coupled with the raw emotions in the second building have led some parents to focus on academia alone without moral values. These parents have no clue that academic education only enables people to add up, divide, subtract and multiply but never equips one with the ability to share. They do not know that individuals who boast of academia without moral values are like a beautiful place of worship with demon worshippers, as their only interest is 'me, myself and I'.

This is why there are many 'fat cats' today, happy to be offered and accept millions of pounds in bonuses whilst many people in the same establishment cannot afford to pay for the roof over their children's heads. These fat cats at times have the cheek to justify their self-fixation by 'make believe' statements such as, 'The country would be deprived of high calibre Chief Executives and Directors as people would leave for greener pastures elsewhere.' But who truly is responsible for the success of Chief Executives and Directors? The men and women on the shop floor! The self has become so dominant that human beings are starved of peace and harmony because each person, community and nation is only interested in feeding themselves with the metaphorical 'long spoon', located in hell as described by the brain above.

The little bird has sent human beings in this building on a wild goose chase. As a result, people have gone into war against people they ought to be working together in partnership with for the good of everyone. The term 'ethnic cleansing', tribal and intertribal conflicts and in some cases 'religious' wars are all located in this building. What is not to be underestimated is the huge influence and impact of latest gadgets in the first building on this second one which was highlighted during the 2011 London riots. Looters never broke into places of worship and libraries. They chose locations where all the latest gadgets could be found. The incessant human quest for the latest gadgets and the need to grab, steal, amass and hoard resources, mainly money or anything in the skyscraper that can generate money, which offers a route to almost all the other items in the skyscraper, is overwhelming.

Yes, there may be laws prohibiting the trading of human beings but today there are baby factories and human trafficking going on across the globe. To the extent that, after abolishing slave trade in 1833, in December 2013 Great Britain introduced the 'Modern Day Slavery Bill'. Legislation is good, however it has its huge limitations as it is only reactive and therefore plays a second fiddle to the underlying problem.

Legislation can only deal with leaves, branches and at best the stem, legislation can never deal with the root cause of any problem in this building. Apartheid may have gone physically but emotionally it is still around and within us. No one leaves a place completely, if emotionally they are still there! The killing of twins in some cultures has ceased, the killing of people in the name of witchcraft may have been outlawed and stopped in some places and in some areas multicultural co-existence has been encouraged. However, trading of babies, including 'miracle babies', promised and delivered in some churches, kidnappings, hostage taking, ethnic cleansing, terrorism, killing of children in the false belief that they are witches or possessed by evils spirits and, human beings' hatred of whatever they consider different are still with us presently and booming.

In this building, multicultural co-existence may seem a great idea but without proper emotional development and understanding that, one cannot be tall unless there is a short person within; this is likely to amount to a recipe for disaster. Multicultural co-existence can only work well where there are 'feel good' factors for example, the economy is doing well, the national football team are performing well and there is no pressure on social amenities like housing, healthcare and education. In fact nations are known to encourage migration when in need of sustenance or growth for all sorts of reasons. It is very rare for migrants to be praised or seen as contributors, let alone pivotal to the good state of any nation even when it is very obvious. Immature emotion would rarely ascribe any credit to the contributions of minority ethnic groups within any society but wait for something to go wrong, for example unemployment, housing, increase in crime, economic downturn or any political unrest. See how quickly raw emotions start apportioning blame on those perceived to be different and at times with dire consequences as witnessed in Uganda, Kenya and many other places.

Nations have been known to enact laws in order to expel and forcibly remove foreigners. For example in 1969, Ghana enacted the 'Aliens Compliance Order' and in 1983 Nigeria enacted the 'Explosion Order' which brought about the catchphrase 'Ghana Must Go!'. In both case these were mechanisms used to flush out those perceived as creating whatever negative climate existed in the particular nation. This raw emotion has no barrier when it comes to human beings and their social interactions. Even in England where massive strides have been made and multicultural co-existence is encouraged and 'celebrated', traces of immature emotion often rear its head. Consider the fact that England throughout history has only won the World Cup once and that was in 1966, since the inception of the competition in the late 1920s. They have never won the European Nations Cup since the tournament began in 1958. However, the influx of foreign players began following the inaugural Premier League season in early 1990s. In spite of these facts, the undeveloped and irrational emotions of some people have led them to believe that the failure of England in international football is directly linked to the number of foreign players playing in England. There is no evidence to show that England had been performing well and winning trophies until the influx of foreign players in the early 90s. In fact, the influx of foreign players has benefited the premier league and helped in the quality development of English players. It goes without saying that when one plays with someone better than them, they learn some new playing techniques. The problem with poor performance in international tournaments has everything to do with coaching at the grass root level in England and nothing to do with influx of foreign players. This immature emotion is so childish and can be so extreme that at times it can cause the teeth to bite off the hand that feeds it, as was the case in Uganda, Zimbabwe, Kenya and many other places across the globe.

Here is the story of Harjit Bansal, a Kenyan born Asian, in her own words.

'I was born in Kenya, to parents who migrated from India. My grandfather, who was born in India (in Punjab), came to Kenya to work as one of the skilled workers required to build the first railway line at the time, under British rule. As this was a long-term project,

he decided to carry on living in Kenya and was later joined by my grandmother and four of her siblings. My grandparents had eight children (five girls and three boys). The four older children were girls and were married in India before my grandmother migrated to join my grandfather in Kenya.

I am one of three siblings, and was educated in Kenya in a Catholic School. In those days, the missionary schools were considered to have strict discipline and good education. Kenya was my only home. We hardly visited India or any other country. In fact, my first visit to India was when I was six years of age. We went as a family, having had to carry out a bereavement ceremony for my grandfather in Kenya before we could visit the family in India. We travelled in a passenger ship and remarkably that was the last passenger ship in the history of Kenya.

Kenya was my home, and most of the heritage in terms of cultural norms and values I inherited from my community in Kenya. The values around dignity, community spirit, love and respect are part of my cultural and religious heritage. These are still part and parcel of me. I remain proud of these values and heritage that have helped in defining me as a person, daughter, sister, auntie, wife and above all a mother. Whilst growing up in Kenya, I was very much part of the African community. However, things dramatically changed, and there came a time when the actions of others brought to my attention for the first time in my life that I was different... that I had assumed wrongly and my beliefs around being a Kenyan were 'false'. Without having any part to play in the matter, I was brutally made aware of this in no uncertain fashion.

In 1982, Kenya witnessed the first coup, in an attempt to overthrow the government of then President, Daniel Arap Moi. A group of military personnel from the Kenyan Armed Forces took over the communication channels and announced that they had overthrown the government of Arap Moi. This caused commotion in parts of Kenya, where people went onto the streets to initially celebrate this. However, there was rumour that this celebration had turned into a

*vendetta against Asian people, who were considered to be much bet-
ter-off economically, owning shops, houses, businesses and jobs in the
city, Nairobi. We also got news that the looting had extended from
looting shops to looting people's homes, rape, beatings and in some
instances, killings.*

*I recall my grandmother gathering us all together. We lived in a
Veranda (open space), with 6 other families. She asked us to have
plates full of red chillies that we were to use, when 'whoever they
were' – came to our house, and use the chilli to blind them. She said
it is not if they come, it is when they come! As it was rumoured that
women were being raped, she asked all the women and girls to hide
in the water tank at the top of the roof. In Kenya, we had houses
with large water tanks that were filled when there was a supply of
water, and the majority of the time, these tanks were empty, due to
shortage of water supply. Luckily, the water tank had been empty
for a couple of weeks. So that was exactly what we did: when
we heard the banging and breaking of doors, my mother and the
rest of the girls all hid in the water tank until the commotion was
over downstairs. They searched and couldn't find us. We were all
petrified, I couldn't say how long we were in the water tank for in
panic, but it seemed like ages and was extremely scary. When we
eventually came out, we were confronted by total devastation these
bandits had caused, our hearts were broken but we remained grateful for our lives; but all our belongings and valuables had gone. We
had nothing left. My grandmother informed us that the people who
looted our belongings were people we knew. People who were our
friends and comrades! These were our gardeners, the cleaners, the
security guard, the woman who brought us vegetables every morning, the man who collected old tins and newspapers, the man who
owned the kiosk down the road, the woman who roasted maize cobs
at the end of the road and… these were people we considered our
people, but they turned against us due to political instability, envy
and because they perceived us to be different. We had done nothing
wrong other than worked hard as citizens and helped in sustaining*

the economy of Kenya. We hadn't prevented anyone from working hard in contribution to the same goal.

The shock of feeling a stranger in a place I had always known as home depressed and confused me as a child. The psychological trauma and shock, I couldn't put into words. I cried but couldn't describe my emotions as I felt so vulnerable, always looking over my shoulder and waiting for the next instruction to rush for cover. I had nightmares then and to this day, all those images have not totally left me. My lifetime brothers and sisters, my kinsmen and women, had suddenly become foes. I didn't know who to play with any more, my home, my streets and my place had become a place of terror to me.'

This is the voice of Harjit Bansal who is the Equality & Diversity Manager (London Integrated Care Directorate), North East London Foundation Trust. A true reflection of the dangers of multicultural co-existence without well nurtured emotional growth and development. In order for multicultural co-existence which is what the world needs to flourish, every individual, family, community and nation needs to self-identify, recognise its peculiar attributes, be it strong and independent. But then, just like the various parts of the body each person, community and nation need to bring their peculiar attributes in one accord for the service of the 'body' our world.

In Summary

The real advancement of humankind and the posterity of the world will not be fully achieved through human ingenuity, in terms of science and technology. Though science and technology have done wonders to humanity and turned what was once a mere foundation into a sky-scraper; they have also proven to be capable of generating and instigating the demise of human beings. Humanity needs to realise that, this building has become extremely hazardous because, the propelling factors here primarily are academia and materialism. Humanity has built beautiful roads and superb vehicles here but it is the quality of the drivers that will determine what happens on these roads.

The real advancement and posterity of humankind can only be achieved with the development of human emotions, in terms of their social interactions in the second building. This is unlikely to occur until humanity understands and claims ownership of the fact that, no colour will exist if there is only one colour, no creed will exist if only one religious group existed and there will be nothing called gender if only women or men existed on their own. Here humanity is desperate for the quality drivers that will reasonable use the great but hazardous inventions in the skyscraper wisely and productively. The unfortunate thing here is that, humanity still wants to depend on academia and materialism to yield these humane and well trained drivers. Looking at our world metaphorically as a tree, humanity is looking at the top of the tree for answers without realising that the answer can only be found at the root of the tree. The top is where the leaders, academically sophisticated and materially wealthy reside. At the root is where the ordinary reside. It happened that the two individuals that made the greatest impact on humanity and the most followed in the history of our world (Jesus Christ and Prophet Mohammed) come from the root. Both are not academically educated, one was the son of a Carpenter and born in a manger; the other was an orphan and as poor as can be. Yet they both made the most remarkable impact on humanity. The advancement of the second building is key to the posterity of the world.

One World, One Entity

In his new year's message of 1ˢᵗ January 2014, The Archbishop of Canterbury, Justin Welby stated:

'Nelson Mandela said that dealing with poverty is not an act of charity, it is an act of justice. He said every generation has the chance to be a great generation and we can be the great generation.'

But how can poverty be addressed without the most basic needs of a baby; healthcare and nutrition because health [they say] is wealth? The woes of our world can only be felt when human beings pay closer attention to the healthcare and educational infrastructures serving or de-servicing millions of our children across the globe.

Being the great generation would not come about just because it is on the New Year's wish list, neither will it come about based on good intentions or as part of what nature offers. It would not also happen as an event. Rather, in order to be a great generation, a new way of thinking and new way of carrying out the world's business has to occur. And it would require a process well thought out, well understood and clearly mapped out. It should not matter who thought of the new way or suggested it, what matters is who subscribes to, develops and implements the new agenda. Those that subscribe to, develop and implement good practice are the wise ones; for they are the ones that make things happen. Our good thoughts and words will always count for nothing without action.

The only thing certain in our world today is that the status quo has lingered on for far too long and has damaged most of the children of this world who are the future of our world. The status quo has not only failed but has also become unsustainable and toxic to humanity. Anyone who thinks that everything is alright or believes our world is a safer place now must be suffering from a total lack of insight. Such people represent a part of the problem, not solution, to the world's crises. Nothing would change if human beings continue to prefer the devil they are hosting inside to the angel waiting to host them outside.

For real change to occur, a proper, not meagre understanding of the state of our world currently and what needs to change has to happen. This would have to be followed by the willingness and bravery to invest in the work needed to achieve the change for the better, for this and future generations. In this work and walk towards change, metaphors such as football, the human body, aeroplane and the tree with its various parts need be properly examined because until human beings appreciate and view the world as one entity with deferring parts needing to independently function to the best of their ability but render service in a complementary fashion to one another, until human beings understand and appreciate that, no part of our world should be allowed to degenerate, because such degeneration would certainly adversely affect the world as an entity in ways unknown to mankind, human beings would continue to self-destruct and the consequences would be dire.

Therefore, let us embrace the challenges and work towards being that great generation. It is our work to do and no one else's. In addition to these, those born with feet must not depart without leaving a footprint? The only question is; what type of footprint are they leaving behind?

The world needs to be viewed by its occupants as one world and one entity. Our world is round like a football, and it is ironic that everyone around the world recognises football. If one were to take a vote on the most admired, most entertaining and the most watched team sport around the world, the 'beautiful game' of football would win easily. Throw a football or anything with a round shape to a crawling baby and watch the baby try to play with it. Throw a ball at a crowd and watch someone either catch, kick or play with it. Everybody, including those who do not want to take part in it, can relate to football. But most importantly, players do not choose which part of the football they catch, kick or play with. There are huge lessons coming from the shape of football, players and teams, in relation to human beings' social interactions and the world they reside in. These lessons have huge bearing on the development of the second metaphorical building, housing human emotions.

Look at the rounded shape of a football, there may be demarcating lines but the lines must be interlinked, seamless and knitted together in order to form the rounded shape. Take a football to any part of the world, one may not be able to communicate with another person in their local dialect but would find many people to kick football around with. If one assembles eleven players from different parts of the globe with different languages, even without a coach, they would play together against another team and know when a goal has been scored. The football would serve as the common denominating factor, the thing that unites them. No individual would be able to play on their own in a team. The individuals within a team would have to work together with each position playing its part for a goal to be scored and when a goal is scored, the celebration is not restricted to the scorer but the entire team. The player who scored, if humble, would recognise that without the effort of the team, they would not have been able to score. It is rare that a player picks up the ball and scores on their own, without the contribution of another player. Yes, a player may receive a pass from kick off and proceed to score a wonder goal through solo effort, but the player couldn't have done that without receiving the pass from kick off. The only way a player would be known to score on their own is if, following the kick off whistle, a player hits the ball straight from kick off without passing to anyone and scores. These are very rare events and almost impossible in top flight football because, first of all, the player would not be able to generate the power required (whilst standing next to the ball) to beat highly talented goalkeepers, from the centre of the pitch which is at least fifty yards from the opposition's goalpost. Even if the player takes a run up to the ball, the goalkeeper would be able to adjust themselves to prevent the goal because of the travelling distance.

Since no one can score from kick off, any other form of goal must have something to do with team effort, even when a goal keeper hits a wonder shot that beats the opposing goalkeeper. This is because the ball could not have reached that keeper without the contribution of one of his or her team mates on the pitch because, by rule, goalkeepers do not take part in kick offs. Just as the brain reminded the other parts of the body, no matter how good a striker is, if the goalkeeper concedes more than the striker scores in any particular game, the striker can only celebrate his or her goal but could never celebrate a win. The best teams are not teams with brilliant individual players who play for themselves, but teams with brilliant individuals in all positions playing together, working hard and covering for each other as a team. In teams where a particular position is weak, other people playing in that team overcompensate and the overall output of such team is likely to reduce.

In strong teams, everyone understands their role; is efficient and effective in their role; respects other teammates' roles; covers for one another; and brings together their collective effort in one accord, for the benefit of the team.

In football, individual players at one time or another, for one reason or another, may begin to feel they are more important than the team or even the club they play for. This is usually borne out of ignorance, short sightedness and a lack of insight. No one can be a great player on their own. When such thinking becomes obvious, such players are often moved on or else they stand to destroy the team spirit. No single player can be bigger or more important than the team, no single player can be called a team and no single player can represent or play as a team. No matter how important a player or group of players are, the overall interest of the team would be more important and central to decision making. In the same way no individual, family, community or nation can claim to be more important than the world they are only a part of, or claim to rule the world. In football, success and failure are not individually based but team based. No disorganised team, no team that fights amongst itself and no team with factions within it can succeed.

The same applies to our football-like rounded world; everyone, through their actions or inactions, contributes to the status quo. Our world is the way it is because of factions, conflicts, wars, discords and infighting. It has unfortunately traded on the ideology that in order to win, one has to subdue, conquer and dominate. Winner takes all, survival of the fittest, he who dares wins; top dog and underdog are the important ideologies/principles. This is as good as the hand subduing and dominating the leg or other parts of the body, rendering the leg impotent or less effective. No wonder our world has weakened and is unhealthy as a result of chaos and conflict.

Contrary to the prevailing ideology, in human life the 'winner' should not and must not 'take all', because Usain Bolt can never win or lose a race against himself. It is the losers that make the winners and vice versa. The principle that 'winner takes all' should belong to the jungle where some animals depend on killing and eating other animals for their survival. It is therefore critically important that people understand and remember at all times that we are human beings, belonging to the same human family and with immense faculties to reflect, project, produce, construct, manufacture, invent, share, rationalise, plan, negotiate and compromise. Our survival should not be predicated on killing and destroying ourselves; our language and behaviour should not be based on jungle language and justice. It should only be in George Orwell's 'Animal Farm' where it was said that, 'all animals are equal but some are more equal than the others.' This is a jungle justice theory that suggests that, life is all about the 'survival of the fittest' and 'winner takes all'. Why for example, must the 'winner-take-all' in the world of 'rational' human beings? Can anyone win or lose any race on their own irrespective of how fast they are? It takes the loser(s) to make

a winner. Therefore, a winner cannot 'take all' when it comes to rational human beings.

If we are indeed rational human beings that we are meant to be, we need to know that theories such as these belong to the jungle, in the animal kingdom because, some animals depend on eating others for their survival. Human beings are not in this category as we are productive, inventive, analytical and imaginative.

The analogy best suited for 'rational' human beings is that of the 'five finger' theory.

All the five fingers are not equal but they are all equally fingers. None of the fingers placed itself in the position it found itself and each has a peculiar role to play for the effectiveness and efficiency of the hand. The five fingers need to be strong and healthy in their individual capacity but must work in a complimentary fashion with one another for the hand to function at its best. If any of the fingers malfunctions or ceases to function, the other four will over compensate and the overall effectiveness of the hand, impaired. If the damaged finger becomes cancerously infected and untreated, the entire hand could be rendered useless or cut off entirely. All the fingers are independent but share a common base or platform.

Just like the five fingers are not equal but are all equally fingers and sharing the same base, it will never be a level playing field from individuals to individuals, communities to communities and nations to nations but we can all play on the same field, ensuring that whatever differing roles we play, we play to the best of our ability but in a collaboration with others to make the field (our world) a healthier and better place for all. Nothing in life is meant to be complete on its own. Anything or anyone that is complete is incomplete. No matter how big, independent and efficient a finger is; it cannot perform the duties of the hand on its own. In the same way, no individual, community or nation can survive or be complete on their own without collaboration with different others.

Just like the candle, human beings as individuals, communities and nations need to appreciate that a candle loses no flame by lighting another candle; rather one candle stick becomes more efficient by being used to light other candle sticks, thereby spreading more light. In the same way, the fact that we have helped another individual, community or nation to develop can only be beneficial to the entire system (our world). There is nothing to lose but all to gain. Our fears are unfounded. Why must we leave one to be in darkness, when he or she can share in our light?

The roundness of a football reflects the roundness of our world. Perhaps that is why football is recognisable around the globe and every nation understands football. Now, for a football to be a football it has to be round and filled with air and bouncy. If it is deflated, it won't bounce or bounce well; if it is not round it would not roll properly and cannot be used or called a football.

In the same way our rounded world, though may have demarcating lines like a football, needs to be properly interlinked, seamless and knitted together in order to retain the rounded shape and roll around properly. It would never function properly if it splits in two or any part of it is punctured, 'fractured' or torn apart by conflicts and/or wars. It would never be smooth or function properly if there are individuals, groups or nations that derive pleasure from maiming, killing or destroying their fellow human beings and nations for whatsoever reason. If human beings continue to believe that they can gain by inflicting pain or destroying others, the world will never function as it ought to. For whatever reason, if the brain feels superior and wants to 'lord it' over the anus and fails to understand that it needs the anus as much as the anus needs it; if the brain feels that it has elected itself and chosen its own location and fails to recognise its folly; if the brain fails to show humility or the anus and the rest of the body parts refuse to appreciate the need for mutual respect, co-operation and co-existence, then the body, our world, is quite simply doomed. Robbing Peter in order to pay Paul can never be the answer because Paul would be as guilty in the knowledge that Peter was robbed for him to be paid. Peter, knowing he has been robbed, is very likely to seek to retrieve his goods by all means necessary at one time or another. A vicious cycle erupts.

Sadly, in the game of life, wrong is wrong no matter the mode of execution but right can only be right if applied correctly. None of the body parts chose its location or vocation and like the body parts, no human being had ever pre-chosen their place of birth on this planet. This fact lends humanity the platform for humility, mutual respect and understanding.

Therefore, in this 'one human family', the only 'good deal' is the deal that benefits every child in the world. That deal, at the very least, safeguards the interests of all babies around the world ensuring their basic educational, healthcare and nutritional needs are met. The deal that recognises that no baby nominates the family or nation they are born into, which makes it a matter of luck (good or bad fortune) where each baby finds themselves. It can never be a good deal in the long run, if the 'good deal' is damaging to other parts or members of the human family. The roundness of the world would be adversely affected, just like a football, if any part of it is punctured, torn or bumpy.

Many footballers are well known and recognisable around the world and children enjoy seeing and hearing about them. Therefore, they need to be ambassadors of each country, each community and each family that they hail from. They need to help in nurturing the children of this world, especially young boys, who at times fail to concentrate or even attend school in the hope of becoming the next big-name footballer. When this does not happen (as is almost always the case) and having reached an age where demands are put on them by themselves, families and society at large to pay their way in life and possibly support others, they become vulnerable to fast cash which easily leads them to a life of crime.

Footballers need to arm themselves with the facts in terms of the percentage of footballers that make it big and the chances of good footballers getting the breakthrough, just like there are many good singers but how many of them get the breakthrough? A lot of boys in this modern world are not concentrating in school; some are roaming the streets in the hope that they would be signed up one day by a big club. These boys need to know that many who are playing professional football are not as rich as people think, many good footballers will never grace a stadium because they were never spotted, and some brilliant footballers suffered career-ending injuries before they could be spotted by anyone. The percentage of footballers that earn big money every week is very small compared to the number of professional footballers. These children also need to know how hard professional footballers have to work and the discipline required. The media also need to help in this regard. The impact of information passing from the media to society as a whole, especially to our children, can never be fully measured, estimated or qualified. In my previous books I have consistently maintained and said that 'the power of the mass media in society today is so enormous, it is unimaginable. It is a well-acknowledged fact that the media have the power to control how society thinks, perceives and reacts to any particular situation.' (Nacho 2010 & 2012).

On this planet earth, human beings are confronted by all manner of hazards, illnesses (physical and mental), natural disasters, accidents and natural death. These, and more, create all sorts of psychological trauma to the psyche, induce suffering and generate immense pain for human beings. The question then is, in view of all these things that human beings have to contend with and endure; is it then sensible for human beings to deliberately instigate and inflict more pain on themselves by fighting amongst themselves and killing one another; person against person, family against family, community against community, tribe against tribe and nation against nation, on the flimsiest of excuses arising from selfishness and greed? What 'little bird' sends mankind on this endless pursuit of the wild goose, when our similarities are glaring to the blind and audible to the deaf and our differences the greatest gift for the posterity of the entire world? How and why did humanity get to this dreadful point when all that is needed was for the 'brain' to do its work

and get the various parts to function at their very best, work in partnership and make the 'body' a healthy place? What role is leadership playing in all this, in our 'civilised' world?

How can the world talk about civilisation when it is a well-known fact that many of the world's children, living in certain parts of our world, would be content with animal rights obtainable in some other parts of the same world? How can human beings talk about human rights when animal rights are not even available to millions, in a world which we 'civilised' human beings are presiding over? In parts of our world where all a child is asking for is not that they won't be killed, kidnapped, tortured and abused in the name of practising witchcraft or being possessed by demons, but that someone in authority asks questions and does something to prevent another child from suffering the same fate. Civilisation is an illusion if 'the civilised' are content to stand by, watch, do or say nothing in the pretence that all is well or nothing is happening. The aim here is not for a perfect world but a healthy world where it is recognised that though all fingers are not all equal, they are all fingers, all the same; as such, there needs to be a baseline. The very least the 'world of plenty' should offer every one of its children is good healthcare and nutrition. The world needs to deal with this before talking about eradication of child poverty.

Civilisation is an illusion if the 'civilised' are happy to act as mere spectators or colluders with 'shepherds' who abandon their 'sheep' to the elements and go to feed in other shepherds' fields. How can the brain stand by or collude with the anus knowing fully well that in the long run that it would suffer the same fate? There is no decency outside if the inside is corrupt and rotten. The mentally unwell is not only the insane person but the 'sane' person who watches, does or says nothing whilst the insane destroys everything in sight, including the future of tomorrow (the children of this world).

All those who are in positions of leadership and those waiting in the wings are like shepherds and gatekeepers. No one should offer themselves as a gate man or woman if they are not willing and able to 'man' the gate. How can those whose duties relate to ensuring good standards, monitoring and reviewing public services, ensure high quality standards in the service they provide to those they purport to serve, if they have no vested interest and do not subscribe to their own provisions? This lack of sincerity and commitment is one of society's biggest failings and is responsible for mankind's unseen crimes against humanity in our world today. This in itself is responsible for innumerable deaths of children, pregnant women and vulnerable people across the globe. Many of the sheep abandoned by such shepherds die in their pens as there are no ambulances to take them to hospital; ambulance services in some parts of our world are only for conveying corpses to funerals for those who can afford it.

Some of the abandoned 'sheep' who manage to get to hospital are often not treated because they cannot afford to pay for their treatment; some that are treated are treated with chalk disguised as tablets and mere water perfectly packaged as drips. In some of these places medication for patients is often sold on a 'do you want the original or imitation' basis. In other words, do you want to be cured or do you want to die? This has turned many healthcare facilities into death traps in many locations in the same world we all share. Little children, who never asked to be born, who never elected the families or nations they are born into (just like every other child in our world), are left to perish whilst everyone is watching, turning a blind eye or pretending it is not happening. Those who manage to survive the poisons served as treatment, and the lack of food, end up running on empty with little or no academic or moral values added to their lives. Many turn to lives of crime and become a menace to society in general.

Children born with many talents, perhaps talents capable of rescuing mankind, are destroyed even before they see the light of day because of the short-sighted few who have no clue what leadership means. Just as the brain informed the rest of the body, 'the wise are not only the ones who speaketh wise words but also the ones who understand and act on wise words', in the same way, the thief is not only the one who steals but also the one who knowingly patronises the thief.

As the bush rat said in its anger and frustration at being caught, 'My anger is not only with the person that caught me; my anger is also towards the person who shouted that I must not be allowed to escape.' When one is aware of evil and chooses to stand aside, say or do nothing, in that instance the person becomes a partaker in that evil because keeping silent in the face of evil is another way of condoning and encouraging evil. Is it possible for a 'good' person to stand aside, do or say nothing in the face of evil? Silence can only be golden if it is not cohabiting with evil. Leadership is akin to piloting an aircraft. All that passengers need is a qualified, well-trained and seasoned pilot to take them to their destination. If the pilot that happens to fulfil the criteria is a relative, that's all well and good. Otherwise, such pilots should be hired from anywhere possible to reduce the catastrophic consequences of hiring a relative with no idea where the cockpit is or hiring a misfit on the grounds of positive discrimination, zoning or quota systems. Such a reckless hire would certainly result in the misfit pilot crashing the aircraft and possibly killing all passengers within it. Furthermore, no one can legislate for where a crashing plane would land. It could land on your roof; therefore don't ever think there is much to benefit by instigating or contributing to a non-functional community, nation or continent. Let all human beings view themselves as being in different brands of cars. The most essential thing that would ensure relative safety in one's Rolls Royce is the good conditions of other vehicles on the road. Therefore ensuring that other cars and vehicles are in good condition and their brakes are in good order safeguards the health, safety and enjoyment of the Rolls Royce owner. Only those who do not understand the true nature of evil will instigate, support and encourage it. Those who appreciate the ever-changing nature of evil in terms of modality and terms of reference will never support or encourage evil. The evil one instigates today could ruin them tomorrow.

When one is a leader, they become a parent to all within their jurisdiction. Such leaders understand that the greatest and most valuable assets of any community or nation are its citizens. Any community or nation that does not understand, appreciate and provide an enabling environment for its citizen to flourish and maximise their potential would be deemed to be blind or dead. The impact of such a failure would be felt across the globe as such a community or nation denies the world of their respective contributions towards it; just like the body would be deprived if one of its parts malfunctions. All leaders need to appreciate the need for constructive criticism and opposition because without these, leaders will miss out on important matters that require attention and consideration in a diverse and multicultural world. After all, it was the action of the anus that led the brain to abandon its original plan to come in with a 'bang' in preference to 'humility'.

Regarding the inhumane and at times invisible acts of crime against humanity, the world needs to say to every leader, if the healthcare provision under your watch is not good enough for you and your biological children, then it cannot be good for any child under your watch. If the educational facilities under your watch are not good enough for your biological children then they cannot be good for any child under your watch. The critical question is, if the education and healthcare you, as a shepherd are providing for your sheep (the people who have chosen you to serve them) is good, what then are you running from? If you know it is not good, who do you expect to make it good and are you happy for the people you are looking after to be drinking from a poisonous cup under your watch? Are you able to explain your mission by offering to serve your people, if you cannot eat and drink from the same utensils from which you serve them? Any nation that treats its citizens appallingly has no right to demand patriotism from such citizens. After all, the nature and quality of relationship between a parent and their child is mainly dependant on the parent.

The best way to ascertain the level of decadence in any society is by looking at the standard of educational and healthcare infrastructures within that society. If such infrastructures have decayed, it simply means that the people using them have decayed too. Each and every society should be judged by these. It is impossible for anyone to change the world around them without first transforming themselves. It is impossible for anyone to produce quality material without having quality within themselves. If one wants to move a car and ensure some degree of safe driving, they must first produce a competent driver. No one can transform a society without transforming the sole agents of transformation (citizens). Only leaders who recognise this simple but vital concept and invest in the most valuable asset of their nation (citizens) can transform their nation.

Citizens of this world are free, in fact should be encouraged, to obtain education and healthcare from any part of the globe of their choice, in the spirit of sharing, exchange and partnership so long as they can meet set criteria and are able to afford it. However, this privilege need not be extended to anyone who has offered themselves to be the gatekeeper or a shepherd. This is because when leaders acting as shepherds and gatekeepers seek healthcare outside, they negate the need for quality control and open the doors to substandard healthcare. It is also a sign that they do not trust their own provisions and are running from something sinister. If it is not good enough for you, why offer it to the people who elected you to serve them? This is at the root of mass killings of innocent children, the vulnerable and many third world country citizens of our world. Our world will be better served when they address these dreadful and shameful acts of evil against humanity. If the world cannot provide its own children with good healthcare and education, then what are people parading themselves as leaders, statesmen and women, for? There is no other way of achieving this without ensuring that those who offer themselves as shepherds act like shepherds and are held accountable for every child within their jurisdiction.

It is quite difficult to ascribe words such as civilised, rational, reasonable, considerate, to any human being who does not appreciate the need to safeguard the interests of children who are the leaders of tomorrow. When one looks critically at what many children in some parts of Asia and Africa particularly are served, in terms of healthcare and education, it beggars belief how many people across the globe, even in affected continents address themselves as 'Honourables' in high and low places. One cannot help but ask: 'is there really something called the United Nations?' May I suggest that, what we have is united nations by name only. How united are these nations and if they are, are they there for the good of all nations? It is time for those they serve to know more about their purpose.

Leadership is a 'calling' and must not be taken lightly. When people are called, they represent the interests of those who voted for and against them equally. They fight for the common interest of humanity and they create an enabling environment for their citizens to maximise their potential in all areas of their jurisdiction. Such leaders understand that the greatest and most valuable asset of any community or nation is its citizens. Based on this under-standing, they invest in their citizens and give them every opportunity to be the best they can be. Such leaders also value the voice of opposition, as it helps them to attend to areas they may not have considered or even known to exist. Finally, such leaders appreciate that, leaders are like leaves at the top of the tree. Their stay at the top of tree is tempo-rary. Therefore, such leaders are not too afraid of falling off the tree but utilise the short time they have to give service, build lasting structures and create an indelible legacy that ensures continuous improvement and growth.

When people are not called but call or send themselves, they pursue a personal and selfish agenda coupled with agendas of their cronies. In that state of mind 'me', 'us' and 'we' become all important and 'you', 'they' and 'them' become either less important or completely non-existent. They never appreciate the voice of reason, opposition or contrary views and at times are ready to eliminate anyone or people standing in their way. They turn the business of giving service to humanity, into the business of looting, sharing and hoarding of public funds oblivious of the fact that the hand will suffer with the mouth eventually, if the hand decides not to feed the mouth because the mouth did not vote for it or disagrees with it. They fail to understand and appreciate that the best and most valuable asset of any society is its citizens; any society that does not understand this and in a world where this is not appreciated, that society is doomed and with it the entire world as a body suffers. As leaves at the top of the tree, such leaders are usually afraid of falling off and as a result; they resort to doing whatever it takes (no matter how bad) to cling on to the tree (power).

Society as a whole needs to devise a means by which such people will not be allowed access into a position where their mean and wicked actions and/or inactions put the lives of the world's future (children) at severe risk, because the impact would not only be felt by the particular area but also would be felt by the entire world in ways human beings may never understand, for there are mysteries beyond human comprehension and control as we often witness.

Our world can no longer afford or tolerate irresponsible leadership in any part of the globe due to the pollution it generates in terms of casualties around the globe. Nothing creates unemployment, immigration/refugee crises, housing problems, pressure on healthcare and other amenities coupled with inhumane acts against humanity more than bad leadership.

The best way to encourage excellence and get rid of mediocrity in families, communities and nations is to create a world where, in order to be the best, one has to better the best in their chosen field of endeavour, a world where honour can only be ascribed when one's peers recognise and nominate them as setting the pace in their chosen field of endeavour, even if the chosen field of endeavour is cleaning. For example, in tennis, every tennis player in Britain would not have a problem nominating Andy Murray as the standard bearer and no one would begrudge Andy any honour given to him in Britain because he won Wimbledon in 2012 which was an achievement no other tennis player in Britain was able to attain for seventy-seven years. The same would go for Roger Federer; no tennis player in the world would begrudge Roger any award he receives as the winner of most grand slams in the world currently. It doesn't matter the career or profession in state, national and international levels, let honour be ascribed only to those nominated by their peers as pace setters in their chosen endeavours.

It would not be surprising that both Andy and Roger would accept such honours with humility, especially in recognition that they were nominated by their peers. They are likely to be first to appreciate the fact that, in order for one to be successful, others have to subscribe, contribute and participate in the one hundred percent basic requirement success demands of oneself. Anyone honoured in this way is likely not to even crave for publicity and unlikely to have 'do you know who I am?' as part of their vocabulary. This would not be the case because everyone, especially in their specific area of specialism, knows who they are and that would be more than enough for them to show humility in their achievement.

If one wants to be honoured and recognised, they know what is expected of them. Those who fight for honours and recognition without seeking to better the best would be seen as what they are, empty vessels who make the most noise. No one would be under any illusion about what is required of them before they can be honoured, because criteria are set on the premises of 'how do your peers rate you and what positive impact are you making in society?'

Money on its own must not feature here, because there is no way of objectively knowing who has the most money or the means by which the money came about. Money must remain something useful as a means but cannot become an end to all things. Take a look below and appreciate for yourself what is obtainable in the part of our world where money is made king of all things and worshipped. This place is captioned 'World's most uninhabitable place'. It provides readers with the understanding of the need to put money in its place when in pursuit of honour. The type of carnage and evil that has brewed and continues to brew in this part of our world would certainly affect this global village in ways, shape and forms not conceived by any human being on this planet. This would come either through persistent crises induced by human beings or natural forces (acts of GOD) beyond the control of human beings, if human beings refuse to stop, take stock and change course. See Abiding Legacy Of The Man below.

As people are honoured based on their achievements, they use their gifts and talents to serve, not oppress, humanity. A world where everyone understands that excellence would remain an illusion without humility; a world where as far as possible each position is filled by the best suitably qualified person, irrespective of creed, gender or race, would ensure that the mouth is not doing the job of the nose which might appear to be okay, but in long run costs the entire body (including those that employed the mouth) dearly.

When the job requires an animal that barks, a dog can offer itself or be sought, not a goat. If, in the entire area all that can be found are goats or dogs that cannot bark, every attempt has to be made to find a suitable for the job dog from anywhere possible. Just like in football, all that matters to people is having a manager who can do the job... a manager who can get the players playing well as a team and winning trophies. No one in the end would give a damn whether the coach came from Mars or Jupiter.

An example of this can be found in England with the appointment of Canadian born Mark Carney as the Governor of Bank of England. This employment was simply on the basis that Mark Carney, with his proven track record, was deemed the best-suited for the job and nothing else. This is how sound human beings with advanced emotions need to think for the benefit of humanity, because when employment is given on any other ground other than content and suitability, humanity is denied. This approach needs to extend to every area of leadership especially local, state and national governance because, immature emotion and sentiments have given room to people who are not capable of looking after their little garden; putting themselves in charge of farms responsible for feeing the masses, with catastrophic and calamitous consequences.

It is crucial to note that when a leader fails and damages the prospects of people in a particular nation, it is not only the people of that nation who suffer but other parts of the world, especially neighbouring nations which in turn have a trickling effect on the rest of the world. Our world has seen this in recent memory during the economic meltdown as the impact of Greece's economy affected the Euro-zone economy adversely. Syria's conflict also comes to mind. No individual, community or nation is an island. **Our world expects those appointed as being the best suitably qualified to use their particular talents, knowledge, expertise and position for the service of humanity, not use them to oppress and destroy humanity. Above all, we need a world where every citizen can make their home anywhere in the world once they can show an in-depth knowledge of the**

place and are willing to contribute positively to that area. As there is Afro-American, Asian-American, Nigerian-British let there be American-Afro, American-Asian and British-Nigerian. As the emotion and social interactions of human beings develop, everyone needs to understand that no one, no group, should be singled out for praise or condemnation when things are going well or badly as everyone has contributed to any situation any area finds itself in, and all hands must be on deck to ensure a better world.

All along, the 'little bird' has sought to destroy and confuse mankind by instigating false ideologies and a split between the 'owners' and 'renters' in a world that should belong to all who inhabit it, a world that should be treated as an entity, just like a football. Well, it only takes the forces of nature through the sheer weight of a natural disaster or death, for example in 2013 when nature chose to present Maggie and Madiba with the same vehicle that will one day approach our doors, irrespective of our status, creed, gender or race, to take us to that 'common' place reserved for all for the human mind to appreciate that no one, no community and no nation owns the world. Each time nature threatens to present this vehicle through a severe illness, natural disaster or by one being in an aircraft that is showing severe signs of malfunction and threatening to crash, the mind that thought it 'owned' the world quickly switches to 'renting' mode and becomes only too happy to accept help in pursuit of survival from anyone including those who are renting the world. The little bird instigates and many a time succeeds to switch the mind once settled and recovered back to 'owner' not 'renter' mode. How ironic that at various points of one's life, the mind goes through different kinds of emotions influenced by many different factors.

In the actual sense, every human being should feel part-owner and renter of the world. The sense of ownership revolves around the fact that life is a continuum; the fact that each life must end means that everyone is renting. There must be no split; everyone would benefit enormously by firmly understanding this fact.

As such, the world needs to be viewed by all its occupants as belonging to everyone who inhabits it. The differences in culture, religion, gender, location and ideology are there to enrich, not impoverish the world because without these differences the world would be stale and dull. The world is well resourced to meet the needs of all those who inhabit it, with different resources in terms of human and natural resources spread in different locations across the globe. Just as the various parts of the body, nations, communities and individuals have to be different and play peculiar roles, but remain in harmony with one another, for the body (the world) to be healthy. When all parts are healthy and functioning at their optimum levels, the entire world will become healthy. However, if any part is damaged or becomes ineffective, the entire body shares in the discomfort.

When human beings fail to bring their unique differences (like the various parts of the body) together in a complementary fashion for service, when human beings fight amongst and against themselves with the aim to destroy that which is different, or segregate themselves by building imaginary or physical barriers and bubbles with emphasis on 'them and us' and driven by irrational emotions, we damage ourselves in the process and place our world and its occupants in severe danger, as it is now.

In order to redress this, human beings need to encourage and challenge themselves and one another, to understand that no one ingredient can be served as food. Without the mix, there will be no food, for I am manufactured in Africa, refined in Europe but still in pursuit of excellence which may be found in Asia, Australia, North or South America. Furthermore, as human beings with cognition, the important thing to appreciate is, if men seek to eliminate women on this planet or vice versa, the gender that succeeds in eliminating the other would no longer exist. If Christians eliminate all other religious groups and the non-believers, Christianity would automatically cease or at best would not identify or recognise what it represents. Everyone should feel special, appreciate and understand that others are special in their own peculiar ways too. Anyone can feel the whole world belongs to them but only if they understand that the world also belongs to the other people too. Everyone should subscribe to human rights so long as they appreciate that the other person is entitled to human rights too.

Any moment an individual, family, community or nation begins to see only themselves and no one else, they have lost the plot and become a huge liability and a problem not only to themselves but to the entire world because within everyone lies the next generation. The best of humanity is as good as humanity's weakest link. The brain can be as useful as it wants to be but would become useless if the leg ceases to function. The only person entitled to feel special above all else, own the world above all else, and covered in glory is the one who chose the seat they are currently occupying prior to their arrival here on Earth and who is guaranteed to remain on that seat forever. The only other person who can fit into this special place, is the person who never subjects themselves or allows themselves to be subjected to the call of 'the majestic toilet seat'. If, as human beings, we fail to appreciate that though all fingers are not equal, they are all equally fingers, equally important and each having their peculiar role to play in making the hand effective and efficient, and most importantly, that none of the fingers chose their own size or location, then we are doomed and our cognition a waste.

One does not need to be a rocket scientist to understand that one cannot ascribe to being tall without seeing a short person, rich without seeing a poor person, female with no male around, Republican without knowing there are Democrats, clergy without a congregation, Protestant without Catholicism, queen or king without subjects, president without the people, non-believer without seeing a believer or call themselves Muslim without seeing people from other religious backgrounds. This means that life in itself would lose its meaning if there was nothing to compare something to. All the values that individuals, communities, religious and non-religious groups and nations' human beings have are relative and in comparison with something different; otherwise there is no value and everything would become stale.

This is reinforced by the notion that no individual, community or nation has everything within it, making it imperative that the only way to have everything is by sharing; hence human beings are inter-dependent on one another. The word 'independent' becomes an illusion. None of the body parts owns the entire body and none can do without the rest of the body parts. All the body parts own the body and each part needs to be strong, healthy and functioning at optimum level and working with the rest in harmony, for the body (our world) to be healthy. This is what is required in each individual, community and nation in this world; that only the best in each of us pulled together in harmony, not against one another, will make our world a healthy place to live. Upon this premise, is it then right, sensible or justifiable to seek to destroy that which is different but responsible for the value we know and enjoy? Aren't we as human beings still wallowing in ignorance amidst our sophisticated intellectual abilities? A typical example of human beings ignorance amidst cognitive intelligence can be seen in religion where, all religious groups pray to an Almighty God (Allah or Jehovah) for help. They sit, bow, kneel, sing and lift up their heads and hands to the Almighty, seeking help, praising or thanking the Almighty for help in the past, help presently and seeking help for the future. This is usually done from a position of weakness and vulnerability, in the belief that God is capable of taking care of all things, for He is an omnipotent, omnipresent, omniscient God. Professing to love God for who and what He represents means believing and accepting that God is all powerful, all knowing and able to do all things seen and unseen but most importantly believing that life and death are in His hands. In other words, it would amount to a state of confusion for any human being who is capable of doing all things to 'waste' their time worshiping God because that person and God are equals and would not need each other. It would be odd for a king to worship another king. This is why, I take the view that the worship of God is not primarily to do with 'love' of God but primarily linked to vulnerability which is mainly associated with one not being in control of all things; because no one in control of all things seen or unseen would have time for God.

To believe in God, one has to accept their weaknesses and believe that by worshipping God, He, as the Almighty, will take care of those issues generating concerns and worry to the individual. Most importantly, believers in

God believe that He is Father of all mankind. It is then contradictory, confusing and senseless that the same people seeking help from God doubt God's own ability to protect and defend Himself from His 'enemies' or fend for Himself. The question is, if God is incapable of protecting and defending Himself, if He is incapable of fighting His own battle, how on earth can He protect, defend and help those seeking help from Him? How on earth can He take care of all things seen and unseen? Isn't your worship of Him worthless and senseless? How do you and how would you appreciate your particular persuasion without other persuasions in existence? Though a woman can give birth to a baby, in religious terms, life and death are believed to be in God's hands. Is it therefore logical, based on this belief, that those seeking help from Almighty God should be 'helping' God by killing themselves and/or their fellow human beings in the name of God and in the name of differences? A baby cannot provide physical protection for its parents. In religious terms, you and I are the babies and God the parent. Those destroying humanity in the name of God or anything relating to God, in the name of power, control or whatsoever, fail to realise that without differences, they would never know who or what they are themselves. They fail to realise that the killing of one is the killing of all. They also fail to realise that all the values they have about their persuasion, for example, rest with the fact that there are other religious doctrines and also those without faith. Instead of appreciating the values which only differences bring, instead of giving and taking in the spirit of sharing to enrich one another, instead of teaching with a view to win souls or convince others based on ideology or agree to disagree, some people (out of sheer ignorance) seek to destroy that which is making the difference in their own lives.

The most potent thing to consider and understand here is that no genuine father would welcome and thank any of his children who goes on a killing spree of his or her siblings because they insulted or disobeyed the father they all own. If our earthly fathers would not praise us for killing our own siblings for their sake, then how much more would God, who is capable of doing the killing Himself if He so wishes? What the loving and merciful God requires of all His children, irrespective of their persuasion is tolerance, forgiveness, encouragement and at most condemnation of the act and not the person, who has thought, said or done something against God or any prophet, saviour, saint, clergy or layperson (dead or alive); say a prayer for those that have rebelled and then, leave the rest to God to administer 'punishment' or 'forgiveness' as it pleases HIM and HIM alone. Having said that, mankind must learn to hate hatred. Therefore, any ideology of hate from one toward another individual, family, community or nation is an ideology of hate toward the self. No priest, imam, rabbi or religious leader of any kind has died and come back to prove that they were welcomed by virgins for killing others by suicide bombing stemming from religious ideology. Parents and society at large have a moral responsibility to enrich the children of this world with sound moral values, so that they won't become like waves which will be tossed about by any wind that comes their way. Any uncultured and unloved child stands vulnerable to exploitation of all kinds including being lured to a suicide mission or becoming a cult and gang member.

When one jumps in the mud to catch the pig, they begin to share something in common with the pig and differentiation between them and the pig becomes difficult. When one gives a careless chase to a psychotic person who has snatched their towel whilst in the bathroom, they are likely to be seen as more psychotic, because the psychotic person is in possession of a towel.

For all have sinned and fallen short of the Glory of God! Therefore all must acknowledge their sin, for no one is immune from sin which flows from thought, word and deed. Blaming one another and playing 'holier-than-thou' will get human beings nowhere. Human beings have often been told that, if they were to be judged based on their thought process alone, they would all end up in prison. No person born of a woman is qualified to punish sin because punishment for sin is deserving of all mankind. As a result, where there is sin, let the one who is Holy, God, deal with it at the appropriate time, known and chosen by Him alone. Where there is crime, let the law deal with it. No one should take the law into their own hands; rather we must keep working and 'fighting' for justice and equality before the law. Never presume someone's guilty or innocent based on their looks, creed or gender. Let academic and moral education help us moderate our negative instincts, emotions and reactions.

Oh, if I were righteous. If I were righteous I would never go anywhere near a place of worship, for I do not like to stand out or appear strange; neither do I want to do anything with anyone nor people I have nothing in common with. I attend places of worship because, I am a sinner and I meet fellow sinners in places of worship. I attend because that is where the likes of me attend each with their little baggage, and all afflicted. From top to the bottom we are all

fellow strugglers, strugglers in faith and seeking, not to be perfect, but trying to attain some level of excellence in the hope of salvation which is out of our hands. If I were perfect, I would not have been able to exist on this planet because I wouldn't be able to understand, let alone relate to anyone nor would anyone be able to relate to me. There is no perfection in an imperfect world. Night and day can never cohabit. Therefore it is not my place or any of my fellow strugglers... the imperfect human beings to punish sinners for we would end up punishing ourselves. Whether you believe in God or not, all human beings need to do is to share. Try to convince me as I try to convince you but in the end if we cannot convince one another, we must agree to disagree and tolerate, respect, value and work in partnership with one another. This would represent the 'humility of the brain' being that we are all made different for complementary purposes. No one ingredient can be served as food.

Anyone who sets up or joins an organisation... indeed anyone who secures employment with a personal motive other than motive geared towards service to humanity will be doing a disservice to themselves, the organisation they purport to represent and humanity in general! The over-arching questions in our relationship with one another are: how can anyone who calls themselves a human being become immune, desensitised and disconnected with the systematic abuse, neglect and killing of other human beings, especially children and vulnerable people? How can anyone claim to be a full-fledged human being when they cannot see glimpses of themselves in another human being irrespective of status, creed, gender and race? Can the brain say to the rest of the body 'what I do or say is solely my business, and no one else's?' In a world where no one, no community and no nation can survive on their own; a world where independence is an illusion and inter-dependency is the order of the day, can any of us really say 'what I do or say is no one else's business but mine alone?'

Finally, let it be known that any individual, family, community or nation without shame is as good as dead. Such can be likened to being in a psychotic mode. If I were a leader in this current climate, I will resign. It is virtually impossible for any objective person to wear a smile in this world considering the crises within it. A world where human beings, including some so called leaders plan and plot evil against the same world they are said to be leading? How can humanity be waging war against itself? Can the body survive if the body parts are at war with themselves? It is worth noting that, none of us as individuals, families, communities or nations is complete on our own. No culture, gender, creed or ethnicity will know what it stands for or represents without the oth-er(s). In spite of all the differences in individuals, skin colour, culture, gender, creed and national-ity, there's only one race (the human race). The same way we have different parts doing different things for the human body to function, so we have differences in one human race. Each individual, community and nation represents only a part of the jigsaw needed for our world to function. Never

ignore or undervalue the other, for they may hold the key to your desired needs. With humility in the brain, the human race can restructure this one body (the world) for the benefit of humanity.

If Only

If only one could imagine seeing themselves everywhere they go, having discussions with themselves, everyone they see looking like them, saying what they say, answering the same name, eating the same food, wearing the same clothes, go wherever they go, sitting wherever they sit and repeating everything they say; human beings without reservation would appreciate, embrace and celebrate differences. Must human beings get burnt before they appreciate that fire is dangerous? Must we, as 'thoughtful' beings, experience living with ourselves and only those that look and do everything like us before we appreciate how frustrating and terrible it would be?

If only we as human beings can learn to trust ourselves and trust others and learn to share without cheating. If only human beings could understand that in the other person lies our learning and development because one cannot learn much from themselves and one cannot be taller and shorter than another at the same time. If only we can learn to appreciate and celebrate our similarities. If only we can learn to value the importance and understand the immense benefits from our differences, then it would be possible to come to a new dawn where weapons that threaten humanities may no longer be required. What a massive IF and what a massive ONLY? Having heard of yet another killing of service men by a service man in April 2014 in America, if only human beings could see more of themselves in times of trials and trouble and less of others; less of themselves and more of others in times of triumph and victory; someone would have perhaps noticed the little tell-tale signs which are inevitable when one is becoming mentally unstable, and these types of disasters may have been averted or at the very least reduced. People are also more likely to locate the heroes and heroines within them and a lot of the social ills seen below in the section captioned 'World's most uninhabitable place' would have not been there or curbed.

If society is serious about tackling the ills of this world, especially child abuse and child poverty, and ensuring better prospects for all children, then a 'root and branch' approach needs be adopted. The root should be nothing other than the education of child bearers (girls and women). This does not mean that the moral and academic education of boys and men is not of equal importance. However, the focus on girls and women will automatically transmit that the same to boys and men. Once the base is set right, everything will fall into place. The branch would be how creative society is in dealing with and providing support for poly-substance abusers, the mentally unwell, perpetrators of domestic violence and paedophiles. If society is not prepared to focus on this 'root and branch' approach then it should be expected that cases such as Victoria Climbie, Baby P, Hamzah Khan, Aniarael Macias and the extraordinary case of Andrea Yates (who drowned her five children, including her six month old, in her family bathtub in 2001 in the United States) and all the overt and covert slaughter of innocent children by some 'leaders' would unfortunately continue to happen, irrespective of how many inquiries are carried out and the number of social workers, police officers and laws enacted to protect children because 'horses are for courses'. Statistic after statistic reveals that the real abusers of children are those who are closest to them (family members and their associates). Professionals, nurses, doctors, social workers and police are essential in detecting child abuse and safeguarding the welfare of children. However, these professionals often are involved only at a secondary level, being that they are likely to get involved where and when there is an existing problem; at times prior to their involvement it is already too late. These professionals are not around people's homes 24 hours a day, 7 days a week or 365 days a year. Last but not least, from statistical evidence, professionals are not identified as the primary abusers of children.

In recognition of these facts, it is very important for governments to adopt a 'more carrots and less stick' approach when dealing with parents and parenting. Over reliance on the law and the quest to criminalise parents might alienate parents from seeking and accepting help and support for fear of being criminalised. A heavy-handed agenda would not offer parents new parenting skills but is more likely to be counterproductive as human beings are naturally equipped with the ability to move the goal posts and mask inadequacies in fear of punishment and shame of being branded as bad parents. This can put children more at risk. What parents and parents-to-be need is encouragement, guidance, help and support in their parenting roles. It is essential to appreciate that some parents were failed by society in general and their own parents in particular. These parents may not have had the best of upbringings themselves and therefore are more likely to replicate what they have obtained from their own parents. An orange tree can only produce oranges not mango. Before devising more punitive measures against parents whose parenting skills are deemed as detrimental to a child's welfare, should the government consider making parenting classes available and mandatory to all new parents and optional to every parent? As someone who had worked in homes for looked-after children and knowing how 'mechanised' life can be for these children and the rewards given to bad behaviour, it would be good to carry out proper research into the current success rates of looked-after children. Yes, it is a well-acknowledged fact that there are some extreme cases where the welfare of children is under threat within their own homes. In such case, those children need to be protected from emotional, physical and psychological harm. However, the state is not a good parent either. The state is simply the 'better of two evils'.

The brain needs to be fully engaged here because the world's crises originates primarily from families, as none emerged from Mars or Jupiter. Parents and everyone need to keep in mind that the candle loses no flame by lighting other candles; instead the candle benefits from spreading more light everywhere. Did you know that as a parent, you get more reward by seeing your child's friends as your children too? That friend of your child may only be looking for someone and some place to belong to and if you capture that child in a positive way, that child may be the one to deliver that advice your child had failed to heed. That child would respond better to your child and know that you are interested in all their well-being. Take time out to learn about your child's friends, show them you are involved and interested in their well-being. Plant in them, the same good seeds you plant in your own child. Feed them with not only food but advice; ask them how they are getting on in school and remind them to focus more on the things that are proving difficult because when something is easy, there is often no dividend as anyone can do easy things. The detrimental cost of driving away your children's friends or trying to cut your child away from having friends can be incalculable. Keep in mind that your well-behaved child remains at risk if your next-door neighbour's child is unruly.

If only, we understood how afflicted we all are, as illustrated by this old story which was brought to my attention by a good friend and an old boy during my days at the Seminary, Ven. Dr. Onundu, Amatu, Christian-Iwuagwu, (The Vicar at St Marys The Virgin Church, Harmondsworth, England) who, narrated during one of his sermons 'One day, a Sunday school teacher died and was shocked when he ended up in hell. He was shocked because, he believed that the mere fact that he was a Sunday school teacher would guarantee him a place in heaven. Whilst on earth, he drew up a list of those he believed would end up in hell. In his list were all the drunkards, illicit drug users, unbelievers, hypocrites and many others. His personal disappointment and shock was nothing compared to when he bumped into his 'holier than thou' vicar who died a year before during his tormenting tour of hell. As he screamed when, he saw his vicar, 'Vicar! What the hell are you doing h...?' His vicar very quickly rebuked him and said 'Shh!.. Keep quiet! The Bishop (who also died a year before) is coming behind me.'

If only we all appreciate these, we may then come to experience living in 'World's most inhabitable place' as detailed below.

World's Most Inhabitable Place

In the course of my work carrying out a Mental Health Act Assessment, I came across a street in Barking and Dagenham, London where in the company of three police officers, two Section 12 doctors and a locksmith, an execution of a Warrant under Section 135(1) of the Mental Health Act 1983 (as amended by the 2007 Mental Health Act) took place. This is the part of the Act that gives power of entry to mental health professionals either by invitation or force into an accommodation believed to be accommodating a Mental Health client where entry had been previously denied.

This particular case relates to a woman who lives alone with her three cats and has no relatives or carer. Mental health services would not have known of her relapse had people on that street not known each other by name. One of her neighbours, who had been helping her with shopping, noticed that all was not well when she attempted to find out if she needed her shopping done. The neighbour alerted us that the woman was not her usual self. As a result, mental health services tried to engage with her with a view to assessing and treating her in her own home. When all attempts to engage her failed and all least restrictive options had been exhausted, a referral was sent to me with a view to engage her with the use of the Mental Health Act (which is always the last resort.) This is because; engaging anyone with the use of the Mental Health Act carries a threat to the person's liberty.

In order to maintain a low key approach and offer the client another opportunity, I sought a less restrictive option by attempting to carry out the Mental Health Act Assessment without the use of a warrant. Therefore I went with two Section 12 doctors (doctors with specialist experience in the diagnosis or treatment of mental disorder) in accordance with the Mental Health Act 1983 (as amended by the 2007 Mental Health Act). However, because of the client's limited insight into her condition and the level of deterioration in her mental state, she still refused us entry. I then had no other option than to seek the aforementioned warrant.

On the day of engagement and following the execution of the warrant, she was detained under a section of the Act. However, we were not able to safeguard her cats because none of the cats was in the premises when we carried out the assessment. It was very moving how neighbours rallied round, taking care of the cats and asking about the patient who had no relatives.

As I was still in the process of fulfilling the obligation of the Local Authority I represent, to protect the property of the detained patient, which included her cats, by liaising with catteries and neighbours to find a means of getting the cats into a cattery, neighbours were telling me the names of other neighbours who were helping in feeding the cats. I was shocked. In London people hardly know the names of those they are sharing the same blocks with, let alone people on the same street. The plan was called off on the day I went to the street and one of the neighbours who had had the cats came round, took me to another neighbour who showed me the food she had bought and the plate from which the cats fed. The client herself made it clear that she did not want her cats to go anywhere as she was confident that her neighbours would look after them. This is what it is all about: people looking after, not working against, each other.

One of the neighbours informed me that they would organise themselves and take turns to visit the client who had no relative in hospital. This is the sort of community spirit one at times, rarely finds in a family let alone, in London, as well as many cities where many people often prefer to mind their own 'business.' The neighbours ensured that this 'lone' woman without relatives never felt alone or lonely. The neighbours seemed to understand that loneliness is an illness in itself. Human beings, being social animals suffer and/or achieve less in isolation or on individual basis but collectively achieve more. What can the hand achieve on its own without the contribution of the leg and other parts of the body?

These neighbours were paramount and contributed enormously to the client's recovery. And, for the client to be confident that her cats were safe in the hands of her neighbours spoke volume. She left her keys with one of her neighbours and it would not surprise me that, they must have rallied round and ensured that her flat was clean and tidy prior to her discharge from hospital. I was so moved because, in my over one decade of practice, I never came across such warmth, love and co-operation between strangers who happened to live on the same street. If I had a say on the matter, I would nominate the residents of this street for an award.

Best Practice Hepworth Ward in Focus

Replication or bettering of best practice is the answer.

As someone who has worked in the social care industry for more than two decades and in the mental health sector for over a decade, covering a number of Local Authorities such as Camden, Greenwich, Barking & Dagenham (twice), Haringey (thrice), Waltham Forest, Slough, Surrey (twice) and Newham; and having worked across many client groups, I was made to understand by one of my ex-supervisors that, I may be the record holder in the whole of England and Wales when figures are compiled of the Approved Mental Health Professional with the highest number of Mental Health Act Assessments including Community Treatment Orders. This was because at a point in my career I was averaging between 100 and 130 of such assessments in a single year. Having amassed such a record in the mental health field, I could not hide the fact that I had attended, seen and experienced varying forms and manner of practices as they relate to support, care and treatment of mental health patients in both the private and public sectors alike.

In my career, I had played a part in admitting numerous formal and informal patients in many psychiatric units across England. However, I couldn't help but notice what I believe is the best in-patient practice in Hepworth Ward, located at Sunflowers Court, Goodmayes Hospital, run by the North East London NHS Foundation Trust based in Essex. I noticed the 'humility of the brain' in action, from the Consultant Psychiatrist and the Ward Manager to the cleaner. In this in-patient ward, everyone worked in harmony with a common agenda to ensure that service users, who may already be traumatised, were to have a good welcome, feel at ease and were as comfortable as possible. The difference was so clear when compared to other in-patient wards; I felt moved at the third time of asking as I approached the entry door when admitting a patient with the police and ambulance crew, having executed a warrant under Section 135(2) of the aforementioned Act that. I said to the consultant who answered the door, welcomed us in and introduced himself to the patient, 'It is surprising that a consultant can answer the door with such humility and welcome a patient and it is the third time I have noticed this.'

In humility, he replied and said to me, 'The patients are the reason for the work we do here. Opening the door and welcoming the patient is the least of what we do and it also does not take anything away from me.' The saying that 'one can never have a second chance to make the first impression' is totally true but this wasn't a first impression, this was the culture on this ward. Each time I attended this ward it was the same. Hepworth Ward staff are masters of patient care. There was not the usual excitement, anxiety and slight panic which at times is associated with bed pressure, limited number of staff and high turnover of patients. There is no confusion as to whether a patient is expected or not. Each time I walk in with a patient, I notice their readiness to accept the patient and everyone is geared towards receiving and settling the patient. They would engage the patient immediately, offer them a drink and ask if they had eaten. They would gently let the patient know that they were in the right place and would be looked after and they would check whether the patient had any concerns and address them. All the staff are friendly and courteous. When patients knock on the office door, they are quick to take their queries in a very calm and polite fashion. Their manner and approach are very receptive, reassuring and accommodating compared to the 'we are busy, don't disturb us or why are you disturbing us' approach I have seen in many places. The patients seem to respond accordingly.

As a professional working in the mental health field and having worked in it for numerous years, it was almost shocking to my system. Having paid many visits to this ward, I have never heard a panic alarm set off seeking staff assistance to control a patient or send them into the seclusion room. I feel so at home admitting patients into Hepworth Ward. It is, quite simply, refreshing. I have felt so at home that I intend to write an advanced directive, in the knowledge that no one is immune to mental disorder, requesting that should I require a psychiatric bed in future, Hepworth Ward should be my destination. However, as the ward is a female only ward, a gender change would suffice for me to meet the criteria.

If one is in public service, and customers feel worse off after encountering them, they are in the wrong job and should consider quitting.

World's Most Uninhabitable Place

'To be, or not to be: that is the question: Whether 'tis nobler in the mind to suffer the slings and arrows of outrageous fortune, Or to take arms against a sea of troubles, and by opposing end them?'

William Shakespeare

This is the common state of a reasonable mind confused about 'something', a right state of mind when evil descends. It is crucial to fully understand all attributes of bad practices and the devastating effect of these on a noble and blessed country.

Sustainable social mobility and emotional development requires human beings to be able to understand good practice with a view to replicate and further improve on it and, in the same vein, bad practice must also be understood, discouraged and challenged to ensure it stops and is prevented from being replicated elsewhere. It is noble to challenge bad practice as, if left unchallenged, it will become the norm and etiquette of the society which then quickens the decline of a state. The Roman Empire was never conquered; rather it imploded due to bad practices.

The stillness and acceptance of this bad practice drastically increases its effect as the victims are not even aware of the symptoms and hence are not seeking help and inadvertently drown in their ignorance. People have become so immune to evil because of the frequency and fear. As a consequence, all they can offer when evil strikes are prayers and well wishes but no condemnation of evil. The problem with inaction is "silence in the face of evil is itself evil: God will not hold us guiltless. Not to speak is to speak. Not to act is to act." – Dietrich Bonhoeffer (A German Pastor during WW2)

Many in positions of leadership have vested interests in evil and therefore turn a blind eye when evil strikes, and many consider as norms the evil they see on a regular basis.

A case in point was the shooting of a two-and-a-half-year-old girl in 2014 by armed robbers who attacked the girl's father in broad daylight as he made his way out of a bank. This girl was the only child and her parents had been in a relationship and marriage for three and seven years respectively in search of a child. One can only imagine the joy of a parent who waited ten years for a child. The child they had waited a decade for was then nearly killed, not by accident, illness or natural disaster but by a deliberate action of a 'human being'. The little girl miraculously survived this hideous and despicable act of terror. The reactions and comments that ensued were troubling as they revealed the state of minds of the citizens of this most uninhabitable place. In this place children cannot even exercise the rights accorded to animals in the Western parts of the world; people have given up on government and 'leadership' that do not care about the security of life and property of its citizens, coupled with lack of will to bring about real change; consequently every bad thing people do is ascribed to 'Satan' and when something good happens, people take credit for it or give thanks to 'God'. It is good and proper for believers in God to give thanks and praise. It is also good for people to wish the little girl well and offer support and solidarity to her parents. However, there was no condemnation of the evil act, the outrage that led to what happened to this little girl. People commented in line with their expectations, because it is almost a norm for such things to occur. People commented with prayers and well wishes as though it were an accident. They were celebrating the fact that this incident was the only shooting that had happened in a long time. These bad practices have become the normal way of life in this particular part of our world. The place was classified as the 'world's most uninhabitable place' because some of the evils that take place are, for most part, not obtainable in a war zone. These are evils committed in peace time, at a time when most people claim to be religious, from the same country and even now from the same ethnicity and speaking the same language. However, people in this place have managed to create a climate where a person's home is no longer a sanctuary but the most uninhabitable place for the individual. The deluded bird has sought to destroy its own nest. The bird's nest has become its greatest threat. Peoples' houses are now occupied by ants, lizards and cockroaches.

People have managed to create a climate which saw a nursing mother broken hearted and distraught as kidnappers in broad daylight snatched from her grasp (at gun point) a two week-old baby whilst breast feeding. The purpose of this is either as ransom or for ritual practices, which are rife in this place. They have created a climate which saw a qualified medical doctor who trained to save lives embark on holding young girls hostage and converting them into baby producing 'objects' for his 'baby factory'. People have managed to turn this place for the first time in human history into a place where the biggest threat to a bird can be found within its own nest. What goes on in this part of our world is at odds with all human assumptions and belief systems. The main perpetrators of the evil gripping this place are, for the most part, the leaders (elected to serve the people) at federal, state and local levels.

The perpetrators of this evil and their supporters use all sorts of tactics to convince the rest that 'things are not too bad here, what is obtainable here is also obtainable elsewhere.' The question is: even if these heinous crimes are obtainable elsewhere does it make it right that people can no longer even bury their loved ones in peace? Why can't the good things obtainable elsewhere be obtainable here as well? The perpetrators have sought to mask their peculiar evil with all sorts of colourful labels and excuses, such as 'this is a revolution, it is a kind of armed robbery which is obtainable everywhere, it is the by-product of poverty and unemployment, it is political, it will stop one day, nothing lasts forever, it will fizzle out or it is not as bad as it used to be.'

Well, they are either in denial of the true state of things in this place or they are deliberately deceiving their citizens. I believe the latter is the case, as these excuses cannot possibly be reasonable. Revolution is an action by the people against the authorities and not authorities against its citizens or citizens against themselves. Thomas Jefferson said that, '...when the people fear the government there is tyranny, when the government fears the people there is liberty...'

Kidnapping (hostage taking) is an evil crime against a person and humanity in general and armed robbery refers to stealing of goods and property. Although both crimes are felonies, in other parts of the world where there is kidnapping, people usually have a 'cause' they are pursuing (rightly or wrongly); on the other hand in this most uninhabitable place, there is no cause being pursued other than self-destruction and extortion and total destruction of trust between people of the same ethnicity. This has brought the economy of this dreadful place to its knees as everyone metaphorically is 'on the run' and in fear of investing in or developing their businesses in a bid not to attract kidnappers.

Poverty and unemployment cannot be the theory, or else we would see such levels of carnage wherever there is poverty and unemployment. And of course unemployment and poverty are not new but the brand of evil within this place is astonishingly strange, new and evolving all the time. People are now estranged from their own homes and people. If one cannot arrange, meet up and discuss with his or her kinsmen and women, what is left in life and whence cometh posterity?

The perpetrators of these crimes and their supporters will often pretend to be patriotic by acting like psychotic parents who, in their deluded state of mind, feel that it would be shameful to accept that their child is terminally ill or seek help by letting the world know. As a result, they keep their child indoors and prevent them from telling anyone they are ill or going to hospital, in pretence that 'all is well'. At times, this could also be a dubious means of laying a trap so people are oblivious to how bad things have become in order to give them a false sense of security, and as a consequence fall prey to their evil and deadly acts. They stand ready to wave their 'patriotic flag'; to criticise and argue with any right-minded person who ventures to let the world know that people are sharing not only the same rooms but the same beds with deadly pythons determined to destroy anyone who stands in their evil ways. Deadly pythons that would also end up destroying themselves, as no human being is immune to the adverse impact of evil, including the evildoers themselves. They act like some mental health clients who oppose and fight anyone seeking to admit them to hospital due to their lack of insight into a condition that is likely to destroy them in the end.

In a world where people have different talents and gifts, and these are often hidden from individuals yet, many people in this part of the world believe that someone can steal their 'destiny', use unconventional methods to stop one from achieving anything and make another person commit an act they wouldn't have ordinarily committed. Their courts contradict this belief system by finding people guilty of their offences but not on the ground of diminished responsibility. When one cannot look within themselves for answers when they fail, how can they improve their life or correct their behaviour? The route to one's improvement is firmly closed when the fault is ascribed to someone or something else. No one finds what they are looking for in the wrong place.

Everything that holds value to a person's or nation's life is hidden from the gaze of the human eye. No one can pick gold or oil from the surface. One has to dig deep to find these; the same rule applies when it comes to each individual's gift or talent. One has to dig deep in order to locate their talent, even when the talent is glaring, one still has to work hard and others have to contribute in order for one to harness their talent. Now, if one has to dig deep to find their talent... if one cannot even see the talent that is located within them, how can someone else outside find, let alone steal one's destiny? This is absurd, weird and only of use to those who do not want to work hard to succeed

and those who want to milk from these 'confused' minds. Those that have become experts in chasing shadows, anything that is unquantifiable and baseless. No wonder there is never any advancement or development in areas where all these have become norms, as people spend valuable time chasing thin air and planning all manner of evil against those they believe to have stolen their destiny. This is total madness; there is no other word to qualify it. These people fail to appreciate that those deceiving them have not folded their arms but are working hard to convince them, by lying to them. Through this means, they secure their earnings and living. How they then think that, they can fold their arms and manna will drop from heaven, only heaven knows. The truth is that, anyone who tries to reap where they have not sown is a thief, nothing comes from nothing and one (in the main) gets out of life what they put into life. Miracles do not happen without effort. Even winning the lottery is not possible if one has not played the lottery. Many people in this dreadful place build networks empty handed forgetting that, one must first develop their product; be it one's talent, business or item of value and then build a network in order to succeed. Many in this place build network only for gossiping purposes and delude themselves praying for miracle to come from it. When the miracle fails to come through, they start saying aimless vindictive prayers and consulting with devious characters to identify individuals or an individual 'blocking' their miracle. It is then not surprising that these evil people will identify family members or member as responsible and pocket the cash for their efforts. How can anyone identify someone they have no contact with, not met before or someone they do not know?

From today, if you are a parent and you feel you have fallen short of your expectation or your children have not achieved as you anticipated, please ask yourself this simple question: 'What did I do or fail to do and what did my children do or fail to do that resulted in this situation?' As long as there is no medical evidence suggesting that you or your children have been poisoned or physically attacked by someone, the failure lies within. No one else is responsible. Life is like the 24 hours in a day. Everyone has theirs, no one can borrow or lend any part of their 24 hours to someone else whether spent wisely or wasted. If someone has taken something that you believe is yours and you have exhausted every means legally possible without success, it means that thing is not yours to keep and you are challenged to dig deeper to find that which is yours. The fact that someone took what you believe to be yours does not imply that they have stolen your destiny. Don't be a champion in chasing shadows, be a champion in real life events. Let the humility of the brain, which is objective, run and remain king in your life from this day onwards. This will end the senseless attacks, mistrust and killings in families as a result of false doctrines. Just beware, Healthy individuals make healthy families, healthy families make healthy communities, healthy communities make healthy nations and healthy nations would deliver a healthy world. There will never be a United Nations without United Families.

It is my take that, failure has two siblings; an older brother named (Blame) and a younger sister called (Excuses). If this is not true, why is it that 'successful' people do not subscribe to 'stealing of destiny' or do they?

In this part of our world, just like a child's reasoning, it is a popular view that their world is comparable to their contemporaries'. They believe they are the most intelligent ethnic groups, the wealthiest, and the best in everything, including the most educated. Just like a little child whose father is not even the strongest in their block of flats but in the eyes of the child, their father is the strongest man on earth. In this place, it would be uncommon to find a parent in 2014 whose grandparent is or was a graduate. However, an objective comparison reveals that other contemporaries boast of some grandparents who are not only graduates but master and doctorate degree holders.

The reality is that, in this part of the world, things have degenerated to a level where people can no longer differentiate good from bad. This is the place that highlights the reality that the foundations in the second metaphoric building are decaying. There is no better way to illustrate this than using Christianity because, in this place almost everyone claims to be a 'Christian'. Each year during the celebration of the 'passion of Christ' as is customary in Christendom, people condemn all those who took part in the suffering and crucifixion of Jesus Christ especially 'Judas Iscariot' who took a bribe and betrayed Jesus. However, the sad reality in this part of our world where every Christian knows this story is that if the same scenario were to occur in this place, I would bet with everything at my disposal that Jesus Christ would not witness His twentieth birthday. So long as people can see that His father is a carpenter, they are more than likely to say, 'Isn't this the son of Joseph who cannot afford a loaf of bread? A small boy of yesterday! How dare he talk to our elders like that... how dare he stand in front of our elders, law makers and important people to condemn our traditions without fear or respect. We will teach him a lesson!' Jesus Christ would certainly have had more than one disciple willing to collect the money and betray Him anywhere else in the world but in this most uninhabitable place, Jesus Christ would have struggled to have one disciple who would not betray and carry out the killing by themselves through poisoning or assassination, so long as the money was right. The story would be about the one who did not take a bribe... who refused to betray Jesus, not about the one that betrayed Him. In this part of the world today, all the Judases would have spent their money, given the ten percent and received blessings from their various places of worship. If, by miracle, they regretted what they did and rejected the money, the elders and churches would be only too happy to collect the money and put it into 'good use'. Our world, if anything, has progressively gotten worse and failure to recognise this, or any attempt to interpret it wrongly, would amount to a lack of insight which is usually one of the main components responsible for the detention of mental health patients.

An interesting aspect of the lives of people living in this dreadful area of the world is that all their 'leaders', both spiritual and temporal, for example title holders, pastors and ordained priests, all accept that they have many within them who are bad eggs, but none can say who the bad eggs are or what should be done about the bad eggs. They happily share the same platform and criticise one another behind them. Exaltation of one another based on money (of which they do not have more than their contemporaries) is an accepted norm. On the other hand, most unions, family units and associations are based on the identification or manufacture of a common enemy formed on propaganda, point scoring and a 'unity in failure' platform, where people exonerate themselves of all responsibility in their personal and collective failure and heap blame on someone else.

Be warned that any 'peace' and/or 'friendship' with one which is based on creating a common enemy is false, deceitful and immoral. Such 'peace' and 'friendship' do not last and one can never be safe in the hands of people who achieve 'peace' by destroying other characters. Such people have no moral values, integrity or principles. As a result, they can trade in any friendship or relationship once they calculate their 'weird' personal 'gain' at the expense of the rest. They hardly can handle peace without an enemy to facilitate their weird 'peace'.

Valuable time one should utilise to work out strategies for oneself and collective development is wasted on discussing others, nitpicking and witch-hunting. People are so quick to camouflage themselves as victims when they are perpetrators and often can only see what someone else has done wrong. Just like their seers, prophets, prophetesses, pastors and native doctors who only see people with negative plans against someone but no positive plans for anyone. A climate covered with negativity. There is simply a one way negative traffic system in operation. Imagine a place where traffic signals are red-red-red, no amber and, most importantly, no green.

The things obtainable in this part of the world are frightening to imagine and before going into them fully, it is crucial that everyone (within and outside this place) works together to get things right. Any part of the world that decays would certainly adversely affect the rest, in ways no one can ever anticipate or legislate for. Therefore never say, 'This is for them out there, nothing to do with us down here, my bubble is safe, and I don't care whether other people's bubbles are busting, it is not my business.' History and current events suggest otherwise, as someone's business can easily become everyone's business, once someone's bubble can burst, ours can burst too, because whatever burst, their bubble is capable of bursting ours, irrespective of how strong ours is. There should and must not be 'us and them' because we are all in this world together, just like the body. As such we need to be open-minded and seek to appreciate what is happening elsewhere and intervene where necessary.

The warning is, no matter how much is revealed here, it would only serve as a tip of the iceberg when compared with the real magnitude of the evil obtainable in this place. This is a place where leadership has nothing to do with the content of character of the individual but primarily based on a 'zoning, gender and quota system' which indicates that something (MONEY) is being shared and service has no room in this brand of leadership. It is all about people taking their turns in cutting what they presume to be their share of the cake. Based on this agenda of grabbing and sharing without service, some 'leaders' in this part of the world use all anti-civilised and anti-democratic means, including kidnapping and killing of opponents, in order to get in and retain their positions. To reasonable and responsible people, all they crave is service, it does not matter who gives that service so long as the person is not only the best qualified but has all it takes to give such service.

We are told that the root of all evil is MONEY. However many people believe that the root of happiness is

MONEY. The truth is, money is good for so many reasons but has never purchased happiness, love or life itself. Most people in this place associate momentary excitement with long-term happiness, momentary affection (infatuation) with love and a momentary high with lasting joy. In life, sane people like money and when people like money which is an object, they are likely to understand its value and appropriate it well, meaning, 'Putting money in its place, ensuring at all times that it retains its status as a servant not the master'. In other words 'good slave, bad master' status. Therefore, when people like money in the actual sense, they would never place money above the person in possession of it. Problems begin to arise when people begin to associate love, which is meant for human beings, with MONEY.

Unfortunately that is where many people across the world have been and continue to be today, resulting in a broken society as people are at each other's throats due to all the attractions in the first building, 'the skyscraper', which are associated with money. Having said that, people might think it couldn't get worse until they discover the world's most uninhabitable place, where the love of money is no longer the issue but the worship and adoration of money. Worship and adoration, words reserved and ascribed to God only, for those who believe in God. This is the only place in the world where everything is equal to MONEY. Traditional religions and cultural values equal money: justice, healthcare, education, politics, friendships, family relationships, prayers, ethics, morality and values all equals MONEY.

Come with me to this place in our world where MONEY is worshipped and adored... where money is king. Come to the place where human beings have devised titles not only in their local and autonomous communities but in places of worship, for the highest bidders. Come to the place where the front row seats in places of worship are reserved for people known for how much money and financial contributions they have made and can make, with no one questioning how the money was made or where it came from. The donor is not even the subject matter; the main focus is the money because once they stop bringing the money the person becomes irrelevant and unnoticeable in public.

Welcome to the place where even a bishop conjured up an idea to confer knighthood on anyone who could donate a minimum of 1000 dollars. This strategy led the bishop to travel to the United States to canvass for such a deal. A place where, priests request cash in envelopes for attending and carrying out their funeral functions. Welcome to the place where people request money for offering prayers to someone and a place where people are inclined to request money for saying even, 'Good morning sir'. This worship of money seems to have turned many people into psychopaths as they have no insight into what is happening in and around them. It is usually the mentally ill person who is the last to know how bad things are for them. In the same vein, people in this part of our world have no insight into the nature and degree of their peculiar problem.

A place where everyone claims to be a Christian and understands the concept of 'little cross for every little child for Jesus', but many cannot see the little they can do or give but the much they can take and demand from someone else. This includes siblings; many have defined their relationships with their brothers and sisters based on what they are getting. Once there is nothing to get, the relationship ends. Some would only make contact when in need and once they have no need, contact ends. They would never see anything to offer or give. Evil does not visit; evil resides in this part of the world. This place has become so bad that, many who cannot manage their little gardens have placed themselves in charge of other people's gardens, and farms that cater for the needs of the masses.

The level of delusion and paranoia gripping people in this place is so bad that, amidst the kidnapping and hostage takings for a ransom, the snatching and killing of innocent babies (for ritual purposes) by people who ought to love, defend and protect them, coupled with the fact that people resort to lying through their teeth in order to deny even family members information for safety reasons, people still come up with irrelevant and thoughtless slang such as, 'nothing de happen, nothing mega' (meaning, nothing is happening, everything is fine), 'no shaking, *owu ujo?*' (Implying there is no fear), 'carry go, everything is fine no problem, God is in control' as though for believers around the world that had ever been in doubt. Just like someone who is floridly psychotic dancing and saying 'nothing de happen, God is in control' whilst their houses were set ablaze with their children inside. This is their coping mechanism; subconsciously they know they are living in danger but they do not want to believe it. Therefore they seek to profess positivity in hope of comfort and reassurance. However, in reality they are only in denial.

This is the only place in the world where one is better off being a door mat than being poor and if one is financially well-off, they have to always sleep with one eye open in fear of that dreaded knock by criminals whose mission is either to steal, wreck and take lives or steal and wreck lives. Therefore, either way, no one in this part of our world is safe. If you are rich you are in trouble and if you are poor you are also in trouble. People here mostly oper-

ate from a confused state of mind and platform and rational thinking is usually a 'few and far in between' thing.
Therefore, if one is poor in this part of the world, they are
a sinner and if one is rich, they are likely to have stolen
the destiny of other family members. Observing the decay
in the educational and healthcare infrastructures servicing
people in this part of our world would reveal the level of
decadence in the people using these subhuman amenities.

The evil activities in this part of the world is uncommon
and the perpetrators have succeeded in recruiting many
supporters who support their evil deeds at times, and act
on their behalf, including some law enforcement agency
personnel (officers whose primary duty is to enforce the
law and protect all citizens) who receive some form of
income (bribe) and fake protection from them or waiting
in the wings to join them. Many corrupt law enforcement
personnel members supply these fellow criminals with
arms and protection, in return for a percentage from the
proceeds of their evil activities. This is a place where victims are further victimised by those whose duty is to protect and defend them.

One would think that if someone becomes a victim of
a crime such as the kidnap of a relative or armed robbery
in this 21st century, the state apparatus would be deployed
immediately in response to the crime. But in this place,
the victim is often told by law enforcement agencies to
provide some form of financial aid to activate a response.
Many a time the victim is given false hope just as a way to
encourage them to bring more aid, whilst little or no effort
is being invested towards solving the crime. And if the
victim becomes frustrated and starts to complain, it is not
uncommon to hear the law enforcement agency respond
with words such as, 'eh Oga or Madam, Abi na only you
way this kan thing don happen to, na wetin! Man no go

rest for you?' This means, 'eh Sir or Madam, are you the only person this type of thing has happened to, what is it! People won't rest because of you?'

In this part of the world, no life is priceless, including the life of a mother. People have been known to offer the lives of their mothers for money, for fake protection from evil cults, as such in 2009, a young man physically killed his mother and cut off her breast for ritual purposes in the belief that his 'suffering' would be over. When he was caught, all he could say was 'I have suffered enough'.

It is endless, the manner and nature of evil committed in this part of our world. Evil that ranges from people kidnapping themselves, a man turning his nieces and nephews into fatherless and motherless children by killing or organising the killing of his brothers and sisters-in-law, turning his sister-in-law into a widow or brother into a widower and kidnapping the bereaved during the period of a funeral or planning of a funeral, kidnapping of the dead at times, setting up baby factories and terrorising brothers and sisters in their own homes through armed robbery, to a point one can no longer bury their loved ones in peace because those that are meant to mourn with the bereaved currently view the death of their relative as an opportunity to commit heinous crimes against the bereaved in the name of making money. All these uncommon and unthinkable activities (devilish) have been classified as 'business' in this part of our world.

Young men and women intoxicate themselves with illicit substances, carry guns and knives and await instructions at times from their political masters to go and kill or kidnap political opponents. Some wait for relatives to come and pay them to go and kill other relatives either because of envy or because they want to annex their relative's property.

Once the money is right, the request is granted because in this place money is worth more than the person who made the fortune. The ancient 'Nwakaego' (child is more than money) has been turned into 'money is more than the person who created it'.

In this part of our world, people are so myopic and narrow-minded to believe that segregation, division and individualism are more important and productive than working together as a team or community. Everyone knows it all and wants to be in charge. Those wishing to be traditional leaders would fight for their own autonomous communities, those wishing to become local government chairmen would fight for their own local government areas and those wishing to become bishops would fight for their own diocese. They pretend they are fighting to bring development and salvation to their people when their whole intention is to 'better' their individual selfish ambitions and permeate hatred, bigotry and discord within their own ethnicity and community.

This is a place where every advantageous opportunity is used for the intimidation and oppression of others, for example, a young man wishing to join the army would not necessarily be enlisted because he wants to defend and protect his country but as a means to come home with uniform and 'deal' with his uncle who is having a problem with his father. A place where the 'powerful' maltreat their elders and classmates because they managed to become a local government chairperson and a place where people see public service as a private enterprise and the fastest route to 'millionaire road.'

A place where a ticket to governance means a ticket to embezzlement, sharing and looting of public funds hence relatives, friends and associates quickly wave the flag of 'this is our time'. Not 'our time' to serve but our time to oppress, steal and loot public funds at the expense of those who elected them to serve. This is why everyone wants to be in authority and wants to do anything humanly possible, including kidnapping and killing, to stop the other person because it is a game of oppression and stealing, not service. This is one of the places in our world where people in authority patronise criminals, seers and fake prophets because, in this place, the cultural and traditional values or norms are anti-civilisation and anti-families, as these values and norms have nothing in them to benefit the common person or posterity of the people, and as a result many families are in disarray and without cohesion.

Most families in this part of the world including those in diasporas are broken and many interest groups have developed within it in pursuit of deferring negative hidden agendas at odds with family cohesion and values. That is why, no matter how wrong one's behaviour is, one would not be short of support and supporters, each with undisclosed game plans intentionally or unintentionally geared towards the permeation of family discord and lack of cohesion which is at the root of the disaster in this place. People are either in camps or indifferent about whatever is going wrong and everyone adopts the position that neutrality provides the best solution to a problem. Wherever there is progress in life, cohesion in communities and nations, it is because people work together, share a common vision, plan and execute together starting from strong family units. However, in this most uninhabitable place, it is the attack on family unity from all and sundry that is at the root of the crisis going on here. Divisions and separations are, if not encouraged, supported in this place either by proactive measures or through deafening silence and indifference. All institutions in this part of the world, including family members, work against themselves so long as there is something with monetary value to gain. Many are often praised and held as achievers by their 'loved ones' not because of their performance at work, academia, invention or business but because of their opposition to their wives, husbands or partners, so long as there is something to benefit and many have used the discord in their immediate family to solidify and mend outside relationships. The biggest trading commodity in this place is gossip and people spend valuable time that should have been utilised for posterity and improvement in their personal lives to discuss others and blame others for their own failure.

This part of our world is full of 'seers', 'prophets' and 'prophetesses' (almost everyone is a seer) and their only job is to plant seeds of discord and hatred in families because they can only 'identify' a family member responsible for any misfortune that someone suffers. They never see anyone responsible for fortune or success in someone's life. In this place, human beings are not only born to 'succeed', but they are born to be always 'healthy' and 'live forever'. Therefore, people never go in search of who is responsible for anything positive, for those are 'standard' and expected but answers are usually sought at the slightest glimpse of any negative occurrence in a person's life. The answer to the negative occurrence will never lay with the individual themselves but a relative would be identified who planted the evil seed in the person's path. Even the death of an elderly person in this part of the world cannot be natural. No one goes to the seers, prophets and prophetesses when the going is good because everyone claims responsibility for any success in their lives. Therefore seers can only see those who are causing bad luck to others and those are usually family members.

People have killed or driven their partners away because

they were informed by seers, prophets and prophetesses that their partners were sent by an evil spirit or they are the source of all the bad luck in their lives. Many families are like battlefields with an invisible warfare going on in this place; hence the entire place is in disarray. My family would have been one of such families if we subscribed to the fiction teller's tale that my mother's illness was 'a spiritual attack' by my uncle. The truth is that many have died and are dying, many have been tortured and are being tortured and many have been injured and are currently being injured because of all these money-driven 'prophets and prophetesses' telling fibs to vulnerable, emotionally unstable and weak people. My mother met her early and untimely death through this terrible 'make believe' gimmick. In this place evil has grown because most people turn a blind eye to it and at times do whatever it takes to mask it or pretend it does not happen. If people cannot review their mistakes... if people cannot identify errors and if people ignore their mistakes, how on earth could they correct it? Well, instead of correcting it, they are more likely to repeat and normalise evil. In places where things work better, when things go wrong every attempt is made to review and learn lessons from the problem. This way, though one cannot remedy what has gone wrong, there will be things put in place to prevent such a thing from happening again or reduce the frequency at which it happens. In this place rather, sentences such as 'hapu ihe ahu' meaning 'leave that thing' became the order of the day and led to a situation where (in metaphoric sense); the nest of the bird became the bird's greatest threat. 'hapu ihe ahu' because he or she is old, a sibling, an in-law or a friend. 'Hapu ihe ahu' no matter how bad the deed, the thought or the saying. Everyone embarked upon 'leave that thing' until, evil gripped all facets of this community and today no one is safe.

This is a place where people happily celebrate failure. A place where people have become so empty, they are only too desperate to obtain 'local' titles from village Chiefs or places of worship to mask their inadequacies. People who cannot compete with their contemporaries in their places of work... people who are not the standard bearers in their chosen profession... people who have not invented or manufactured anything... people who are mere consumers and people who cannot even make positive impacts on little children through their behaviour or utterances contributed immensely in creating the world's most uninhabitable place. This is the place where the saying 'empty vessels make the most noise' comes to life. A place where people take pleasure in encouraging others by telling them to 'scatter' or 'destroy' if someone says or does 'this, that or the other'. They forget that scattering is an offering of nature and the masters of the art of scattering are children, because that is how children explore and learn. They delude themselves by thinking that an act which anyone including children can perform is an achievement... an art that does not require learning or teaching. People generally believe in this part of the world that one can obtain 'good' by doing 'bad', without an inkling that any 'good' obtained through 'bad' would generate more bad in the long-run. The same way that a good looking building built on weak and faulty foundations is subject to collapse with the possibility of destroying everything within it. **The biggest problem in this part of the world is that there are many adults who are stuck in the mindset of a child... in the mode of scattering and destroying but very few builders. This means that those who scatter easily find many people who scatter and they begin to encourage,**

support and hype themselves up in the weird belief that they know what they are doing. They never plan on how to build or unite and whenever they are seeking to bring people together, it is always for an ulterior motive with evil intentions. They are also masters in jumping from camp to camp; always calculating which camp favours them the most. They are always carrying propagandas and fabricated lies as a means of gaining entry into their desired camp. All they know how to do is to scatter.

If people are too old to learn the skill required to build, they should, at the very least, learn to support the builders. The one who scatters has more impact as no skill is required and anyone can scatter, but very few can build. Please teach and equip that child with the knowledge and skill of mending fences and do not leave them with their scattering ability which nature offers every child, or at the very worst, encourage them to scatter. That way, the child will develop the skill and know how to mend fences when the inevitable challenges of life occur in their lives.

The evil in this part of the world has strived and continues to strive because the perpetrators and their supporters seek to brand anyone who tries to do or say anything against the status quo as 'talkative or over critical'. They act as cancer which prefers paracetamol as mode of treatment, forgetting that evil is like weeds which do not seek permission from the farmer before appearing in greater numbers than the planted crops, but would never depart without the willful and persistent actions of the farmer, otherwise the weeds would stand to destroy the potency of the planted crops.

In most places, if not everywhere in the world, the act of killing is mainly applicable when nations are at war; people are fighting over something, this could be power, money, a portion of land, woman, man or because someone has wronged them. Though none of these should warrant the killing of another person, in this evil infested place, envy and jealousy is enough for one to seek to eliminate the other. The quest to be the first can cause someone to eliminate anyone seen to be better, therefore second best becomes the 'best'. This pattern is at the root of the level of decay, mediocrity and backwardness in this place. How can anyone attain excellence with this manner of approach... when sane people understand that the only way to achieve excellence is by seeking to better the best? An uncle who is not happy that his own children are not working hard to succeed in life might seek to eliminate his nephew who is progressing in business, education or career. This is the only place in our world where someone would complain that his or her office is dirty but has no regard for the cleaner whose job (assigned through 'division of labour') is to clean. The same person can be seen saying to the cleaner, 'What are you still doing here? Will you get out of here; I have an important meeting now. Get out, ordinary cleaner.'

This is the birth place of people who attribute collective success (even when their success is an act of luck) as their own individual achievement but any failure, no matter how small, they attribute to others. As a result, people seek reasons and there are many 'seers', both in the places of worship and black magicians, who quickly confirm who is responsible for their failure within the person's family set up. If no one has seen a state of anarchy or anomie in time of peace, this is the place to see it played out in real life. If anyone is in doubt of what human beings can turn into when money becomes everything for them, this is the place to preview the consequences. The psychology of people living in this part of our world needs to be studied and understood in order to find solutions, as well as to ensure this is not replicated elsewhere in our world. In the words of Wayne Dyer, PhD, "If you change the way you look at things, the things you look at change." This place holds the key to the understanding of how evil evolves and confirms that human emotions and social interaction have not changed; rather they have taken a turn for the worse due to all the attractions in the first building. People are not interested in the division of labour and are only willing to pursue something, irrespective of what it entails, so long as there is money in it. Everything is obtainable as long as the money is right. Even criminals would join the band wagon and mask their evil acts by claiming they are doing whatever is 'in vogue'. This whole evil took hold with the inception of the 'business' called 'clearing and forwarding', then '419' (a trade mark code exported around the globe in support of a head of state) and now the final nail on the coffin of Igbo people, 'kidnapping' – where they now eat from their own flesh and steal from their pocket and terrorism (carried out by BOKO HARAM) in the north (at least for now?). Prior to the 'clearing and forwarding' parents, indeed mothers in particular, always advised their children with these words as Igbo ethics and culture demands: 'chetakwa ebe isi, emenyekwala anyi ihere, ezi aha ka ego' meaning 'remember where you come from, don't bring shame to your family; good name is better than money'. But following the inception of 'clearing and forwarding', and the crowning of criminals in the name of 'clearing and forwarding' businesses by corrupt local title holders and church leaders, parents' advice changed to 'lekwe ihe ibegi mege. Ihe ibegi mege, soro ha mewe. Ino n'ulo emegini?' meaning 'look at what your mates are doing, whatever your mates are doing, go and follow them and do it. What are you doing at home?'

The damage in this place has primarily been caused by the people inhabiting the land but in their confused state, they point at others as responsible for their woes when they have carried out more killings and miseries on their own than any outsider has done. Instead of dealing first with what is inside, they pretend it is not happening and point at others. They forget that one cannot build without foundation and one must always count one before two in mathematical terms. Things have gotten so bad that a vicar, in seeking to justify the reason some churches have chosen sombre funeral services as opportunities to invite donations and pledges from mourners said, 'Oh well, funeral services are now the only time one can guarantee the availability of those who can help the church financially. Crime and fear of crime have driven many people away.'

This means that it is not only the criminals who see funerals as an opportunity for financial 'gain' but places of worship too. The places of worship have become trading arenas with the highest bidder getting the highest title. The leaders in some of these places of worship have either no clue or have forgotten that without truth, love and faith it is impossible to please God. They have no understanding that the way they revere those with the biggest donations and confer them with titles, irrespective of the sources of their wealth, encourages criminals and others to acquire money by all means possible in the weird belief that their money would 'cleanse their sins'.

As children of God, we need to only preach and deliver the Word, the right way (salvation message) and trust with faith that God's words are more than powerful, more than sufficient to do the work. Tell people of God to give generously with joy, as God appreciates cheerful givers. It is a good practice for people to give help (financially or otherwise) but this must be done in secret, so that God, who rewards in secret, would reward them accordingly. Never single out anyone for a special praise, because of the worth or value of their gift for which you have no clue where it came from. Rather, just like the Author of Christianity (Jesus Christ), encourage the least who is giving their all, as Christ did in relation to the 'widow's mite'. As the Curate at All Saints Church, Edmonton, in London (Reverend Meymans Sala) told his congregation on the first Sunday of 2014, 'I encourage all of you, indeed all Christians, to always read and be guided by Psalm 141.' The entire verses are great but verses 4 and 5 note, 'Let not my heart be drawn to what is evil, to take part in wicked deeds with men who are evildoers, let me not eat of their delicacies. Let a righteous man strike me. It is a kindness, let him rebuke me. It is oil on my head. My head will not refuse it. Yet my prayer is ever against the deeds of evildoers. Their rulers will be thrown down from the cliffs.'

This is a place where many have lost their lives simply because they visited and wanted to stay with their own people in their respective villages. Their own villages should represent their safety net and safest place, yet some are butchered and slaughtered in ways unbefitting of an attacking wild animal. Yet the following Sunday, a relative who took part in the brutal murder, the child kidnapper, the baby factory owner will carry their bibles with their hefty gifts and dance towards the altar as their pastors dance with joy in anticipation to welcome a hefty present and give 'blessing' from 'above' as the congregation celebrates with murderers, rapists and kidnappers and eats from evildoers' delicacies. Even a wild bird would never destroy its nest but here people are engaged in wilful destruction of their own homes with limited or no insight.

People have become so confused in this place that, even though no one trusts the other person and will rarely give information or about their whereabouts, some people would still say, 'Oh I had a great time there, things are improving or everything is okay,' even when they visit this place in hiding.

People are so gullible that one single act of 'recognition' or 'praise' they received in an event they attended or the sight of some good roads would make them forget that they had been playing 'hide and seek' in order to survive their visit. If one pushes them to gain a little insight that things are really bad, at worst they will start to tell you how to survive the place. 'All you need to do is not give anyone information about your movements, if people ask you how long you are staying, tell them you still have three weeks, even though you are leaving tomorrow.'

How on earth could one pursue posterity if all they are doing with their own people is playing a fatal 'hide and seek'? People in this part of the world have no under-standing that the real yardstick to judge the level of devel-opment and decadence in any society is by examining the state of healthcare and educational infrastructures. They will not take out time to examine these infrastructures to appreciate how damaged the psyche of the people using them has become, when they visit the place they call home. The evil in this place is so masked that at times the only way one can hear about it is if it happened to them directly, or they are within the scene where it is taking place, or it has happened to someone very close to them because the media in such places are government propaganda machines. Therefore it may be happening next door, yet if you haven't heard or seen it, it hasn't happened. However, the evil going on in this place has affected almost everyone in one way or another. Those who are the perpetrators of these evil crimes would leave no stone unturned in seeking to convey the message that all is well, in an attempt to carry on with their evil ways or to lure those who are running away to get into their evil net. **What they do not know is that they are acting like the 'proverbial snail' which thought it was extinguishing the fire by releasing bodily fluids without knowing it was fastening its own death in the process. No evildoer will go unpunished; what awaits them is perpetual pain and suffering with serious generational consequences. This is a guarantee unless they genuinely confess and repent of their sins and their offspring, siblings, relatives and friends condemn these evil acts and repent of them.**

The way things are in 2014, anyone can occupy another person's land so long as they have enough money to bribe that person's traditional ruler or elders in the rightful own-er's community. Instead of losing the case in court they will bribe members of the judiciary and delay justice until the true owner of the land runs out of money to pursue the case. And if they choose, the person can hire killers to assassinate the true owner of the land and usually in this part of the world, the word 'redress' is nonexistent. The way money controls everything in this place, including securing of a 'passport to heaven', has led many people to pursue it at all costs, including killing their nearest and dearest. Elders in this community move from camp to camp, holding different viewpoints on a singular issue and giving to each ear what they want to hear depending on what is on offer. If all parties become present at the same time, the same elder will choose to be absent, quiet or support the person they have taken more from or likely to get more from.

Words such as 'principles', 'truth', 'integrity' and 'justice' have no place in this part of our world; people do not even know the value of these any more. They have forgotten, or never really knew, that when one loses wealth, nothing is lost, with health, something is lost, but when one loses honour everything is lost. In this place currently, integrity, principle and etiquette have disappeared from the elders' dictionaries. An uncle who never wanted to even accept your greetings, let alone have a chat with you because you were a student in need, would start querying your whereabouts once they feel you have something (material) to offer. They would lay all sorts of fictitious claims about what they did and did not do when you were growing up, simply because they believe you have some assets.

Some would use still pictures to describe their involvement in your life but would never produce any documentary evidence such as a receipt to prove they paid your school fees or even visited you at school. They have no understanding that anyone can concoct any story of choice around still pictures, including, 'This was when I used to fly with my hidden wings or when I used to walk with my head'. Depending on whom this is being told to, who would argue it did not happen? If some of these elders have no story to tell, they might seek to convince you by telling you how close they were with your late parents. None of these they remembered or cared to tell you when you were a struggling student. Some would set their children up against you by claiming that all the money they had, they used to train you with, no singular proof. Everything is based on fairy tale, fiction and fantasy. It would all be well and good if it remains a fairy tale but in this case people are dying because of all this nonsense.

As they narrate their lies over and over, it begins to make sense to them and they begin to believe in their own fabrications along with others who share in the same delusional belief system. The central theme here is nothing else than MONEY.

One singular 'monetary benefit' is enough in this place, for elderly parent, an uncle, auntie, a pastor or native doctor to destroy a family by encouraging hatred, separation and even killings in the family. A place where the majority of parents see their children as their insurance and would use all forms of tactics including emotional blackmail to maintain and achieve their selfish goal, irrespective of whether the tactics destabilises their children's immediate families. Parents have been known to say, 'If the marriage is not working, you can go your separate ways,' instead of looking for ways to keep the family together. These parents do not give a damn about the impact of separation on their grandchildren. All they are interested in is how such separation would benefit them with the central theme, MONEY; nothing else. They have no clue that reasonable parents do whatever it takes, including giving all they have to build up their children who are starting a family and invest their experience in making their children's union a successful one. Honour, integrity, straightforwardness and principles have vanished from the dictionary as far as most people in this part of the world are concerned. The few who believe in doing the right thing have been suppressed and oppressed by the sheer volume of the noise makers and their intimidating tactics. However, just like in the words of Steve Jobs, 'Don't let the noise of others' opinions drown out your own inner voice.'

Children growing up in this place are being conditioned to learn that all that matters is money, irrespective of how it comes about. Knowing that children can only replicate, reduce or advance what they have seen, heard and touched, one can only imagine what the future holds in a decade or two if this trend continues. It is, however, very critical to understand that, when it comes to evil, they are very likely to advance the acts because nothing comes easier than evil; teaching and learning are often not required. It is usually copied and the 'copycat tendency' in them is higher. Imagine what this place would look like in the next decade if this status quo is retained, as these children graduate, still replicating and enhancing these evil practices?

In this part of our world, the worship of money has led individuals to believe that they can survive as branches without being connected to the tree. This adoration and worship of money has turned many sombre funeral proceedings into military processions, as some human beings, who are deprived of morals, intoxicated by illicit substances, rise above the serenity of death and view funerals as an opportunity to kidnap, rape and at times murder the bereaved.

In this part of our world, the true revelation of what nature offers, when human beings have no morals and are uneducated, coupled with the dire need to have the 'latest' whilst in possession of firearms and under the influence of illicit substances, has been laid bare for all to see. This is the part of our world where rags are preferred by many to anyone without money. This then contributes to the desperation to have money by all means necessary, as everyone deserves respect. In this part of our world, brothers negotiate with kidnappers to have their siblings kidnapped and on a regular basis. The 'baddies' eliminate the 'goodies' and gradually the baddies, like weeds, are outnumbering the goodies and people generally either hail these baddies as heroes or provide excuses for their evil acts as they themselves lie in waiting to join the baddies. The act of carrying guns, which any physically able person can do, becomes something to be glorified, with no insight into the psychological damage these acts of evil generate to victims and their real relatives. These are people who may not even be able to write their names, let alone manufacture a gun or its bullets. But a trigger, which anyone including little children can pull, becomes an achievement for them, and terrorising the people they ought to protect gives them a sense of achievement. The baddies can never be seen as the baddies so long as they are making huge donations to the church and local communities. They kill, steal and destroy their own people and at the same time use their evil 'proceeds' to buy their people over. They feed the rest with their money made from killing their relatives and everyone then eats from the delicacies of the evildoers.

Things have gotten so bad in this part of our world, people are known to kidnap themselves in pretence that someone else is holding them at ransom so relatives can send money to pay for their release.

People merely exist here, not live, and many of the 'patriotic people' of this land act like confused parents who refuse to accept that their child is in a coma, therefore denying their child medical attention by masking the illness. The saddest thing about this place is that; children have taken and are taking note, children are have copied and have gradually been conditioned to believe that these evil ways are 'normal'. Children in this part of our world are being conditioned to believe that it is okay to render one's nephew or niece fatherless, motherless, turn one's sister into a widow and one's brother into a widower so long as enough money is made to purchase titles from the church, buy over the local community, government and build a massive house in the village with a fleet of the latest cars and gadgets.

Our world needs to wake up and study what is happening in this part of our world for two reasons. Firstly, the citizens of this place are on Earth for a reason. Keep in mind the anus which was always belittled because of its position yet other parts of the body failed to fully appreciate that the anus held the key to the overall health of the body. Remember the rejected stone can sometimes become the corner stone. It might not be obvious to the eye right now, but the decay of this part of our world where citizens cannot even bury their loved ones in peace anymore, or travel and stay in their villages without fear of being kidnapped or killed would adversely affect our world in ways the world never seen or anticipated before if our world turns a blind eye to this uninhabitable place. Secondly, the world needs to be mindful and understand what can happen to the human psyche when deprived of academic and moral education amidst total breakdown of law and order, extreme consumption of drugs and alcohol, confused leadership coupled with all the attractions in the skyscraper and worst of all, the worship and adoration of money.

It is important to keep in mind that human beings, indeed children, do not invent in isolation. They invent based on that which is seen, heard or touched. Therefore one must ask, what are the children of this place seeing, hearing and touching and what else is there for them to replicate and enhance other than the WORSHIP of MONEY?

American exceptionalism is rooted on their founding fathers declaration of independence which reads '... **we hold these truths to be self-evident, that all men are created equal, that they are endowed by their Creator with certain unalienable Rights, that among these are Life, Liberty and the pursuit of**

Happiness...', so I invite readers, citizens of this uninhabitable place and the whole world to an uncommon anthem that holds the key to turning this place to be the best inhabitable place on earth:

Arise O Compatriots, Nigeria's call obey
To serve our fatherland
With love and strength and faith
The labours of our heroes past
Shall never be in vain
To serve with heart and might
One nation bound in freedom, peace and unity
O God of Creation, direct our noble cause,
Guide (thou) our leaders right,
Help our youth the truth to know
In love and honesty to grow
And living just and true
Great lofty heights attain
To build a nation where peace and justice shall reign.

Brothers and sisters, remember that Nigerian exceptionalism is rooted on the forgotten declaration of independence by our founding fathers – '... to build a nation "and a world" where no man, woman or child is oppressed and so with peace and plenty, Nigeria "and our world" may be blessed...' and effective use of the humility of the brain. All hands must be on deck with no fear or favour so that together, we can walk towards a better tomorrow. No good thing comes easy and according to a dear friend, Mr Charles Oham 'one is better die for something than live for nothing'.

Men Are The Problem, Women Are The Solution

If indeed children are the future, mothers are key to that future because, no matter how well or how badly behaved, no mother alive has ever, or will ever, be able to miss the birth of her baby, but there is always a possibility, a real chance, that even the best fathers can miss the birth of their babies. Due to the inseparable link between the womb and the baby, mothers or 'mother figures' on average spend more time with their children during their formative years (0-5 years) than anyone else. These formative years are pivotal to every child's development.

Children only learn through observation; what they have not heard about or seen simply does not exist. All their imaginary friends and/ or foes they grow up to know are not real. Only what they see, hear, and touch will make real sense to them when they reach the age of reason. How important are these facts to the 'organisers' and leaders of this world who happen to be men? Do they really understand and appreciate these? If they do, how much investment have they made to support mothers in this most critical role of spending more time, and nurturing children in their formative years? And what are the author- ities doing to ensure that the right morals and values are inculcated in mothers and would-be-mothers to equip them to be ready to nurture their children positively? This question is necessary because, with or without fathers, mothers are more likely to be the ones nurturing the future of our world (children). Isn't it shameful...isn't it a lack of insight that, in view of these glaring facts, some places in our world today have laws and traditions prohibiting women's education? This is as good as leaving one's future in the hands of a gambler. No wonder some of the children in this world grow up devoid of morals and standards which leave them vulnerable to all manner of exploitation. No wonder some of them turn into 'waves' which can be tossed about by any wind that comes their way. Some become vulnerable to exploitation by gangs, crusaders of hate who turn them into suicide bombers or cult members. Because they are not deep-rooted in positive values, everything that glitters becomes gold in their eyes.

It goes without saying that every child is likely to observe and copy good morals from an academically and morally sound mother.

Good fathers are products of good mothers and/or fathers who benefited through a lineage or association where a good mother 'planted a good seed.'.'.' Even when someone had become a good father in order to counter the effects of a bad father, it still requires a good mother primarily to guide that thought process. The genesis of good fatherhood is simply good motherhood; for example, traditionally, within some cultures in the past, boys were not brought up to be 'domesticated'; therefore, for any boy to be domesticated in such places, a mother must have begun the process somewhere. As a male, I am able to cook today because, I saw my father in the kitchen cooking. My father was able to cook because my grandmother defied a 'males never go into the kitchen' tradition... a cultural norm that prohibited male children from entering the kitchen. She insisted on taking my father into the kitchen risking the wrath of my grandfather and the community elders. Her suffering and punishment then, for defying this tradition, have today made a positive generational impact because my sons cannot relate to a world where sons are barred from entering the kitchen to cook. As it is for cooking, so it is for every other thing that children observe and are privy to. It is unlikely that we would find a good father if a good mother had not begun the process somewhere because everyone is a product of the womb. In addition, caring and nurturing are primarily and historically roles that nature has bestowed unto women while men have to be nurtured to do follow suit. The caring and nurturing expertise of women should not be restricted to family situations but should be utilised in governance too. It is expected that fathers would play their roles and commit themselves to the development of their children especially, their sons during their formative years. However, a father's role becomes more critical during his children's teenage years (especially his sons) in order to prepare them to become good fathers, husbands, and civilised and responsible adults. A father's role during his children's formative years is important, but it should be mainly supportive of mothers. A Father is unlikely to play this critical role in his children's teenage years effectively if, during their formative years, a proper foundation was not laid primarily by mothers or mother-figures who spend the most time with the children. In teenage years a mother's role may need to switch to supportive and, within that period, an academically and morally sound mother who goes into politics or any leadership position is likely to do a better job of it than a man. Without adequate investment into girls who later become mothers, our children will not have the proper foundation to develop into the reasonable adults, parents, and leaders they are meant to be. Why have I said this?

In the course of my work as an Approved Mental Health Professional I have come to know many families and have seen various dynamics at play. The most pertinent factor in most of the cases I came across is that, at least three quarters of over one thousand assessments I carried out under the England and Wales Mental Health Act of 1983 (as amended in 2007) had a background that read, 'his or her parents divorced or separated when he or she was...' There was a case of a young man who was under 25 years of age. He was living with his mother who was identified as his nearest relative on the legal grounds of 'living together and providing care' which takes precedence over the older parent who is not residing together with the client. When I was collecting information about the client's background from his mother, she said, 'the main reason my son got involved with drugs and went mad is because of his father. His father refused to help him; he was never on the scene and abandoned us when our son was only 9 years of age. I tried everything to get him to help in controlling this boy, but his father was too selfish and left everything to me.'

I happened to meet the client's father unexpectedly much later on the ward during one of his visits to the ward. Without knowing me, and because I was dressed in my traditional attire, he greeted me with, 'Good afternoon, sir.' I greeted him back and then he asked me, 'Are you an Igbo man?' I replied 'Yes' and he said 'I am too.' He then asked 'Please can I talk to you for a minute?' I obliged and took him to a quiet room. He then told me that he is the father of the young man I applied for his detention the other day. He said to me 'I am an Igbo man like you and I thank God I met you. My brother, I had such a nice family back home before we came to this country. When we arrived, my wife and I were both doing menial jobs to make ends meet. However, my wife was very fortunate to get a very good job whilst I struggled to get one. I am a professional but it was difficult to find a job. I even considered retraining for something else. However, I carried on doing menial jobs whilst my wife became the bread winner in our household. I was shocked when she suddenly changed overnight. She made sure that my children knew that she was the bread winner and reduced me to nothing before my children. This boy you see here was such an intelligent boy when he was much younger but my wife made life so difficult my children were not listening to me anymore. They saw their mother as their god who provided everything they need. She would buy all manner of games for them, leave the house whenever she wants and come back whenever she likes. She even began to attend a different church. If it is not what her friends advised her, it is what 'my pastor said' she would confront me with. She called me all sorts of names and told the children that I was a useless, stupid and hopeless man. I literally became impotent in all ram-ifications overnight. I was no longer able to say anything to my children and they would listen to me.

I remember one day, I commented on a particular violent game she bought for the boys. That day, I was told that my presence in the house was disturbing the family peace. She asked me to say how much I contrib-uted to the family upkeep. The situation in the home became so difficult and unbearable, I could no longer function. She called the police numerous times for me and in the end, I just had to leave.' You won't believe this; but on the day I left, she organised a party. I was told by one of her friends (who she did not know was in contact with me), that my children and their mother were saying that the devil in their lives had gone. This son of mine was then nine years of age.' At this point he became a bit emotional. After a short break he went on to say, '…when this young man was 15 years of age, she suddenly realised she could no longer control him. She then called and for the first time, wanted me to come and perform a miracle, but it was too late. I remember coming around but my son would not sit and talk to me. All he wanted was for me to give him money to feed his drug habit. He walked off on me several times. Once I say anything he does not like, he walks off and will never come back no matter what I say. He was no longer listening to his mother either and she could not control him. I was not surprised because his mother cultivated the idea in his mind that I was nothing. He grew up with that and believed that to be true. There was simply nothing I could do. I made it clear to her that she was reaping the fruit of her labour but everyone is now sharing in that fruit. She continues to blame me but cannot see that anything she did was wrong.' I asked him whether he had told his wife then, what could happen if he was not able to control his children. He replied, 'I told her, but she would not listen. She believed she could do it all by herself. She had many friends advising her, plus her pastor who was also advising her. She simply was not listening. Instead she was threatening me with all sorts of things.'

This story says it all; it is usually the case that parents blame one another when things go wrong. The truth of the matter is that the problem here is situational. From an African perspective it is almost un-cultural for a woman to be the breadwinner, though this is changing now. It may also have been very difficult for the man to adjust to the situation and revert to a house-husband. They were not prepared for the culture clash and the switch in responsibilities and roles. Having said that, if society invested in girls both morally and academically situations like this are unlikely or less likely to occur. If society which is mainly run by men understood the importance of family cohesion and the need to set children on the right path to become leaders of tomorrow, human beings would be more prepared to retain family cohesion in various life situations, especially when migrating to a different country such as England. Both parents would be more likely to prefer doing what is right, instead of doing what they can do. As my late father who was a teacher said, 'In order to operate within the realms of humanity, one must prefer what is right to do, to doing what they can do.' He cited an example 'If one cannot visit someone they know when they are bereaved or ill because of a disagreement (unless the bereaved made an advance directive or the unwell had indicated they do not want to see that person), then, the person is operating outside the realms of humanity.'

Boys in particular are usually able to listen to both parents when young. However, as they grow into their teens they naturally begin to develop into young men and, at that stage, there is only so much a mother can do, especially for a boy who decides to go the wrong way. A mother who is not aware of this could easily fall victim to what happened in this case and many cases like it. Though ignorance of the law is not an excuse, people can only do what they know how to do. There is no way one can expect an orange tree to produce a mango. If they don't know the law, they cannot and will not do it. Any mother or father in the same frame of mind is likely to do the same, and, at the time of doing it, they would not see anything wrong with it. People rarely notice what they are doing wrong, they might not do it. They are likely not to appreciate that life is not about doing what one can do but all about doing what is right and proper to do. The problem here has something to do with the couple, but it has everything to do with society (engineered primarily by men) which failed to empower and invest in girls through education in this most vital role.

As a young boy growing up, at the age of 12, I knew I could out-sprint my mother. I also knew she could not discipline me. At that time I knew I was stubborn. Then, I was only interested in activities such as; sleeping, eating, playing and hanging out with friends. However, nothing kept me on the straight and narrow...nothing got me to do what my mother (who usually was at home) wanted as much as when she said 'Wait until your father gets home.' Each time she said that, I quietly checked with her about what exactly she wanted done and got it done. I knew then as I know now, that without that line from my mother, it would have been both practically and theoretically impossible for her to get me to do what I didn't want to do. In most cases the things children do not like to do are often useful things. Mankind cannot say the problems of the world are beyond it when most of the problems are man-made. The quickest and most effective way to destroy the world is to bring chaos in families which remain the bedrock of society.

In order to start the process of fixing this world, and for mankind to genuinely advance the second metaphoric building above, all emphasis needs to be laid on family cohesion. Children are central to this because no one goes on to become anything good, bad, or ugly without first being a child. Once this is acknowledged as a fact, then issues of upbringing, parenting, and particularly mother-hood become critical. It must be understood and acknowl-edged that the massive problems and crises seen in society today did not originate from anywhere else other than the family, and the way in which children, who become our future leaders, are brought up.

Trimming around the edges, and coating over the cracked walls cannot provide lasting solutions or answers to our world's crises. The 'first principles' of engineering (which are: 'going right back to the guiding principles, theories, formulas or science upon which whatever calculations are made') need to be applied in order to get to the root causes of our world's crises, which have never gotten better and will progressively get worse if mankind continues on this dangerous path that has put everyone at severe risk. This is now even more critical in view of the interplay between the two metaphoric buildings described above. The designers of this world (predominantly men) since time immemorial have pursued everything on the basis of cheating, class division (superior and inferior, master and servant), 'us and them,' and the 'goodies-and-the-baddies' approach to life. This is as good as parts of the human body waging war against themselves, which wreaks havoc on the body (the world) itself.

There is no doubt that from the moment of creation or 'big bang', leadership has been the domain of men. To date over 90% of our world is still run by men. Men have gradually brought our world to this current state where, safety has become an illusion to the sane. Therefore, it will not be an exaggeration or unsafe to say that men are behind the mayhem we had seen and are witnessing in this world today but, in women lies the solution we desperately need.

In order to get things right, the focus should and must be on the families of this world.

If human beings manage to get all families right, communities and society at large will become right automatically. Once the root of a tree is healthy, the stem, branches, and leaves are likely to be healthy as well. The time has now come to trace the problems of our world to their likely origin.

A whopping ninety percent of three hundred adults of varying racial, cultural, and religious backgrounds surveyed for this book, who had the experience of having both parents around in childhood, agree that their mothers (or mother figures) spent more time with them from the time they could remember to the age of ten (that's five years on top of the accepted formative period of a child's life, which currently stands at between zero and five years) and had more impact on them in their formative years than their fathers or anyone else. The survey did not include adults from same-sex partnerships as they were difficult to come by.

From the result of this survey, it is not surprising why Mother's Day has an edge to it compared to Father's Day. The ideal hope is for fathers to play, if not an equal role to that of mothers, a significant role in the upbringing of their children. However, even with the best will in the world and no matter how far human beings take social engineering, on average, mothers are likely to have the upper hand when it comes to time parents spend with their children during infancy. There are and will continue to be some exceptions to this rule where the reverse is the case due to factors such as, mental and physical illness or death of a mother. The truth is that fathers are strangers to their babies from the day of conception to approximately nine months later when their babies are delivered. Mothers always have two options in terms of the mode of feeding their babies, whereas fathers have only one option, the less important option of the 'feeding bottle.' Fathers may be the 'pillars' but mothers are the 'live wires' and keys to all families. Therefore, mothers cannot be expected to perform their work empty-handed, or without a fuse. Men may be the owners of the shop, but women are the shop-keepers as well as the customers and, without these two, the shop would not exist. If women are not supported and equipped to keep the shop, or if they stop shopping, the shop will close down. The key to sustaining a shop lies in treating the shopkeepers and customers well. When the owner of a shop does that, they can sit back and watch their business grow.

If society invests in girls and women by ensuring sound academic and moral education, the world will take a different turn for the better. The brain needs to be activated here and humility is required in order for this to be properly understood and implemented.

It is critical to examine the failings of men and appreciate why girls who later become women and then progress to become mothers hold the key to positive change in this second building. An investigation into and an understanding of this would cast shame on society as a whole, and men in particular, because of the lack of investment in girls and women who are the bearers of our world's future (children). This should have been of the utmost priority.

This is not a religious book and was never intended to be; after all, I am a failed seminarian. The story that unfolds here is not intended to be believed as a 'gospel.' The story is not chosen for any particular reason, other than the fact that the lessons from it are beneficial to mankind irrespective of one's background.

In order to appreciate how men have historically gotten things wrong, a critical examination of what is said to have happened in the Garden of Eden may help. It is important to emphasise, irrespective of one's persuasion and/or the interpretations given to the events in the Garden of Eden, that there is a pivotal lesson to be learned from these events by all human beings (believers and non-believers alike) that illustrates what is at play and the major reason why human beings' emotional and social interactions have not positively altered. What happened in the Garden also provides humankind with insight into what needs to change in order to progress to the second metaphoric building, which can be likened to a five-year-old, due to its emotional immaturity. This story is indicative of what is still happening in modern-day society.

It was said that in the Garden of Eden, Adam was the only person there at first. He was in charge; he was the manager. Prior to the arrival of Eve, Adam was charged with the running of the affairs of the Garden and made to understand the rules and regulations governing the Garden. He was told to do as he pleased and eat from every tree except the 'forbidden tree' from which he must not eat. When Eve arrived, the forbidden tree was no longer forbidden because of what had transpired between Eve and the serpent. Eve violated the rule even though she was told not to eat from the tree. This happened on the day when Adam was away and the serpent came and tempted Eve who yielded to the temptation and ate from the forbidden tree. She did not only eat, she then proceeded to offer Adam the fruit when he returned, and Adam ate it as well. Some people, including women, have sought to blame Eve for not only succumbing to temptation but also for encouraging Adam to eat from the forbidden tree. This story epitomises what is going on in the world today. People, at times, fail to examine things properly and rush to conclusions, driven by raw emotions. We have the lines in the general context; we have what is in between the lines and we have the small print. However, people often concentrate on the lines only.

The truth of the matter about the incident at the Garden of Eden based on this story was that, Eve did what came to her 'naturally,' based on raw emotion, and, of course, she was responsible for her actions. However, she was driven, like many people in her position, by curiosity. However, questions need to be asked about Adam's contributions (as a person in charge) to Eve's transgressions.

Eve may have failed once, but Adam failed at least three times and the overall responsibility was his. In the first instance, how much induction and education (nurturing/investment) did Adam put into the newcomer (Eve) in relation to the forbidden tree, considering the importance of the tree and, as the one who was instructed in the first place? What measures did Adam take to ensure that Eve did not tamper with the tree, let alone eat from it? Could Adam have done more in terms of theoretical expression and practical measures to ensure protection of Eve from the tree, which was the only hazard around, and given the fact that Eve was likely to be spending more time around the garden as Adam was not always present at home? Did he not anticipate that the serpent might come around when he was not around?

Secondly, there was nothing to suggest that Eve forced the fruit from the forbidden tree down Adam's throat. Adam happily accepted the fruit and gobbled it up. It could well be that, either way, Adam would still have had a price to pay because no one knows what Eve's reaction would have been had he refused to eat the fruit. As the saying goes, 'You are damned if you do and damned if you don't.' However, Adam should have lent Eve a hand out of her predicament by insisting that she not eat the fruit and suggesting they seek for pardon from the owner of the garden. Had he done this, the penalty for Eve's offence and Adam's inadequate provision in protecting Eve from the tree is likely to have attracted lesser punishment than that prescribed. It is also likely that Eve may have been disappointed at first but later may appreciate the reason/s Adam turned her offer down. She may also have felt grateful that he had not accepted the fruit but rather, helped her to obtain forgiveness. At the very least, Adam would have retained some integrity. Most people in today's world believe that in order to be husband and wife, be members of the same family, in a relationship, and belong to an organisation or group; one must join in even when what is being pursued is fundamentally wrong.

Instead of lending a hand to rescue Eve primarily from her derailment; Adam showed his inept nature, immature emotion, and poor judgement by joining in and eating the fruit from the forbidden tree that he was warned not to eat.

In the third instance, and worst of all, instead of accepting responsibility for his own failings, Adam chose not only to point at Eve, but to God as well, as being responsible for his failings when he said, 'It is that woman you gave me.' This re-echoes the statement we are all too familiar with; in modern times that was made when a sitting President tried to run away from responsibility by referring to 'that woman.' Adam could not see that anything he had done was wrong. He had no clue that he had failed to prepare Eve well enough for her role. He forgot that Eve did not force the fruit down his throat, and that he voluntarily accepted the offer and happily consumed the fruit without posing any questions to Eve, his wife. If Adam had done what he ought to have done, Eve may not have even had the courage to offer him the fruit and may not have even eaten it herself. Therefore, the overall responsibility rested with Adam, and the real failings were his. He tried to attribute his failure to not only Eve but God – 'that woman you gave me' – and apportion the blame to God and Eve. In that process he sought to declare himself a 'victim of circumstances.'

It is a known fact that the easiest thing in life is to blame others for one's shortcomings. Blame is usually associated with failure. This is a mechanism human beings use to absolve themselves of any responsibility, to ensure they are not standing alone in their shame and to seek vindication. Blame very rarely occurs when success is achieved, as human beings are very quick to point to their achievements in a successful venture. The reverse should be the case because, as stated earlier, success demands one's one hundred percent commitment and effort as a minimum, but relies heavily on other people in order for it to happen. In order to achieve that percent, one must sacrifice a lot, for there is no success without sacrifice.

It is important for everyone to examine what they consider as their success. Is it in academics? Could they have achieved it without being taught or without being in good health? Is it in business? One could own all the shops in the entire world, but one would never count them as successful if customers did not patronise them. Are you the owner or chief executive officer of a company? Are you the brain with all the ideas behind the success of a company? The truth is, your ideas can never work or be useful if people do not buy into or implement them, just as if 'the brain' had said to the rest of the body parts, 'I could have given the best advice, but if the rest of you rejected it or refused to implement it, the advice would have meant nothing.' Is your success in politics? No one can hold any elected office without others helping them and people voting them in. In fact, some of the best politicians cannot make it into government because they do not have the right people around them and cannot package and market their brand properly. Examine the history of one of life's celebrated individuals, Nelson Mandela. As the world honours, celebrates, mourns, and recounts all his achievements through personal sacrifice in service to humanity, Mr Mandela in his wisdom and humility was the first to share his achievements with all those who made it possible, including ex-president F.W. de Klerk. He recognised that without this kind of person/s, none of what he set out to achieve would have been possible. He was also not oblivious to his failings as a human being; hence, he said, 'I am a sinner who kept on trying,' as he reminded those wishing to make him a saint.

Is your success being a football star? Many of the better footballers have not even been noticed by the right people, let alone signed up by a club. Is your success to do with an appointment? One very rarely appoints oneself but usually one would rely on someone to appoint them. What is your success? Examine it properly and discover that it is not something an individual can achieve alone. However, success demands one's, one hundred percent effort and commitment as a minimum. This effort and commitment (on its own) will never be enough to achieve success, but it will form the basis upon which success is achieved when others subscribe to it. Hence, humility is required in order to be really successful, as it is not all about the individual's effort. Failure is one of those things in life that one happily achieves on one's own, either by doing what comes naturally or doing nothing at all. Failure is resident within everyone, that's why one does not need to do anything or go anywhere to keep it; but success lives far away and one must work hard and obtain other people's help in order to reach where success lives, let alone obtain it. Therefore success is what should be shared as it is not solely individually attained like failure, which is individually owned. Success is a team effort and failure an individual's lack of effort or effort others did not subscribe to. However, immature and undeveloped emotion led Adam and many people today to turn this glaring reality upside down; people are quick to attribute their well-earned failures to others and collective successes to themselves. In other words, there is no such thing as a self-made person.

Adam was quick to attribute a well-earned failure of his to Eve, having failed to equip her in her role and he tried to push the blame onto her and to God. Men have continued in the same vein since time immemorial across cultures, creeds, and nationalities. Men, generally, have done the ultimate damage to society at large by seeking self-gratification at the expense of women, children, and vulnerable people, who ought to be the priority. Men have always sought traditions that safeguard their interest in all places and stages, and at all levels. When one considers the battles women fought around the world, and the suffering they endured just to be able to vote, and when one looks around and sees many countries in the world in which girls are prohibited from going to school or seeking employment, one can begin to appreciate why the second building will be easily recognisable by the ancestors of this planet, were they to return. These are girls who become women and then bear the children who grow up to become mothers, fathers and leaders in our communities and nations. These are girls who end up as mothers and are likely to spend more time with their offspring during their formative years than fathers would in many circumstances. Men have constantly acted with limited insight and upon these formulated ideologies, cultures, and traditions to suit their primary 'needs', without fully understanding the dire consequences of such myopic ideas.

Examine your own tradition/s and it will be glaringly obvious that historically men have sought to create and design norms for their sole benefit. They sought to make rules sometimes that were superstitious in nature and cannot be quantifiable or measured if violated by women and/or children.

For example, in Igbo land, an eastern part of Nigeria where I made my entry into this planet, Earth, without my consent; certain special parts of a chicken like the gizzards are reserved for fathers and men alone. Women, mothers and children are forbidden from eating those parts. However, this does not mean that men will not take part in consuming other parts of the chicken, but, no matter how much they consume, those reserved parts will remain for them and them alone. And, under no circumstance, would women and children touch them. Another example that springs to mind has to do with alcoholic drinks. Women are forbidden from drinking the bottom part of any alcoholic drink. There is no recognisable mark indicating where the bottom part starts. Therefore, it is up to individuals, and mainly men, to decide where the bottom part of the bottle starts. This part is reserved for the father of the house, the eldest or designated male who, also, is not barred from taking part in the consumption of the rest of the drink. Therefore, no matter how much this individual drinks, he can rest assured that the bottom part will still be waiting for him even if he went away for several hours. Ndi aruruala! This means, 'crafty or cunning people!' They would then justify this practice by saying, 'It is our tradition,' without explaining the basis for it. They would also seek to fabricate a fictitious punishment that would befall anyone who violates this practice. These may be trivial practices but the consequences and the impact of them are huge. Examine your own culture properly and you will discover some similarities. This selfish drive is a contributory factor which propels most of the leaders of this world, who happen to be men, to be so greedy, so self-centred and atrocious, to a level at which they do not care what happens to the rest of society... a level where they become psychotic due to lack of insight as they embezzle, steal, hoard, and share public funds at the expense of those who elected them. They forget that if the hand hoards everything and refuses to feed the mouth, it may celebrate momentary victory, but the consequences of not feeding the mouth will, in the long run, affect the hand.

In order to appreciate the immense power nature invests in mothers particularly to do wonders through their children. Through this wonder our world can be transformed; one only need to look at the generational impact of my grandmother forcing my father into the kitchen, in order to appreciate this.

Since there is no doubt that children (the leaders of tomorrow) are more likely to spend more time with their mothers or mother figures during their formative period (though exceptions may apply), and that they can only learn through observation, and bearing in mind that the leaders of today were once children who may have spent more time with their mothers during their formative years, it beggars belief that men who have been and remain in charge of this world are blind in terms of recognising the importance of motherhood and the critical role it plays in raising the children of this world. If the brain is dormant, how will the hand know when or how to do its work? The brain needs to wake up now because there is massive congestion, especially in view of all the hazards currently obtainable in the skyscraper (looking at the two metaphoric buildings above), it would amount to psychosis of immense proportions for mankind not to understand and appreciate that in girls and women lie the answers to the world's problems! When one does not know, one can plead ignorance as a mitigating circumstance, but when one is aware and still acts stupidly, one becomes foolish and the ultimate penalty is incurred. Humanity needs to start investing in all girls, mothers, and mothers-to-be so that they are able not only to guide their children, but also to equip them with the skill to navigate all the minefields capable of destroying them and the entire world, which are located in the skyscraper.

Currently, a lot of children are left to navigate this minefield on their own. Some are picking up ideas from their peers, and some mothers who are spending more time with their children are either not equipped to guide their children, or have bad habits of their own to add to what their children are already picking up. For example, the use of bad language and/or abuse of alcohol and illicit drugs even in the presence of their children; perhaps that's all they learnt from their own parents. Their children observe and pick these habits up and are likely to replicate, minimise, or enhance them depending on other influences. The impact of this can be felt and seen on our streets today; many of these children have turned into 'boats' that are tossed about by any wind that engages them, because they are not deep-rooted in sound, well-informed, ethical and moral values. Do not forget we are now living in a world in which mobile phones can detonate bombs, and almost everyone has a mobile phone.

Imagine a world where all parents, especially mothers who are spending more time with their babies during their formative years, are academically and morally equipped to face up to the challenges of parenting. A world where all babies from day one are taught to appreciate the importance of life and the responsibilities everyone has to the self and others to preserve life. A world, where children are made to understand that, they are not only vital components of their families; but also of their communities and the world as a whole. A world where all children are nurtured, the contents of the gadgets they use are vetted, their time is structured, and they are made to separate fiction from reality at an appropriate time. Imagine a world where all children are nurtured to understand that though all fingers are not equal, they are all equally important to the efficiency and effectiveness of the hand and each has a purpose and peculiar role to play; and that the deficiency of one finger contributes to the reduction in efficiency of the hand, and that if the mouth feeds alone and the rest of the body dies, the mouth will have no dwelling place and will consequently die. Imagine, also, a world where all children from an early stage understand the importance of respect, love, caring, sharing, patience, and, above all, understand and appreciate the 'all-important' need for 'differentness' or diversity; no one would ever have known who they were or what they represented if everyone was the same. Hence, seeking to destroy that which is different and only accepting one's own values, identity, and peculiarity as an individual, group, community, religion, or nation can be linked to total ignorance. Yes, there would still be differences in culture and other attributes; however, these are basic human factors that should form part of every culture, race, gender, and creed.

In the modern age, many children are being indoctrinated by violent, sexually-explicit video games and music full of foul language via high-powered computers and internet systems that also have all sorts of predators surfing them—and these hazardous gadgets in the skyscraper, which they have at their fingertips, are capable of destroying mankind. They also provide a child or any individual with the ability to have multiple identities and live false lives that are locked up behind individualised passwords.

In view of all these things and more, parenthood in this modern era, especially motherhood, cannot be a 'natural' thing! Modernity, in view of the huge danger now posed by the skyscraper, means that mothers- and fathers-to-be or persons looking after children during their formative years would need some specific or baseline skills in parenting. Imagine assembling paedophiles, rapists, drug addicts, alcoholics, gangsters, murderers, thieves, and musicians projecting violent lyrics with bad language and sexually explicit videos inside your home to indoctrinate your baby. This is what is likely to happen if one has no clue about the contents of gadgets or sites that one's children are using and watching. Imagine a world where all mothers are well-equipped to deal with these things, a world where every mother understands the immense forces which enhance nature over nurture, which would help them to intensify the nurturing of their children as forces of nature would at times pull them back. Do not forget, if one thinks training is expensive, they can invest in ignorance and see which one is more expensive.

Consider how many laws are being enacted on a regular basis in England alone to regulate human behaviour, including the behaviours of law-makers themselves, but still, the forces of nature creep in, in instances such as the 'cash for questions' incidents and the abuse of expenses. This is why nurturing (training) is crucial; and ignorance, which is extremely expensive, will never do! Imagine a world where all mothers appreciate that the makers of most of these gadgets are not likely to be interested in their children's morality, but are only interested in the size of their bank balances. The gadget-makers play on the psychological fact that children enjoy action and so they overload the gadgets with scenes that are likely to create sensational reactions in a child.

A lot of men have become 'useless' fathers and each day women complain about how some men have turned themselves into 'sperm-donor' fathers. At times, women complain that their husbands or partners do not help in the day-to-day domestic chores. This cannot be far from the truth, but the irony is that a lot of these 'useless' men are by-products of their mothers, who did everything for them when they were growing up, based on the age-long belief that domestic works are exclusively for the females.

How many times have there been such 'loving' mothers who are only too happy to say, 'John, your food is ready, come and eat,' or, 'John, come and take your clothes, I have finished ironing them'? John is only allowed to see and consume the end product, and remains oblivious to the process. How many times has there been an over-eager mother, rushing into her son's room to tidy it up for him? By doing these, John's innate ability to attain independence is gradually eroded, reduced, or destroyed. The ability that requires nurturing becomes trapped, underdeveloped, or undeveloped in John. Every 'normal' child will always, naturally, want to please their parents and get involved in adult activities, especially when these are done in partnership with their parents. This is usually at a particular point when children are seeing more of their parents. But at times, impatient and lazy parenting get in the way. Parents who are pressed for time, fixated on their own way of doing things in pursuit of perfection, or lacking in understanding that no 'normal' child should be brought up to become a liability to others, turn a blind eye and refuse their child's offer to help out at home. This, then, probably reduces or eliminates the child's desire to help out in activities such as cooking, ironing, washing and tidying up. A child's willingness to help at home is likely to reduce when they begin to engage more with the outside world.

Every parent needs to inculcate the tree metaphor into their child in relation to relationships inside and outside the home. Because no matter how big and spread out the branches of the tree are, the roots hold the key to their survival. Therefore, no matter how interesting relationships outside the home are, well-organised and supportive families are the roots. John will possibly grow up looking good and being intellectually clever, if the emphasis is on dressing him up in expensive outfits and being academically excellent. But beneath all that, John will be bereft of daily living skills and/or interpersonal skills, and will be looking for another 'mother' to live with, but sadly, in this case, as a wife or partner. It is this other woman who is likely to bear the brunt of John's inability to participate in activities of daily living; hence the question, 'Your child, my child, whose child?' Who suffers the consequences of the input or lack of input you make in your child, in the long run?

The biggest irony is, no matter what level of frustration shown by John's future wife or partner, his mother is likely to be the last person to admit to or to accept the failings of John because admitting this would mean admitting her own failings. It is very likely that she would rather complain about John's wife or partner: 'John, my son, is such a lovely man; it is unfortunate he is living with such a horrible woman who cannot see how good my son is.' She would be the last to notice that she has created in John exactly what she had detested in John's father. This is emotion at work, and there is a level of irrationality attached to it. How many times have there been mothers or sisters who describe their sons or brothers whom they cannot objectively (sentiment and emotion apart) recommend as husbands or partners, with words like, 'My son or brother is such a lovely man. He has no problems and would not cause anyone any problems. All he needs is a woman who can look after him.' They completely forget how they themselves would perceive such a man if they were to have him as a husband or partner. In fact, they might even think their son or brother has done the woman a favour by living with her. This is emotion and sentiment at its most dangerous level! How many times have there been mothers in particular who refuse to see what their sons have done wrong, or seek to minimise it and simply project their subjective emotional feeling about their son: 'But my John is such a lovely, lovely boy'? Even if they are able, for some reason, to acknowledge what John did, they are then likely to say, 'It is just the bad people who have led him astray.' They forget the saying, 'Show me your friend and I will tell you who you are.'

Children who have been shown how to value themselves and their families, children who have been taught the lesson of not eating alone because they cannot survive alone, children who understand that all persons have to function to the best of their abilities for the world to be healthy, children who understand that their families would not support them if they do the wrong things would not only think twice, but would think long and hard before going the other way. Such children would not consider the law and law enforcement agencies as a first priority, but the feelings of family members, especially their parents, before deciding whether to engage in activities that could bring shame to their families. The quest for real change will be attained when the education of girls, including teaching them sound morals, becomes a priority in every corner of the globe. This would increase every mother's awareness to such a degree that they would not create in their sons what they detest in their husbands or partners, whilst each father would help his daughters to avoid creating in themselves what he detests in his wife or partner.

When a job requires barking, dogs need to be employed, when letters need to go to someone far away, the post box has to be used, and when the job has to do with nurturing the future of our world (children), emphases need to be laid on girls and mothers because, anywhere there is a good father; a mother started the process somewhere in his lineage.

A well-rounded mother is likely to appreciate the various interpretations her child will give to a particular scene or act, witnessed or observed. She is able to debrief her child following anything witnessed or observed that is likely to plant a dangerous seed in the child. Parents who understand the danger of anger and the destructive nature of anger which is propelled by raw emotion will not allow their children to develop a habit of, 'That is just how I am. Everybody knows that when I am angry things happen. I just do stuff, I don't mean to do, I just lose it. That is how I am and I cannot help it.' Any child who is allowed to develop with this notion is likely to become a menace to society, especially when they come into contact with illicit drugs and/or alcohol.

When children ask a question or express a view based on their understanding of what they have seen or heard from someone or from a gadget, a well-rounded mother is likely to deal with the issue in a way that either nips the problem in the bud or moderates the child's thought in order to eliminate a wrong interpretation which may cause a lasting problem. Each question asked or each view expressed by the child, creates an avenue of learning for the child, and the child, through observation, will automatically mimic the behaviour of the mother who is usually present during his or her formative years. Such mothers will automatically pass on the qualities they have and their children will, by the same token, copy, because that is what children do. If all mothers did the same (though it is practically impossible), where will the peer pressure come from? Even those who produce violent and dangerous video games came from a mother's womb.

Quite simply, until human beings understand that the key to a healthy world lies with the education (morally and academically) of girls and women who are mothers and mothers-to-be of the future of our world (children), and invest, empower, and equip them for their critical roles, humanity will continue to suffer! If all women and girls are given the opportunity to go to school, if all women understand the fingers, tree, aeroplane and body parts metaphors, especially as they relate to the mouth not eating alone (even though it is the source of nutrition) and the dire consequences of the mouth eating alone, then our world will become safer.

It is vitally important to note that, the greatest crime against humanity is the non-education of the 'girl-child' who would grow to become the mother of our future leaders (children). This is because, all the evil in society from bad leadership to terrorism stems from the non-education of girls and woman. It does not matter how much education or level of exposure one get through travelling and/or by association; certain bad seeds sown during the formative years of a child are irreversible once they become parts of a belief system cannot be taken away. This is why, some educated and well-exposed men still believe that the woman's place is in the kitchen.

It is important to appreciate that, the best

way to brainwash a child is by brainwashing the child's mother. And the best way to brainwash a mother is to ensure she is not educated. Men of evil have used this means to inflict untold mayhem upon this planet earth. An academically and morally sound mother is likely to advice their children to tell a preacher of hate who says 'the angels will be celebrating you and your family in heaven if you carry out suicide bombing in the name of whosoever', to ask the preacher why he and/or his household would not want to be celebrated in heaven first.

Let it also be known that an academically and morally sound woman makes a better leader than a man of similar standing because, the female species are naturally equipped with not only the 'multi-tasking' gene, but also the ability to distribute goods accordingly. Hence a hen with 12 chicks has no problem sharing food to all her chicks no matter how small the food is.

The Vision

Far away lay the most beautiful house which contains everything human beings need inside it; the peace, love, comfort and security that humanity craves. Men are the pillars of that house; children the doorway into that house but women hold the key into that doorway (Children) that would lead humanity into the peace and comfort , longed for. Humanity need to appreciate that the moral and academic education of the girl-child and all women is key to open that doorway that leads to the 'promise land'. Human beings need to appreciate this quickly and take necessary

steps to get into the safety and protection that beautiful house guarantees, otherwise humanity will remain outside in the bitter cold weather, high wind and/or temperature and would likely implode.

Mothers are the bedrock of families and families are the bedrock of society. The hand that rocks the cradle should rule the world if not directly then, by proxy. The cradle holds value to every child that enters into this world and that hand is often a mother's hand. It is said that, when a woman is education, a nation benefits but when a man is educated, it is likely that only an individual benefits. An educated woman inadvertently transfers her knowledge and skill to her children (boys and girls) and this can have a generational impact as her children transfer same to her grandchildren.

Even in governance, morally and academically educated women have made their marks when given the opportunity to serve. The German Chancellor, Angela Dorothea Merkel is one of such women as the German economy is not just one of the best in Europe but in the world. The Nigerian Minister for Finance, Dr Ngozi Okonjo-Iweala is another example because under her watch, Nigeria was listed as the third fastest growing economy in January 2015 behind China and Qatar by CNN Money. However, it is with special affection I introduce, Senator Oluremi Tinubu.

Below is an example of Senator Tinubu's service to humanity as rendered by one of the beneficiaries (Alexander Ezenagu) with befitting curriculum vitae to prove it!

'Last Sunday was Mother's day. It didn't hold any special appeal for me since I lost my mother barely a year ago. However, I found myself reluctantly boarding the train from Cambridge to Letchworth

to attend a Mother's Day church service for two reasons: I'd been invited by the Pastor whom I met at an event last year; and in deference to someone I'm honoured to call… "Mum".

Upon arrival, it was a small congregation comprised of seven adults and seven kids; and the church itself was nothing fanciful or particularly appealing. The thrust of the sermon that day was how special mothers are – and the pastor's wife did a good job of drumming that message into the hearts of the few men present.

It wasn't all negative, I must say, because I do agree that women are the most special people on earth. And, as though fate thought to buttress this belief, right in front of me was this beautiful, petite lady in charge of the IT – I was certain to make an introduction after the service. I suppose she also noticed this fine brother sitting right behind her as I could feel the uneasiness in her actions.

To save you the boring sequence of events, I walked up to her after service and introduced myself. Lo! And behold! I was standing in front of my neighbour back in Oshodi, Lagos State, whom I last saw some 13-odd years ago. This chance meeting brought a few tears. Back in Oshodi, we all lived in a beautiful compound of 3 attached apartments, with a Boys Quarter (BQ) for the helps. My family of 14 occupied the BQ, while this old neighbour of mine (and her family of 4) occupied a 4-bedroom apartment.

I attended a Nigerian public school, where the school fees per term were a little under 60 pence, depending on the exchange rate. Sadly, my parents couldn't afford to send me and my siblings to school, so four of my siblings dropped out of secondary school in rapid succession. To remain in school and buy books to read, I had to hawk petty goods, wash cars and clothes, carry goods for people and run myriad errands. Thankfully, I had shoes to wear because my dad traded in shoes.

Fast forward to 2004, I was in my final year of high school. For some reason I do not quite understand, I was adjudged the best in the school and selected to represent it at the regional qualifiers of a Spelling Bee Competition organized by the New Era Foundation – the pet *foundation of Her Excellency, Senator Oluremi Tinubu. I won that competition, and was selected to represent the local government at the State Finals, competing against 56 other contestants. Well, I did not win that competition. I came third. However, the ceremonies and prizes were extended to those who came 2nd and 3rd place.*

That motherly extension is the reason I am standing before you all today.

2005 was an important year for me. It was the year I resumed at the University of Ibadan to study law, and, the year I boarded a plane for the first time. The Foundation honoured its promise to give the winners of the Spelling Bee Competition some global exposure; so that year saw us spending Christmas in South Africa. You can imagine my excitement about visiting the great homes of Nelson Mandela, Desmond Tutu, the Apartheid Museum, and other notable places there.

In 2010, I graduated from the University of Ibadan with a First Class Degree in Law. Guess who was at my graduation? Senator Oluremi Tinubu and some of the guests here today travelled to Ibadan to share in my joy.

The Nigerian Law School was next. I must say that after begging and working my way through the University, I never dreamt of going to the Nigerian Law School. The reason? Law school tuition fees at the time were about 1500 pounds, and maintenance didn't come cheap as the law school I was posted to be at the centre of Victoria Island, Lagos. However, my law school bills were completely bankrolled by Her Excellency, and maintenance was covered by a scholarship scheme established by the then Chairman of Oshodi Local Government, Honorable Ipesa Balogun. I graduated with another First Class Degree, and was called to the Nigerian bar.

Today, I am a Masters of Law Student at the University of Cambridge. Come June 28, 2014, I would be a proud graduate of the prestigious University of Cambridge.

I have chosen this narrative path to put things in perspective and help everyone here to understand what a beautiful heart sits in our midst today. Her Excellency, Senator Oluremi Tinubu is Yoruba, I am not. I wasn't born with a silver spoon and quite honestly, we probably do not share a lot in common. Despite this, I and scores of other people, through the New Era Foundation, have benefitted from the acts of a selfless visionary with a keen interest in upholding merits despite all seeming dividing lines. It is a great honour to testify to the immensity of this rare gift to this world; and to follow her example.

In a bid to continue her legacy, I and a handful of friends from Oxford University, University of Cambridge and other London universities, have founded an organisation – The Excellence Movement – aimed at promoting and creating a culture of excellence in Nigerian Universities. Our primary areas of focus are Research, Writing, Reading, Scholarship and Mentoring. I enjoin us all to get involved in promoting excellence in our schools in the little ways we can.

I conclude by asking: "What could possibly go wrong?"

What could possibly go wrong if we all decided to train a child today? What could possibly go wrong if we decided to donate books to that library today? What could possibly go wrong if we decided to take out time to mentor the younger ones?"

May I add by asking, what could possibly go wrong if every child has good healthcare... if every child is supported to maximise their potentials? What could go wrong if society invested in the education of all girls and mothers and what could go wrong if capitalism is moderated in our world?

Alexander went on, 'Mum, beyond making you proud always, I promise to live your legacy; to expand the good works you have started and to give hope to people of all backgrounds, just as you gave me. God bless you now and always.

Thank you Mum.'

The above speech was delivered by Alexander Ezenagu on 5th April 2014. A day, Councillor Adedamola Aminu the Mayor of Lambeth and President of the Association of Nigerian Academics (UK), the executives and members of the Association honoured this humble gem of a human being and special gift to humanity, Senator Oluremi Tinubu. Senator Tinubu in her speech echoed her concerns about the real state of affairs by stating, 'Nigeria still ranks low in the United Nations Human Development Index yet we boast of an increase in our GDP. There have been reports of billions of dollars missing from our national treasury in a country where millions barely scrape a living to survive daily, and unemployed graduates' efforts to apply for jobs have led to extortion and loss of lives.'

ALEXANDER EZENAGU'S CV.
CORRESPONDENCE: Hughes Hall, University of Cambridge, cb1 2ew, United Kingdom
Mobile: +447918138689
E-mail: ape23@cam.ac.uk; paulezenagu@gmail.com

EDUCATION/QUALIFICATIONS:

2013-2014 Master of laws (LLM), University of Cambridge Majoring in International Corporate Taxation, Competition Law, Corporate Finance and Corporate Governance.

2010-2011 Barrister-at-Law (BL), Nigerian Law School – **First Class** (out of **4,891** candidates).

2005-2010 Bachelor of laws (LLB), University of Ibadan – **First Class** (out of **140** students)

Distinctions in Taxation Law, Law of Banking and Finance and Insurance Law.

1998-2004 Bolade Grammar School, Oshodi, Lagos (WASSCE Certificate).

A-grades in Maths, Economics, Commerce and Accounting.

AWARDS AND RECOGNITION

Scholar, Cambridge Commonwealth Shared Scholarship 2013/2014

Scholar, Cambridge Trust Scholarship 2013/2014

Col. Yohana Madaki Prize for Best Student in Environmental Law, Faculty of Law, University of Ibadan, 2010 (out of **140** students)

Gamaliel O. Onosode (OFR) Scholarship Scheme for Excellence, University of Ibadan.

3rd Place Winner, Lagos State Spelling Bee Competition, 2004 (out of 7500 contestants)

Chief Speaker, Tedder Hall of Fame, Faculty of Law, University of Ibadan

WORK EXPERIENCE
September 2011- 2013
Associate, Banwo & Ighodalo, Ikoyi, Lagos

Relevant experiences include:

Advising the **Lagos State Government of Nigeria ("LASG") Debt Management Organisation; Chevron Nigeria Limited; Brass LNG Limited; Enageed Resources Limited; Saro Agro Limited; Kwara State Government; Accenture Limited; Oando; Mansard Assurance Plc, etc.** on various areas of their operations.

From the array of clients I have had to advise in the past two years, I have garnered the following skills and abilities: efficient team work; liaising and dealing effectively with clients; researching in a particular business area and advising the client; managing a project from inception to completion; vast experience in review of agreements and drafting opinions; sufficient knowledge in litigation matters and Civil Procedure Rules of Nigerian Courts.

May 2011-June 2011:

Intern, Femi Okunnu & Co., Victoria Island, Lagos. Focused on everyday client-related legal solutions.
June 2007-September 2007:
Intern, Lere Oyedepo & Co., Oshodi, Lagos. Focused on property law matters.

PROFESSIONAL AFFILIATION
Nigerian Bar Association
Student, Chartered Institute of Taxation of Nigeria
Student, Institute of Chartered Accountants of Nigeria

LEADERSHIP EXPERIENCE
President, Literary and Debating Society, Tedder Hall of Fame, University of Ibadan (2007)
President, University of Ibadan Literary and Debating Society (2008-2009)
President, Literary and Debating Society, Faculty of Law, University of Ibadan (2008-2009)
Team Leader, Students In Free Enterprise, University of Ibadan (2009)
Youth Ambassador, New Era Foundation, Lagos State, Nigeria
Project Manager, Council of One Day Governors, Lagos State, Nigeria
Project Leader, Save Secondary School 1 by 1 (Save Nigeria Group) (2010)

PAPERS/PUBLICATIONS
"The Private Transfer of Oil and Gas Proprietary Rights in Nigeria: Mechanisms for Business Growth" being a Paper delivered at the 2013 Annual Conference of the Christian Lawyers Fellowship of Nigeria held in Lagos, Nigeria.
"Towards a Re-definition of Corporate Gover-

**nance in the Nigerian Banking Sector: A Case
Study of Auditor's Liability"** being an LL.B disser-
tation for the award of LL.B degree, 2010

ACTIVITIES

Tennis, Travelling, Music, Football. I play football for the
law office of Banwo & Ighodalo and I am an ardent sup-
porter of Barcelona Football Club of Spain. Also, I follow,
keenly, the Tennis Grand slams.

REFERENCES

To be supplied on request

Here lies the extraordinary achievement of this young
man. In contrast, the shame and woes of a nation and
many others who have rendered many Alexander Ezenagus useless are laid bare for humanity to see. Who on earth
knows what his other siblings and many others like them,
having dropped out of school due to poverty, could have
achieved in life? Could any of them have contributed to
the discovery of treatment for some of the incurable illnesses confronting mankind, for example? Today, there
are many Alexander Ezenagus who are still wasting their
life in Nigeria and many other parts of our world, children
born with gifts and talents that may provide a cure for our
world's problems, but which are trapped and destroyed
due to 'confused and deluded' leadership in high and low
places. Those of us who are living in our little bubbles
may say, 'Well, this is not our problem. It doesn't matter
because it is not happening within our shores.' Well, your
position is as good as the brain telling the anus, 'Well, I
don't care what you do. I am far away/higher up than
you. It is not happening within my vicinity.' We are all
interlinked for everyone's benefit. Therefore those who
cannot man the gates must not and should not offer them-

selves as gatemen or women! The consequences are grave! Below is an address by the Social Secretary of the Association of Nigerian Academics (UK), Dolapo Ajakaiye, revealing some of the endearing attributes of the brilliant and humane human being, in the form of Senator Oluremi Tinubu, whom many have described as 'a gift of God to mankind'. In the words of Dr Chris Imafidon, who is the Chair of the Board of Directors, an Excellence in Education Programme Scholar and a consultant to governments, presidents & monarchs in reference to Senator Tinubu's selfless contribution to education specifically and humanity in general, 'It is disappointing to associate you and your humane values with politics because I know what politicians do.' It was one of those few occasions everyone felt that honour had been given to a person where honour was due, and no one left with the feeling that honour had been accredited to failure or mediocrity.

"ANA UK SPECIAL RECOGNITION HONOUR ~ WELL DESERVED!

Good Evening Our Special Recognition Recipient, Distinguished Guests of Honour, Ladies & Gentlemen, All Protocols Observed!

Senator Oluremi Tinubu is a Visionary Leader with nspirational Sskills and Qualities. Our first encounter, i.e. Councillor Aminu & myself; with her, started with very Positive first impressions. Mrs Tinubu truly Leads by example; A meeting scheduled to start at 12.00 noon started at 11.57am, 3 minutes before the scheduled time! On arrival, she was set and waiting with every member of her Team in place, including two Local Council Chairmen, from her Constituencies in Ebute Metta & Lagos Island. Before the meeting, we were informed of her respect for time but we took it with a pinch of salt as one assumed Mrs Tinubu to be like other Nigerian leaders who work on Stereotypical 'African time!' But you informed us that, to you time is money! I do wish Nigerians both at home and abroad can take a leaf from that!

Our initial encounter was that of mistrust both ways – we approached her with a bit of scepticism and cynicism, whilst on the other hand she equally received us with some suspicion and caution. Both parties, not trusting each other; that unfortunately is the story of our Nigerian society!

We took Senator Tinubu through gruelling questions, to which she answered every single one, not as a Politician who most times fails to take a stand on issues, but rather as Passionate Educationist, imparting knowledge and truth. She poured out her heart and produced evidences to all our questions where necessary. As a Woman & an Academician myself, I was impressed at her depth of passion and knowledge, She had facts and figures about her Initiatives and Works at her fingertips.

Senator Oluremi Tinubu, when I asked why you were not deterred by the negative press, constant condemnation and judgement, but rather continued doing good, you said and I quote "I know who I am, what I do and am happy to be who I am. I am not out to make 'Political Headlines'. As long as I am able to change just one person's life, then I am fine. My people are the less privileged & the youths, whose generation we have failed; the down trodden, the voiceless in society, the elderly, the 'good boys' otherwise known as 'Area boys'. I identify with them on the streets and they do likewise"

You were asked what makes you different and sets you apart from others – again, you said and I quote "The fear of God, He lifts up and brings down. My greatest ambition in life was to be a School Principal, but God in His mercy had other plans for me. But in spite of my position I have not lost focus, hence my continued passion to Enhance Education and Empowerment. Knowing my calling in life matters a lot. When I see the break of the day, I thank God. All that I have goes back to God. I do not play around with myself or other people's lives. At the end of each day, I reflect and make amends. Whatever we do, let's do it with all our might. This is the day and time, let's do the work"

Counsellor Aminu and I visited the New Era Youth Camp in Aja, Lagos; we saw the State of the Art Structures and Facilities in place, Alternative High School for Girls in Agboju Amuwo by

Festac Town, Lagos and saw similar Structures and Facilities there too. The Principal, Mrs Subuola Akanni and Vice Principal were both interviewed. We substantiated these facts and many other things.

To all of us sitting in this hall tonight, Stephen Grellet once said and I quote "I shall pass through this world but once. Any good therefore that I can do or any kindness that I can show to any human being, let me do it now. Let me not defer or neglect it, for I shall not pass this way again" ~ unquote

Sen Oluremi Tinubu, you are leaving your footprints in the sands of time. No matter the negative publicity, judgements and condemnations from society, friends and foes. I can assure you that the truth of your achievements remains in the heart of those lives you have touched. An example is Alexander from Cambridge University, who is here tonight. The parents and families of children you have provided with opportunities in Education, the women you have given a second chance at Education & Skills Acquisition, who can now boast of a Better Quality of lives for themselves and their families, those whose lives have been Empowered and have been provided Employment though your Generosity, some of the so called 'Area Boys' whom you call 'Good Boys'; you have succeeded in Empowering and taking off the streets, the Disabled and Registered Blind students of Pacceli School in Surulere, whom you recently provided with accommodation after they were evicted from their homes. The less privileged youths you enabled to gain access to your State of the Art Facilities in New Era Youth Camp, etc. will not forget you. You are sowing into the lives of our youths, who are indeed Nigeria's future leaders. I can assure you that, one day, one or some of the recipients will aspire to Leadership Positions and make changes that past and present generations have failed to do.

Some people can be sceptical thinking she's doing what she does because of her position, which is true! But let's ponder and ask ourselves, how many Women have been in her shoes and still are? And how many of them have come up with Sustainable Projects, superseding the tenure of their husbands? If only and I repeat, If only we have more of the Remi Tinubu's giving back to Society, perhaps change can start from the bottom with the government buying into it. Sen. Tinubu's story is that of an 'Unsung' Hero working quietly, selflessly and unnoticed by many.

Senator Remi Tinubu reluctantly agreed to this Recognition & Honour. Councillor Aminu and I told her at the meeting that we believe in John F. Kennedy's saying - "Ask not what your Country can do for you, but what You can do for your Country" You are doing, not asking.

Senator Tinubu, I now speak to you as a woman. After about 5 hours with you and of course sharing wraps of authentic Amala and Ewedu with goat meat from the White house, I tell you now, we look forward to another round of that! I became endeared to your honesty, down to earth attitude, your fairness and firmness and above all your warmth. I realise that most women constantly live in the shadows of their husbands. Our achievements most of the time, go unnoticed and swept under the carpet. To most people you are just the wife of the Asiwaju Bola Ahmed Tinubu! But to me, you are not just a Wife; You are a Mother, Homemaker, Educationist, Politician, Visionary, Inspirational Leader, Philanthropist and above all a Unique Individual in your own Rights!

We, the members of the Association of Nigerian Academics UK, as Professional Colleagues in Education, Recognise and Respect your Human Rights as a person. Your Rights to Aspire and Achieve, Your Rights to freedom of thoughts and expression as an Individual who contributes to Society. On this note, may I call on Councillor Adedamola Aminu, President of the Association, to kindly come forward and join me in Presenting the Plaque. Also Senator Oluremi Tinubu, I invite You to step up to receive this SPECIAL RECOGNITION Honour, bestowed on you tonight. Ladies and Gentlemen, please let's be upstanding to welcome our Most Distinguished, Senator Oluremi Tinubu, OON!

(C) Adedolapo Ajakaiye, April 5th 2014"

In humility and in reverence to her audience, Senator

Tinubu remained standing whilst the association rendered a tribute, in spite of a determined pressure by an over-eager member of the audience who tried to persuade her to sit down by standing in front of her with a chair. A woman full of humility and nobility, Senator Tinubu refused to be served even when it came to dinner. She queued up just like everyone else and went to get her food. Something that may seem so small but means so much, as the brain shows the rest of the body that every part is different but as useful as the rest. Our world has a living legend in Senator Tinubu, and everyone can learn something from this humane soul.

Cohabiting

No two marriages/unions are the same. Never compare two differ-
ent marriages unless individuals within them have the same names,
looks, jobs, dates of birth and personalities. No human being is per-
fect; therefore, it would be an illusion to expect perfection in the other
partner or in any union irrespective of the combination of the union.
People have often destroyed their union in pursuit of perfection that
they are led to believe or they presume exists elsewhere. Every union is
different; all a person needs to do is to make theirs work to suit their
peculiar circumstances and needs. What is obtainable elsewhere is
not likely to be obtainable in your own union due to differing needs
and personalities. However, no matter what the peculiarities of the
relationship are, cohabiting is hard work and requires commitment
and effort; it won't be worthwhile if it is easy. The only easy unions
can be found where one partner's name becomes 'endurance' or where
the term 'folie a deux', meaning 'madness of the two', applies, as
in Ian Brady and Myra Hindley's case. This was a case in which
Myra Hindley, who converted to Catholicism and thus became 'a
Christian', met Ian Brady, a criminal who had come out of prison,
and fell in love with him. Soon after that she gave her heart and soul
to Ian for his absolute control and then began to share in his madness.
They then went on to become two of the most notorious serial killers
ever known in the United Kingdom. Ian Brady might have claimed
that he had a perfect marriage, because he married a woman who

agreed with everything he said and did. But how perfect was the marriage? The test of a pudding cannot be judged on the looks, aroma or 'make-believe' subjective flavour to it; the test of the pudding must be based on the eating and nothing else. Part of the test for a successful marriage and union is based on how the children from such a marriage turn out in adulthood. Choosing a partner who agrees with everything you say or do may not be a good idea, because marriage is a serious business that should include checks and balances. Do not act like a mentally unwell patient who decides not to comply with the medication that is responsible for their mental stability and suffers a relapse in their mental state as a result. It is mainly your loved ones who are likely to tell you what you may be doing wrong. The biggest threat to anyone's development is a crony! A crony can cause one's stagnation, making one believe that there is no room for improvement, even as one slips into a disaster. A crony is what Adam was to Eve and what Myra was to Ian. Therefore be careful when someone is agreeing with everything you do or say and is not making you see or consider other perspectives and not helping you see or, at the very least, take cognisance of the possible pitfalls! Always remember that a coin has two sides and anyone that genuinely loves you, has a duty to remind you of this fact at all times.

It is a commonly-held view in some quarters that happiness is your own business. However, one's family members often hold the key to one's joy and/or sadness. This is because the act of stepping on one's toes is usually carried out by those closest to the feet. This can happen either deliberately or by accident. Understanding this is critical in order not to overreact in frustration but to adopt the position of 'the brain' (come in with humility) when things have gone contrary to expectation. This will help in ensuring that the act of healing, not creating more wounds when conflicts arise, becomes the desire of humanity. In this way, within families, communities and nations the acts of healing, reconciliation and forgiveness will triumph over revenge and retribution. Every parent and/or parent-to-be needs to appreciate the fact that babies come to us like beautifully made 'cars' with forward gears only. However, for a beautiful car (the baby) to be fully functional it must have a reverse gear as well as a brake. But these have to be built in as optional. Therefore there is a cost attached. Babies who are brought up without these additions get stuck in adulthood with no ability to turn back when conflict is brewing. Sometimes they create more conflicts, destroying themselves and others, as they try to turn back without a reverse gear. They also crash into others, damaging themselves and others because of the absence of a brake.

The war raging between parts of the body (the world) stems from *families*. Often the crises in families stems from the 'anus' making decisions meant for the 'brain': I am referring here to the way in which people go about choosing their partners and to people's unrealistic expectations, disguises, and lack of planning in the early stages of these unions. What people do in their teenage years, in terms of who they go out with or befriend, may be taken lightly, but when it comes to deciding who to live and procreate with, the word 'lightly' should and must disappear. This choice can make the difference between 'peace' and 'pieces'. People have often made their choices based on looks, career, wealth, the need for a child, ethnic origin, time pressure, pressure from others or because of someone's heritage. As important as these things are, they should not and must not be the primary reason/s to embark on such an important journey. The primary reasons should revolve around compatibility in terms of shared ideologies and love. However, it is not love that sustains the union in the end. It is understanding, which comes through communication, negotiation, compromise and mutual respect.

One will make their own mistakes, but their mistakes may be less if they learn from other peoples' mistakes; hence experience is often the best teacher.

Marriage is a journey that is very important, useful and exciting. However, just like any useful adventure, it does not come easily or cheaply. A lot of commitment, hard work and determination to succeed is required. When two people are committed and put in the hard work, they usually succeed and reap the benefit that comes from it. Therefore do not expect cohabitation to be a 'bed of roses', or easy, as this will induce a false sense of security and then, when reality hits due to lack of preparation and unrealistic expectations, leaving the marriage becomes the quickest and easiest solution.

Leaving the marriage when children are not involved is not usually a problem, but exiting when there are children may sometimes seem and can be the better of the two 'evils'. However, children caught up in the exit door often suffer, if not immediately then later. Children have often been described as 'resilient' because they can adapt. They are also quick to read other people's countenance from a very young age; they seek to please and at times say or do things they believe will resonate with a particular parent's viewpoint. They may conceal their true feelings in order to keep the physically present parent happy; this is a defence mechanism built into every 'normal' child. However, in the long run the concealed will be manifested, and many a time with devastating consequences.

Having worked in the mental health service for more than a decade, and having been involved in carrying out Mental Health Assessments/Mental Health Act Assessments and written over one thousand reports which include clients' back-

grounds, it is not surprising that I have found that over three quarters of both adults and adolescents assessed came from broken families. This is both critical and fundamental, because much of the carnage seen in our world is primarily linked to broken homes, drugs and alcohol, coupled with mental health difficulties. Ordinarily, mental health patients with no poly-substance (drug and alcohol) abuse are more of a risk to themselves than to anyone else. However, mental health problems have been linked to many serial killings around the globe. In fact, some of the so-called leaders who crave war, who are willing to destroy millions of citizens in order to fulfil selfish ambitions, who cling onto power at any cost irrespective of how old and how unproductive they are, who are fixated on their deluded selfish ambitions without giving a damn about how many human lives are being destroyed and what the level of human suffering is elsewhere, who loot their country's resources with impunity and without due regard to the number of lives destroyed in the process, and many so-called terrorists and those willing and committed to killing their fellow human beings with 'pleasure' are very likely to be psychopaths and/or to be suffering from a form of undiagnosed mental disorder: undiagnosed! This is because no rational and sound person would fit into these categories. The world, just like the body, should not wage war against itself!

Before going into such a union, ensure that the bigger picture (family) drives the smaller sketches you make. Consider the values of the individual you are intending to cohabit with and ask whether s/he has the basics in common with you. Have you two shared interests? If not, are the two of you able to negotiate and compromise? Consider what principles you need to have in place as a family, as these would be the bedrock of the family that children within it would abide by and follow. If at all possible, study the person's background, because people often repeat what they are accustomed to. A mango tree is likely to produce nothing else other than mangoes.

Everyone needs to understand that, as individuals inhabiting this earth, we are born with different gifts, but no matter how brilliant our talents/gifts are, they cannot reach their full potential without others feeding into them through sharing. No human being can gain much excitement from living in isolation because true enjoyment in life lies in sharing. No one can be fully content on their own without requiring others to play one part or another in their lives. The most beautiful thing in life is the act of introducing new life into the world. This can never happen without a moment of sharing with another person. No matter how good we are as individuals, on our own, we remain only a part of the jigsaw. However, with another part of the jigsaw coming into play, different kinds of challenges may arise because sharing requires skill and an ability to negotiate, compromise and balance. Unions are about giving and taking and not conning and cheating. The objective is to give and take in equal measure; however in issues relating to life, it is not easy to measure a fifty-fifty split. The reality is that sometimes one gives more and receives less, sometimes one receives more and gives less and sometimes it appears as though people are giving and taking on an equal basis. It is all about an individual's perception of things; hence communication is needed in order to negotiate, compromise and understand. Two people living and sharing a life together is an incredibly brilliant and wonderful, but an extremely challenging, thing to do. It is worth repeating that living together is extremely difficult because it is a good thing and no good thing comes easily. Anything that comes easily is never worthwhile and is usually of no value. Everyone needs to understand and appreciate this before seeking to share their life with another person. Each union is different and must not be compared with another. A man or woman who is in his or her third marriage is unlikely to say to friends who are in their first marriages, 'I made a mistake in this third one, my first or second marriage was better, even if they are living in hell.' People generally are slow to acknowledge a personal mistake, which is part of the reason the second metaphorical building has not advanced.

Overactive raw emotions and excitement usually propel people to work harder in their second or third unions in the same way that people behave when they have just bought a new car. They want to make sure it is not scratched and will often clean it more than they used to clean the old one. In the case of a new partner, people are generally keen to show that their ex-partners were at fault. People want to present themselves as faultless, and at the beginning of another relationship, their new partner struggles to work out why the previous partner left or supported the reasons for splitting up. New partners also present themselves as faultless initially and both feel they have met their 'dream' partner. For many people it works out fine, but for other people it is only a matter of time before the cracks start appearing. Human beings are experts in exhibiting behaviour that best suits their emotional state at any given time. So never judge a book by its cover. Just be clear in your mind that cohabitation is not a bed of roses. It is a wonderful thing that requires serious work prior to, during and throughout the life of the union. People should not be tempted into it simply by judging it based on what usually occurs on wedding days, where there are mainly happy faces. The wedding day should serve as a celebratory day before the commencement of a long-term project that will demand the very best of the couple. They must forget about the fifty-fifty division between giving and taking, because there is no way of working that out. Rather, they must value that which the other person is doing that they cannot do and spare a thought for the one at home running the home and looking after the children whilst they are away. And by the same token, they must spare a thought for the one who is away working in order to provide for the family. Problems always arise when people can only see what they are doing and become blind to what the other person is doing well. People need to learn to complement not work against one another in a family relationship. It is odd for a bird to wreck its nest because of internal and/or external forces.

Marriages and cohabitations of all forms would work better if couples concentrated more on the value of the other person than on their own value to their union. From the start, don't let love blind you from understanding what you are getting yourself into. Those entering into a union should view it as trying to build a house. A lot of planning needs to go into it, from the architectural design to the laying of the foundations. Do not allow love, which can be 'blind', blind you from knowing that you have to work hard at making your union a success. It takes two because the best partner is only as good as their weakest link. The two partners need to have a full and clear vision of what the building should look like when completed. If an adjustment to any part of the structure is needed, the two must negotiate, compromise and agree. At times you may agree to disagree, which means you stick with the initial agreement. The burden should be on the partner introducing new change to the initial plan, to convince the other. It is impossible for any union to do well or succeed if one partner sets up a different camp and begins to use words such as 'people on my side and those on your side'. This is a clear indication of opposition and against the core principle of being a couple (one entity). If as a couple, one partner never uses words and/or actions that children within the union cannot understand or relate to as encouraging unity, cohesion and cooperation in the family rather; all the children see are actions and words that are divisive in nature; that union is likely to fail.

Couples need to appreciate that anything said or done that is likely to advance the prospects of one of the couple will add to the fortunes of the family. On the same token anything said or done to sets one of the couple back automatically sets the entire family backwards. Being on one side and the other couple on the other side suggests there is a contest going on for which a winner must emerge. Such contests are detrimental to family ethics, values and principles. Couples win and loss together. In a game of two, one cannot play on their own effectively and the good intentions of one counts for nothing if, the other resolves not to 'play ball' because, the good partner is as good as the bad partner, their weakest link.

If I could change anything in the marriage vows which should also be applicable to any form of cohabiting, it would be in the area of putting 'asunder.' Though 'rational' human beings everyone is expected to respect the sanity of unions; the onus primarily rests with the couple. Therefore, I will suggest it to read 'none of you in this union must put asunder.'

Couples should know that they are putting asunder

when any or all of the following is happening;

1. If one invites a third party irrespective of who that person is into any issues relating to the union without the knowledge of their partner.

2. If one prefers decisions made with their parents, friends or outsiders to decisions made with their partner,

3. If one starts to take their partner for granted in any way, shape or form especially when their partner is making their feelings known.

4. If one fails to communicate their feelings to their partner and,

5. If one starts having an affair.

On the issue of having an affair, it is important for couples to hold the straying partner responsible not the outsider responsible because, no matter the temptation (which is 'natural'), it will always take the consent of an adult partner for it to happen. Other people's intended asunder will never come to fruition without someone from within the union subscribing to it. It is vitally important to remember that, if an act is immoral and/or sinful it can be condemned by human beings but no mortal being(s) has the credentials to prescribe punishment unless the act is unlawful. If anyone acts otherwise to punish such, they will only create more pain and crisis to themselves and their victim(s).

My advice when infidelity (which is one of the many asunder and main cause of separation and divorce) occurs in a union is; the offended partners following all said and done should decide whether to forgive or to walk away. The offended partner 'naturally' will be justified to be angry but must ensure they are not violent in any way, shape or form towards the offending partner and certainly should try not to make the outsider the issue. The out-sider will have nothing to do with the inside if an insider has not made it possible. However, irrespective of what it is, violent must not be an option to be considered or deployed. There is no way one would realistically claim to love someone they are violent towards. Love never cohabits with violence and violence never resolves but worsens situations.

If your children witness your disagreements, ensure they also witness your agreements. They need to understand conflicts and learn resolution of conflict skills. If a union is without conflict or is based on conflicts and disagreements without civilised resolution, the children within it will become inadequate either by lacking in conflict resolution skill and/or suffering emotional damage which is likely to manifest negatively later in their adult lives. Every child needs to be well-rounded and balanced because this is real life and not fantasy. However, and most importantly, in your disagreements, swearing needs to be avoided and everyone must keep their hands and legs to themselves. Conflicts and disagreements can never be resolved physically and can only be resolved through negotiated compromise.

Unions are like embarking on a long journey of 10,000 miles, with glory awaiting those who understood what the journey would be about before embarking on it and who work together in partnership to deal with all the obstacles in order to complete the journey.

No couple who embarks on this journey in their vehicle complete the journey without needing to stop many times, either due to obstacles or to refill their tank and repair breakdowns. Though the number of stops and the length of time spent carrying out repairs will vary depending on the skill of the occupants and the reliability/durability of the vehicle, the durability depends on the quality of the vehicle made by each couple.

However, no matter the quality, every couple in their vehicle on this journey must face some difficulties; otherwise, the journey will not be worthwhile. Nobody has won something without putting in something. Because it is a very important and beneficial journey, it is usually very tedious, especially when children are on board and the vehicle full of luggage which weighs the vehicle down.

In this journey, one of the major hazards is the billboard sign that says, 'If your vehicle suffers a breakdown, if your are tired or unhappy in the vehicle you are travelling in, you can get out and enter another moving vehicle of your choice, as long as the occupant/s are happy to have you.' At every service station at which one stops to refill the tank there are vehicles on their way to various destinations; and at every breakdown there is the temptation to join the vehicles on the move, especially vehicles with single occupants who are travelling light.

It is even more tempting when these vehicles stop to offer a lift to one of the couples that are visibly arguing about their breakdown to prolong the delay, instead of working together to repair the vehicle. Those who did not prepare themselves or lack the understanding of what the journey entails, believing it to be a smooth and easy ride without stoppages, get easily frustrated whenever their vehicles stop. They are then attracted to 'judging the book by its cover' because of the smiling faces of others whose vehicles are yet to stop and are too quick to jump out of their vehicle into another offering them a lift.

They usually struggle to understand that if the occupant of the vehicle they are entering is going on the same lengthy journey then sooner or later, their vehicle might suffer the same fate, though there will be momentary pleasure if there are no children inside the vehicle offering a lift to 'disturb' their peace.

Those who have prepared themselves well appreciate what the journey will entail and the glory that awaits. They work tirelessly together to get the vehicle in working order with the bigger picture in mind. They plan their journey and are clear from the outset about the route they are going to take. If at any point one of them thinks another route could be better, the two partners discuss it and either agree to change the route on the basis of the new information, or to continue on the already agreed route. They expect the car to break down at some stage and are prepared to do whatever it takes to repair the vehicle. They try not to allow any fault to linger and seek to start each day afresh. They are usually very committed and passionate in the knowledge that one person cannot do a job that requires two people and that no matter the best intentions of one of them, nothing would ever work without the agreement and co-operation of the other. They understand that no matter how skilful they are as a couple, if one of them is determined to damage the car or stop the journey, the one who is committed to repairing and completing the journey successfully will fail because the destroyer is more powerful than the 'determined to succeed' partner, due to the fact that no skill is required when it comes to destroying things. As stated earlier, children are experts when it comes to making things untidy because it is an offering of nature.

The couple seek to avoid doing those things anyone can do which are valueless and destructive; for example, causing trouble by looking to deliberately halt the car or turn it in another direction, building demarcating walls inside the vehicle or valuing and finding more pleasure in what is happening in other vehicles around them instead of focusing on their own journey. Worst of all would be finding pleasure in celebrating the malfunctions inside the vehicle with others outside of it who may or may not want to see the successful completion of their journey.

Couples seeking to embark on this journey must see themselves as seeking to build a house. They will benefit by making sure there is proper architectural design of the building they want to have. Building without an understanding that you are building a house or without a clear plan as to what type of house is being constructed leads to confusion and disaster. This results in either the collapse or the non-completion of the building. If one person is committed to building the house and the other is hell-bent on destroying it, the person hell-bent on destroying it is likely to win because there is no skill required for destruction and nothing can stop anyone who wants to destroy from being destructive.

However, many things can prevent a builder from building, and even if the builder completes the house, the destroyer can have the final say if they want to destroy it, and it would take them less time to destroy the house than it took the builder to it. Everything about the development and/or further destruction of the second metaphoric building (above) stems from what is going on in families; this is the root cause of what is going on in our world. No leader in this world, good or bad, indeed no one alive today, came from Mars, Venus or Jupiter. Everyone is routed through the family. That is the first principle and this is where to find the answers to our emotionally broken world/society. Well-informed individuals make for well-informed families. Well-informed families make for well-informed communities. Well-informed communities make for well-informed nations and well-informed nations make for a united world.

As stated earlier, the chaos in this world stems from the

root (family). The rich, poor, weak, powerful and high and mighty all came from the womb and rooted from a family of one sort, form or another. How united is our world? How united is the United Nations? It is virtually impossible to have a united nation without united families. United families bring about united communities; united communities bring about united nations and united nations will deliver a united world. In the mathematical game of numbers, one would always get the answer wrong if one jumped to number ten without counting to it from number one. Therefore, in the game of life as it relates to our world, the family counts as number one and United Nations as number four according to the list I have mentioned above. However, there would be no family without a couple. As such, the word 'COUPLE', which means 'combined or joined together', needs to be respected by those who are a couple and those who are not. Any attempt to separate whatever is joined, linked or combined together at any stage is likely to result in lasting damage. Once a couple have separated or living together but working in different directions, the family is likely to become divided and the negative effects of this would adversely impact on that family, their community, nation and the entire world.

It is absurd to have rules and regulations at places of work without basic rules governing couples, who are the genesis of family life and the bedrock of society. There needs to be order; otherwise disorder will automatically occur. Couples need to be united, even though they may disagree at times and when they are acting as individuals within their relationships. Cohabitation ought to be a complementary not competitive relationship. It pays more to focus less on one's contribution and value more what the other partner is contributing to the relationship. That which one can do is not an issue; the issue is that which one cannot do. Being a couple cannot be turned into a game; a couple who are only a couple on the outside or for a particular event may engage in 'make believe', but will still be miles apart on the inside. The long-term cost of this type of game will certainly outweigh any short-term 'gain'. Let the overall interests of the children and posterity take priority.

Remember, if either party that makes up the couple is hell-bent on not making it work, it will never work because no matter their best intentions, each can only be as good as their weakest link and no skill is required when the agenda is to spoil something. Wanting to spoil something is a natural thing, and children have this 'desire' in abundance; this desire comes with no trophies and it is never an achievement. Only a confused partner destroys their own homes for 'glory' outside; or allows others that have destroyed their own homes convince them that it is a good thing to do in order to have fellowship together. No sane bird destroys its own nest no matter the circumstances. If one hand takes pleasure in weakening and/or destroying the other hand, the hand that weakens the other will, in the long run, suffer too, and the entire body will suffer the consequences. When a couple fail to plan, they automatically plan to fail. If they do not deal with their issues, their issues will become bigger and are likely to consume them and others around them. After all is said and done, it is not about winning or losing, because the couple and society will win and lose together based on what the couple do or fail to do.

Doing as one likes does not amount to doing what is right and proper. Children are also experts in this area, and often what they like most, such as playing, eating and sleeping, can be detrimental to them if these things are all they can do. Children do not need an invitation to do what they like, if that is what their parents do. When 'I am coming', 'I am going to see someone', 'I am going somewhere' and 'I will see you later' become the language of a parent, children who only learn through observation (what they see, what they hear or what they touch) will follow suit. This will mean that neither children nor parents will know where members of the same family are, who they are with or what time they will return. This is a recipe for calamity and disaster!

Couples will be better served when no relationship or activity outside their own takes priority over it unless such a relationship or activity is seen by them as sustaining their relationship and that of their immediate family. A couple need to know that if one of them is excluded then the other is, by implication, excluded too, irrespective of who is doing the excluding – unless the word 'couple' changes in terms of its meaning.

Individuals doing their own thing, excluding one another and not showing interest in each other's activities within their relationships is primarily responsible for many separations and divorces. What people are able to calculate is the number of divorces and separations, but the underlying factors remain mostly unaccounted for. These marriage/relationship breakdowns are the biggest threat to children's psychological and physical well-being. The misplacement of priorities, which occurs when one or both parties in a relationship place outside interests above the interest of both of them as a couple and that of their families, is the agent responsible for destroying a lot of families, which, in turn, leads the community to decay. This is the main catalyst at play in the 'world's most uninhabitable place' above. It is not just peer pressure, the internet age or being disenfranchised that are responsible for youth crime.

The biggest contributor to or the biggest agent of youth crime is dysfunctional families. Looking at London as an example, every well-informed person understands that any issue, be it peer pressure or the internet age, is applicable to all youths across the ethnic divide. Based on this belief, the question then would be; why is it that out of the twelve teenage murder cases in London in 2013 at least seven, that is, over fifty percent of the victims were of African and Caribbean parentage? The same figures are replicated in prison and mental health institutions in London. The proportion of 'black' people represented in these figures is more than all other ethnicities put together. How scary is that? The answer is quite simple: dysfunctional families, absent and non-supportive fathers, selfish mothers and fathers and lack of community cohesion, which collec-tively contribute to many children, especially boys within the 'black' community lacking in direction and purpose. However, at the root of all these are disjointed and 'each-to-their-own' couples. This is the main contributing factor generating these outrageous figures. For more information on this type of crime figures, google 'citizens report'.

In cultures in which children turn out better, it is often the case that families function better and there are functional community support systems. Children can easily get used to their parents, but when they know that they are part of a wider community and can interact with other children from the same community who are achieving and doing well, they are likely to feel a sense of challenge and motivation. Every individual family, com-munity or nation needs to be identifiable by its distinct traditions and values. However, just like the mouth, which at times helps the nose to bring in and let out air when the nose is blocked, everyone must hold on to and value their particular culture and traditions (so long as they are progressive not regressive). The mouth cannot abandon its role and decide to play the nose's part and anus's part. If this happens, the mouth and the entire body will suffer the dire consequences of such an abdication of duty by the mouth. When families are bound by and hold on to community values, the community becomes strong. This is what one can observe in Asian, Jewish and Chinese communities, where families and communities are more united and committed. The British are also very good at this. Wherever they go they study other communities but retain their particular traditions.

It is important that when people fail as individuals, communities or nations they look within themselves for answers, and when they succeed they look outside themselves for reasons. It is time for African and Caribbean people to look within themselves and to stop looking elsewhere or blaming other factors for the state they find themselves in. The cost of this is not being felt by the African and Caribbean community alone but by every community in London. Keep in mind the football analogy: when one part of the football is punctured or uneven, the football will not bounce as expected. Every community needs to self-identify and be strong just like the various parts of the body use their attributes, in a complementary fashion, to service the entire body (society). This will make society (the body) healthier and stronger and will not weaken it. If the anus had not self-identified, the brain would not have come in with humility and the body would not have survived for as long as it did. However, whether the body ended up surviving in the long run, or whether the little bird succeeded with the confusion it brought, is something to discover later.

Everything has to start from the couple. A coordinated

and focused couple are likely to produce coordinated and focused children, and the benefit of this will extend to the community and have a wider impact on the nation and the world in general. Though this may not be applicable in all cultures, where it is applicable, such as in the 'world's most uninhabitable place', couples need to ensure they are not serving as insurance to their parents and should instead focus all their energy and resources on building up their immediate families. No reasonable couple would negate the needs of their parents and extended families, but this should be their secondary not primary consideration. Every child needs to be brought up well equipped to deal with varying situations. Any child who grew up with or was given only a hammer for all situations will use the hammer in every situation, including using it to kill a fly. The adverse impact of one unruly child can be felt more than that of one million well-behaved children. The impact of 'one bad apple' could be seen and felt in Leeds, in the United Kingdom, and across the globe on 28th April 2014 when a 15-year-old pupil stabbed his teacher to death. The 15-year-old did not just take a life but has destroyed (in this singular act of evil) an institution, judging from the length of the teacher's experience and the number of students she has taught. The psychological impact of this unlawful killing on her family members, students and staff at Corpus Christi Catholic College, the local community and society at large will remain incalculable. The real losers here are society in general and the many students who would have benefited from such an experienced, knowledgeable and skilled teacher, but have been denied this benefit because of this individual. May Anne Maguire's soul rest in peace and may peace rest upon all the members of her family and all those who mourn her loss. If couples took care of their families the right way, dreadful incidents such as this would become unlikely. People have become too selfish these days and too pressurised in this 'capitalism gone mad' state of affairs; they have no time for their own individual needs, let alone another person's. In most cases where acts of homicide are committed, one or more of the three major cancers of society is likely to feature: a broken family, illicit drug use and alcohol abuse. Mental health is also a possible contributing factor however; as I have stated, mental health on its own is more likely to lead to suicide not homicide in the absence of drug and/or alcohol misuse. This highlights the failings of society at large with its root located within the family set up. The truth is often the bitter pill responsible for our well-being, but is difficult to swallow.

One of the golden rules in seeking to redress the family set up is that a daughter-in-law must ensure that she does not repeat what she detests in her mother-in-law when her she becomes a mother-in-law.

There must be no conditions linked to what is happening outside the family unit that would drive a couple's relationship inside. How can the two hands provide adequate services to the body if they are disunited? The body will surely suffer. The right hand must not be under any illusion about what the left hand is doing and each must work in the best interest of the other. Anyone who does not understand this or who is unwilling to comply with this will be better off remaining single; otherwise, they will serve as part of the agents contributing to the mayhem in our world. Let the brain take its rightful place and do its work in our bodies, and let the hand not make the call reserved for the brain and vice versa. For all those wishing to go into partnership of any kind, I introduce to you the dangers of partnering with **'Zero (0)'**.

Zero may look empty, undervalued and useless but it is the most powerful and effective number known to man. The absence of Zero will ensure that every number or digit will remain at unit level. There will be no tens, hundreds, millions, billions or trillions. When Zero comes up against any number; no matter how big or great whether in division, subtraction, multiplication or addition the best one can hope for is that, the number it came up against remains the same. Otherwise, it will bring that figure to Zero. Try adding Zero to one million and see that you can only have one million or try multiplying one million by Zero and observe as Zero brings everything to Zero.

This is the lesson of life. Human beings need to pay attention to the all-important Zero and ensure it is accorded the respect it deserves. Everyone needs to avoid partnering with Zero unless they are sure where to place it or seek to add something to the Zero. If one has accidentally run into Zero, either run away or accept the adverse effects of Zero and soldier on. If one has Zero, they have to be sure where to place the Zero for it to be positive. It is clear that the more Zero one has and depending on where and how they are piled up, the better. Having one Zero as a partner and not being mindful how it is deployed could turn one, no matter one's value to Zero.

The saying 'One is as good as their weakest link' seems to be a by-product of the 'Zero' factor. No good football striker who scores two goals per match with a goal keeper who concedes three goals per match can ever celebrate a win. It is important to know that, being a good striker who scores two goals per match requires a lot of hard work but being a bad goalkeeper requires one to do nothing. The builders are more creative but the destroyers are more effective.

The only way out! If man is to survive this earth and not implode parents and parents-to-be, need to heed the following warnings:

If what you, as a parent are saying to your child is geared towards the hatred of another individual, community or nation or you are not sure of the variations of implications relating to what you are about to say to your child; you must stop and remain silent until you are sure about the positive message or teaching you are intending to give to the child. Planting a seed of hatred in your child against an individual, group, community or nation is as good as the brain instructing the hand to hate and destroy the leg whenever it has the opportunity. The brain may have deluded itself by thinking that it wouldn't be affected if the hand succeeds in destroying the leg. We are all in this world together as parts of the same body. The destruction of one part surely will affect the rest adversely in ways never intended or imagined. If as a parent, you cannot quote any words of wisdom from your parent/s, it simply means your parents failed you. You must then ensure you do not fail yourself and your children by repeating the same mistakes as your parents. People can only make corrections when they identify errors. Identify the errors today and open yourself up for learning and sharing. It is never too late to learn and share.

Parents/carers and parents-to-be need to know that, the saying 'it is my life, it is my business how I bring up my child and no one else's' could possibly be more harmful than alcohol

and drugs put together. In a world we all co-ex-
ist and share, just like different parts of the body
living in one body. Can it be possible that only
the hand will feel the impact of the actions and
inactions of the hand? Is it the case that, a child
who was encouraged and conditioned to believe
that violence is the way to resolve conflicts, will
stop being violent when they cohabit? Is it possible that the young man carrying a knife on the
street waiting for someone to stop is targeting
their parent who once said, 'It is my business, no
one else's.'? At these various points, whose business is it?

The truth is that, as other peoples' actions and
inactions affect us, so ours affect others. We are
not only responsible for ourselves but for each
other and one another. As people belonging to
the same world, we need to learn to share, complement and encourage one another. Every child
needs to be taught to appreciate this as a concept
from an early age.

Finally, remember that birds of the same
feather will always flock together. As a result,
it would be odd for a 'happily coupled' man to
enter into a friendship with single men or men
who are always critical of their wives or partners
without negatively portraying his wife or partner,
even though he may be sharing false information. However, as he continues to share the negative and untrue information with his friends,
he is likely to begin to believe it to be true as he
receives reassurances/affirmations from his
peers who are not happy in their relationships,
and those who are single whose views may be

how small has something in common that
unites them. If this is based on negativity, every
member will share in it; if it is based on positivity, the same rule will apply. Couples are better
off with those who value their relationships and
have similar values in relation to family ethics,
as they do. They key principle in today's 'troubled' world should be, for couples to unite and
ensure 'our job is not to toughen our children up
to face a cruel and heartless world. Our job is to
raise children who will make the world a little
less cruel and heartless.'
L.R. Knost.

Being that cohabiting is the main route by which
children emerge into this world, it is my wish to
conclude this section with this appeal to everyone,
particularly teenagers carrying or intending to
carry weapons with the intention to harm fellow
human beings, to do the following; 1. Consider
the pain you feel when you injure or cut yourself
accidentally with a knife and then, imagine the
excruciating pain those who are stabbed, shot
or butchered to death go through. The memory
of this excruciating pain is what will live with
the victim's families and friends for life and, 2.
Approach your mother who is the custodian of
the womb that gave birth to you and ask, 'mum,
how would you feel if someone stabbed, shot or
butchered me to death?' Then, listen attentively
to what your mother would say and with that
please, please, please drop your weapon. Whatever you represent to your mother is what the
person you intend to harm represents to their

mother. If you cannot see a bit of you in someone else then, something is fundamentally wrong with you somewhere. You need to seek help urgently.

Finally, it is better to build/own little or nothing and bring up children who will build and sustain than, own the world and 'drag up' children who will destroy it.

Human Excesses
And Limitations

Below are some of the human excesses and limitations impeding on the humility of the brain, which has resulted in the crises in our world. Why won't our world be in crises when, political correctness, capitalism, religion, science and technology have all gone mad? For example, some people today are afraid of saying that men and women are different, why? Men and women are human beings but they are like 'hand and leg' that are different but complimentary to each other. None is more or less important than the other but each has different but at times similar roles to play for the effectiveness of the body. A father can only have one mode but a mother two modes of feeding the baby.

As important as it is for mankind to keep searching for answers, including answers to how human beings arrived on this planet Earth, humanity will be better served when, in humility, it appreciates its vulnerability, limitations and mortality whilst it celebrates its ingenuity in terms of science and technology. Humanity would need to align humility in every endeavour, 'invention' and achievement. This would aid our appreciation of how limited each individual, family, group, community and nation is and help in projecting the invaluable importance of differences. It is not rocket science to understand that no matter how good anything obtained (given) or made (orchestrated) by a human being is, when that thing is used in excess or to an extreme, that thing becomes toxic and hazardous to human beings. As long as human beings are limited and constrained by the forces of nature, every man-made thing must be limited too and any attempt to stretch or take anything beyond its limits would wreck havoc and represent danger to mankind. Consider water, which is the source of life; however, excessive consumption of water will not give but destroy life, hence there is something called water poisoning, intoxication or dilutional hyponatremia. This can occur when there is a disturbance in the brain functions that results when the normal balance of electrolytes in the body is pushed outside safe limits by over-hydration. People have also been known to die from large consumption of water during water drinking contests. It is not rocket science to appreciate the fact that one of the contributing factors to death by drowning is over consumption of water.

Love is another wonderful thing. According to the bible, love is patient, love is kind. It does not envy, it does not boast, it is not proud. It does not dishonour others, it is not self-seeking, it is not easily angered, it keeps no record of wrongs. Love does not delight in evil but rejoices with the truth. It always protects, always trusts, always hopes and always perseveres (1 Corinthians 13:4-7). The above is true but extremely hard for mere mortals to observe in full. People have often applied their subjective understanding and interpretations to the word 'love'. Therefore, many feel unloved if one refuses to delight in their evil acts or wrongdoings. Some feel loved only when they are supported in masking the truth or turn a blind eye to their evil deeds. I therefore term such as 'excessive love'. Those who protect or support others in their wrongdoings due to a shared belief system, family connection, community and national interests are applying 'excessive love' which becomes detrimental and dangerous to all concerned in particular, and humanity in general. Whilst those who support and encourage cover-ups, manipulations and devious activities in defence and protection of a 'common interest' by belonging to the same group are applying what I term as 'excessive professional or religious nepotism' which lies at the heart of many evils seen in our world today: 'protect me and I protect you, scratch my back and I will scratch yours, 'we cannot allow our good image to be stained', all geared toward 'closing ranks'. It is excessive love that gives room to a mother or father not seeing anything wrong in their children and rather than accept that their child has done something wrong, they seek to apportion blame onto others or something else. Excessive love can also prevent children from seeing anything wrong in what their parents and/or siblings are doing. Excessive love is behind many families and couples living with and protected murderers, rapists, thieves and paedophiles, and at times, conniving with their so-called loved ones to commit heinous acts against their fellow human beings. Myra Hindley is a typical example of this as indicated above. For it to be love, it must be all that is stated above and I would add that it also needs to care, set good standards, rebuke and challenge things that are not right. Anyone who agrees with everything you say or do is suggesting that you are perfect. Therefore, you have no room for improvement and can stagnate. This is a very dangerous position to be in. Love doesn't have to smile all the time. In order for it to be love, it must frown at times, as well. Haven't we heard that in order to be kind, one has to be cruel at times? If all one has is daylight, how would one relate to night or understand the difference between day and night? The main question however is: have we loved ourselves so excessively that everything we do is right but when others do the same thing, it becomes wrong? The answer may provide the basis for the status quo in our world today. It remains my view that the academic and moral education of women and girls will address these excesses which would help mankind to appreciate more, its limitations. This can only happen when the 'brain' at all levels humbles itself.

In the same way, science and technology have rendered and will continue to render enormous service to humanity. Impossible journeys have been made possible and many untreatable illnesses made treatable; impossible connections have been made possible and many more are yet to come. Indeed the question is and will always remain: where would mankind be today without science and technology? Would it not be inconceivable to exist now without the use of mobile phones, let alone automobiles? However, just as with water, over-reliance on and over indulgence in science will not only hinder but destroy mankind. Human beings need to be certain of some limitations of science and technology... mainly those limitations that can only be consigned to so-called possibilities but are factually impossible.

Medical research, for example, may end up identifying the gene responsible for aging but the researcher who locates the gene will remain subject to death in my opinion. Even if medical research provides a solution to death, it is unlikely to bring back to life anyone crushed or burnt to ashes. Science may calculate the speed, direction and the impact of the wind but it is unlikely to stop the wind or pinpoint the exact spot the wind took off or its resting place. Human beings will never be able to physically explore the sun. Science has done a lot but it remains a great pretender with elements of deceit attached to it, which is bringing much confusion and giving human beings a false sense of hope and security.

As the world mourns and commiserates with families around the globe who sadly lost their loved ones through the disappearance of the Malaysia Airline Flight MH370 on 8th March 2014, the limitations of humanity and science have been laid bare. Human beings have been led to think that science can locate a pin dropped into an ocean; but as big as an aircraft with 239 people on board, humanity and science are still searching as at 27th May 2014 and counting. In this instance, human beings are dealing with an ocean that is visibly physical and can be seen with the naked eye. Now, if humanity and science are struggling with this, how much more with the inaccessible and the unseen? The recent discovery of a new planet Kepler-186f, which mankind never knew existed until 2014, provides evidence that there are many things existing which are 'non-existent' because they are currently hidden from the limited human eye.

In little over one calendar month; to be precise, on 16th April, 2014 from the disappearance of the aircraft; came the disaster in South Korea, but human beings with their scientific knowhow initially blamed difficult weather conditions, inaccessible parts of the ocean and poor visibility as hampering effort to provide full answers to the cause of these disasters. The reality would remain that science may predict an impending natural disaster but would remain shy when it actively engages and cannot prevent it from happening. It can also predict the weather conditions but can never change or prevent the weather conditions. Science is a product of man that would remain limited due to the limited and imperfect nature of man. Therefore, as long as human beings are imperfect, every activity of man will also have limitations. Human beings and every activity of man will remain subject to natural forces.

Science may have informed humanity of the theory of 'big bang' and in 2014 we heard of the 'echoes of the big bang' but science has not been, and may never be, able to tell anyone what or who was responsible for the 'big bang' and 'echoes of the big bang'. We hear that 'discovery of gravitational waves by Bicep telescope at south pole could give scientists insights into how the universe was born'. Well, it is hoped that this would also give scientist insights into who or what gave birth to the universe. If this is not done, the jury would remain out and our limitations and that of science would remain vulnerable to the forces of nature. In life, human beings have been led to believe that reaction stems from action... that nothing happens without something pre-empting it, unless human beings have suddenly resolved to accept that something can happen without anything pre-empting it. Could this be another assignment for science: to prove that something can actually happen without anything causing it to happen? Over reliance on things and not understanding limitations of everything and lack of moderation in all things is likely to be at the root of the implosion of human beings. It is also likely to result in the brain deluding itself by thinking that it is in control or it can go it alone without the rest of the body parts. Understanding the limitations of science would help human beings to search for genuine answers towards things science may never be able to resolve, and this may help us to make further discoveries without the aid of science and/or accept certain realities ignored by mankind due to an over reliance on science.

It goes without saying that religion is useful to society. Most, if not all religious doctrines revolve around love, peace and to a great extent freedom of choice. But most importantly, almost all religions and denominations advocate the protection of the vulnerable and strangers. However, the biggest threat to humanity in today's world is extremism and excessiveness linked to religion. Our world has seen and continues to witness the extreme and excess versions of religion from those who are using religion to instigated wars, killings, stealing in furtherance of personal and group selfish agendas, betrayal of the vulnerable and instigation of wars even amongst families. For example, in Christendom, the author of Christianity, the Lord and Saviour of Christians and the one, God asked the disciples (Christians) to 'hear him' meaning 'listen to him', Jesus Christ not Moses or Elijah; instructed his followers with these words "You have heard that it was said, 'Love your neighbour and hate your enemy.' But I tell you, love your enemy and pray for those who persecute you, that you may be children of your father in heaven. He causes the sun to rise on the evil and the good, and sends rain on the righteous and the unrighteous. If you love those who love you, what reward will you get? Are not even the tax collectors doing that," Matthew 5:43-47. In Roman 12:19 comes the promise "Never take your own revenge, beloved, but leave room for the wrath of God, for it is written, 'vengeance is mine, I will repay', says the Lord." But in spite of this clear instruction from Christ, some Christians advocate Moses' 'an eye for an eye' stance. Many preachers today inspire their congregation to a chorus of 'back to sender'. These preachers and their congregation behave like naughty footballers on the field of play who, negate their business of playing football and instead instruct the Referee to issue a card to an offending opponent. They forget that their job is to do what Christ told them to do as Christians and leave Christ to do what He has promised to do. Today some 'preachers' tell their congregation that their husbands, wives, mothers or other relatives have stolen their destiny or are witches blocking their progress. This is a particular cancer that has eaten so deep into the continent of Africa. These extreme and misguided 'religious' views have caused untold damage to Africa in particular and mankind in general.

The same 'theory' applies to capitalism. Capitalism as a concept has served humanity immensely. It has unlocked the ingenuity of man and inspired inventions of all kinds. However, just like water and science, the extremity and excesses of capitalism are not only ruining the world right now but could destroy it. Take, for instance, the area of pharmacology. In recent years many have died as a result of bacterial infections contracted in hospitals. Hear the views of a pharmacist friend of mine, Mr Nigel Uhuaba:

'...the perils of capitalism are illustrated with the current problem of increasing deaths due to antibiotic resistance. The multinational drug companies have steered clear of research into new antibiotics as it does not fit their business model, rather they have concentrated on chronic illnesses which require daily dosing and hence large sale volumes. Gone are the days when drug companies invested in a portfolio of medicines on an ethical basis as part of their duty to tackle diseases afflicting mankind. Drug resistance has got worse today with increasing mortality in hospitals. This problem is exacerbated by the medical profession keen to reserve and protect new agents from exposure and resistance, therefore any new antibiotic would not sell in large volumes, only used in resistant cases. This does not bode well for profit, hence the problem we have today.'

Extreme and excessive capitalism suggests that an individual can be self-made and encourages human beings to have this deadly idea that a 'winner' can 'take all'. It cannot be over emphasised that this concept of 'winner takes all' belongs to the jungle. When it relates to human beings, no one can win alone. No matter what one invents and no matter what talent one has, in order for that person to become successful others must subscribe to the individual's gift or invention. Success will always continue to demand two things from everyone.

In the first instance, everyone must deposit their one hundred percent effort and commitment. However, the one hundred percent deposit on its own will not be enough to secure success, unless people subscribe to it. For example, one may invent the cure for all types of cancer; that would represent their one hundred percent, but if others do not buy into invention and use the drug, the person will never consider themselves successful. This goes for everything. **Therefore, it is in success we need to share but in failure we need to own and keep.**

Failure lives within each and every one of us, and as a result one does not need to do anything to retain failure. As stated earlier, the irony is that human beings have turned this concept upside down. People are quick to attribute their success as individually orchestrated and failure as stemming from others. No matter the idea brought about by a Chief Executive, he or she alone can never harness and turn it into a success without the 'foot soldiers'. Therefore success needs to be shared but people can be as greedy and selfish as they want with their failures. What would go terribly wrong if capitalism is moderated? For example as an inventor, what would go terribly wrong if there is a cap of one billion pounds or its equivalent in other currencies, and anything beyond that trickles down to all the 'foot soldiers' and/or go towards a 'good cause'? How can it and how will it hurt humanity if there is a cap on how much an individual can earn and keep? How can it hurt anyone if all the presidents of this world were to have equal salary, for example, five hundred thousand dollars per year which can be converted into different countries currencies? The hand cannot eat everything it harvests alone because without the leg taking it there, there will be no harvest. And if the hand keeps and eats alone it will not survive. Let us share more reasonably; not equally, but in a considerate manner as rational human beings! There is a beautiful house awaiting human beings.

Football continues to epitomise our world and in football the height of humility was displayed by Tony Pulis, manager of Crystal Palace who became the first manager since the inception of the Premiership in 1992 to keep the club in the top flight. His achievement was more remarkable considering that he took over when all indicators were pointing at yet another relegation story. His side had only three points after eight games and had conceded seventeen goals. He took them from there to finish eleventh on the table, beating the likes of Chelsea and Everton to reach there. The issue here is not mainly to do with Mr Pulis's achievement but the humility he showed. Mr Pulis's achievement drew calls from managers, media and fans alike for him to be named the manager of the year due to the 'miracle' he performed at Palace. However, he was reluctant to be drawn, but was more focused on highlighting that his success wasn't his alone. He pointed at the chairman of the club, directors and his players: 'The chairman and the directors deserve a lot of credit for backing us in January and the players have really bought into what we are trying to do.'

He also suggested (when he was being encouraged by the media to acknowledge his organisational skills in the way that he set up and organised his side) that his organisational skills would have come to nothing if the players disorganised themselves on the pitch. Mr Pulis through his humility and insight has revealed the complementary nature of life. He has illustrated that although his role as a manager is pivotal to the success of the team and club, he is only a part of the jigsaw and he can only be as good as his weakest link. He has shown by practical example that success is impossible to achieve alone. He has displayed the immense power of a 'humble brain' that recognises the contributions of the 'foot soldiers'.

The humility of Ian Holloway who made way for Tony cannot be underestimated. Mr Holloway was the first to acknowledge that he had taken the club as far as he could when he said, 'This club needs an impetus of energy. But I just feel tired to be honest. I'm worn out. I want to give them the chance to stay in this division.' Mr Holloway, through this statement and his actions, placed the need of the many above personal ambitions. It takes humility to do what Mr Holloway did. How many of those who purport to be leaders today can do this? Our world is littered with many who cannot 'tend their little garden' but are in charge of the huge 'farm' responsible for feeding the masses. It is obvious that if Mr Holloway did not do what he did, Mr Pulis's achievement with Crystal Palace is likely not to have been witnessed. This is what can happen when 'the mouth' is left to do the job meant for 'the nose'. Human beings need to realise that, anything that looks good, sweet in taste, exciting and enjoyable can be destructive when used in excess. Therefore, these things need to be engaged and treated with caution and used in moderation. The sooner children are made aware of this fact, the better.

It is clear to an objective mind that, whenever human beings get to these excessive levels in anything, they become psychotic in that area which is characterised by a lack of insight. In psychiatry, people are not usually detained on the basis that they are psychotic only. When one is suffering from a mental disorder and has insight into their condition, they are either treated a home or offered an informal admission. The only time detention into a psychiatric unit becomes necessary and appropriate is when, one is psychotic and the nature and degree of the person's presentation is such that compromises or likely to compromise the person's health and safety and that of others, and the person has no insight into their condition. Insight is key to where and how treatment is given or obtained in psychiatry. Those who for example, are collecting millions of funds whilst others in the same company cannot afford to pay for roof over their heads... those who are using religion to preach messages of hate and revenge are lacking in insight because they have no clue the damage they are generating to mankind which, they themselves will not be immune to.

The true essence of humanity will never be realised until human beings embrace their vulnerability, ignorance, limitation and appreciate the true value of differences.

Problematic Foundation
The origin of the crises in our world also stems from the fact that our world is full of assumptions and misconceptions. There are ample examples highlighting these, such as; human beings' interpretations of success and failure, which I have gone into great length to explain in this book, and which have contributed to the malfunction in human emotions. Some people have misconceived and assumed that it is a man's world, but the reality is that it is a woman's world because there is not just Mother Earth; there is Mother Nature as well as Mother Nurture. We are informed that children are our future, but the truth is; children are not just our future, they are our past and our present because no one gets anywhere without first being

a child. Human beings have also, in the main, assumed that, for evil to abound, 'good people' have to stand aside and do nothing. The truth is that good people are very likely to do and/or say something when they witness evil. Would it not be difficult to qualify anyone who chooses to do and/or say nothing in the face of evil as a good person? Have they not encouraged the evildoer to do more and consequently, contributed to the evil by their silence and inaction? How about the saying 'it is my life, my business and no one else's; how I bring up my child or how I live my life. Do your own thing and I do my own thing'? Isn't this saying more dangerous than illicit drug and alcohol abuse? When parents are doing their own things, aren't children going to copy and also do their own things? Isn't this saying at the root of most things that go wrong in society today? If the parents of the 15 year-old boy who was arrested on 12th September 2014, for the arson attack that claimed the lives of up to 60 dogs at Manchester dogs' home on 11th September 2014, used such language and their son is found guilty; wouldn't it be a question of finding out from those parents, how their own business ended up becoming other peoples' business including the defenceless dogs that perished? A father who uses such language and ends up in prison, as a result of 'minding' his own business would need to be explain how his own business became the sole business of his wife, left alone to cater for the needs of the children they both brought into this world. I wonder what will happen to the body if, the hand tells the rest of the body parts that it is not their business whether it functions or not? We all know that, in this world we share; what other people do or say affect us the same way what we do or say affect others.

It has also been suggested that silence is golden, but is it possible that silence can remain 'golden' when it is cohabiting with evil? It is in the same vein that, society has 'beaten around the bush' for such a long time, chasing shadows without a proper understanding that men are the real problems of this world, and in women lies the solution.

Society has also always responded by enacting laws, and has forgotten that, though legislation helps in deterring people, it always plays a catch-up role as a response to crime already committed. It trims around the edges as a curbing mechanism. Legislation and the enactment of laws have no capacity to deal with the root causes of crime or prevent people from committing crime or going underground with their crime. Moving from a place physically does not mean that one has left the place if, emotionally, one is still engaged with the place. This is why human beings are likely to change course, change their modalities, or move the 'goal post' once they are restricted by law in a particular area. The truth is like a bitter pill that is responsible for recovery, but too difficult to swallow! Mankind will need to swallow this bitter pill (that women hold the answer to our world's crises), irrespective of who is manufacturing, prescribing, or dispensing it, in order to witness some recovery and development in the second metaphoric building above. The truth hinges here: in women lies the solution to our world's crises. This truth will not bring about a perfect world, but real and positive strides will be made towards a better cohesive and united world—as a body belonging to all who inhabit it.

It cannot be over-emphasised that our world (the body) is what it is today because of what the human beings who inhabit it have done, and are still doing, in it. Repeating the same practice over and over will only produce the same outcome over and over. Indeed, everyone has contributed, through their actions and/or inactions, to the status quo in our world today. No one has ever arrived at his destination without knowing his starting point or being confused about his immediate location.

The second metaphoric building housing human emotions and their social interactions can only develop when 'what is known' forms the basis of 'what is thought' and 'what is done.' The problem in this second metaphoric building also stems from the fact that, in the main, 'what is thought' forms the premise of what people believe, know, and act upon. Therefore, assumptions about human emotions have often triumphed over sound reasoning which is based on practical and objective understanding. This is indicative of emotions, which are usually irrational and are based on subjective realities. They act without rhyme or rhythm as the heart rules over the head and produces a reaction before the application of thought and fact. It should be expected that human beings with cognition can induce positive change for the better. It is important to begin the process of focusing on what is known, so that discovery of what is not known can take place through what is known. So the question then is: what do human beings know as facts, and how can what human beings know lead them to the truth that women have the answer to the world's problems?

We know that there is no perfect way of bringing up a child, but there are wrong ways to bring up a child. We know that most 'wrong' things human beings do to one another are propelled by 'natural emotion.' They are usually things other animals do. For example, the response to fear is usually either flight or fight—being selfish and grabbing all the 'lion's share' for the self primarily and for those linked to the self. People do not need to be taught how to be selfish; looking after number one is a natural tendency.

In order not to grab for oneself and those closest to oneself alone, proper teaching and learning must occur, and this is always a process, not an event. The teaching and learning can only happen when people understand that for the mouth to survive it must not eat alone, as the well-being of other parts of the body is key to the survival of the mouth. Having said this, it is important to note that no matter how much nurturing is done, if what is available can only serve the purpose of one and is not sufficient for two, the mouth, given the choice, would grab and eat alone without minding what happens to the rest of the body. This, though, is not, and can never be the case, in a world of plenty and in a world that has the capacity to absorb twice the number of people currently inhabiting it. If everyone would harness his or her potential...if every country would harness all the resources within it, our world, like the body, will be a healthier and better place to live.

Nature is likely to continue to reign supreme over nurture. Hence, every effort needs to be made to nurture at all times, to reduce and ameliorate some adverse impacts of nature on human beings by other human beings. For example, if the ability to kill is natural because everyone possesses it, it is important then to inculcate in children from an early age the importance of life. Society needs to invest in girls and women not only for the purposes of good nurturing for their babies or children, but also for good governance when in politics and decision-making positions. Yes, investment means spending money, but if one says 'training is expensive,' then one needs to invest in ignorance and see which is more expensive in terms of cost and consequences. Society needs to appreciate that; in the main, it is the wrong, valueless and easy things that can be copied. Every important, useful and valuable thing is likely to be taught, studied and learned which involves a process.

We know that nature is inherent whilst nurture is an attachment or add-on. The attachment can help to moderate the inherent but, at times, the inherent still manifests itself, as attachments can fall off now and again, depending on what is at play and the strength of the attachment. Hence, no matter how much training is given to children on how to clean their rooms and the importance of cleaning their rooms; at times the inherent (nature) makes the children not clean their rooms. This is because it is not natural to clean rooms; rather, cleaning rooms is a human orchestrated activity.

Just as the unplanted weeds that appear in the garden and out-number the farmer's planted crops, bad things and behaviour lend themselves to human beings with ease. And these bad things, like the weeds, would never get rid of themselves and so the farmer has to proactively and persistently get rid of them, in order to give the planted crop a fair chance of producing good fruit during harvest. Therefore, waiting in the hope that bad things will suddenly go away, or that someone else will resolve them is as good as expecting an iron bar to produce water. Waiting and hoping that society will suddenly get better without understanding that investment in women is the answer, is as good as expecting the weeds to disappear through luck or by chance.

Still, concentrating on what is known—a close examination of the offerings of nature and what is obtainable through nurture will show that natural activities are easy, but things that are obtainable through nurture are not easy. Similarly, sweet things are likely to do more harm to human beings than bitter/tasteless things. Why do children prefer sweets to kiwis, prefer going to fun-fairs to libraries and prefer fizzy drinks to water, as do many adults? Why is it that hard work is linked to anything that benefits human beings, but things that are worthless come with ease? Building is difficult (nurture); not everyone can do it because teaching and learning is required, but to destroy is easy (nature) – anyone can do it without coaching. Medically, saving life is difficult (nurture); not everyone can do it because teaching and learning is required, but taking life is easy (nature) – anyone can do it and no training is needed. Starting a war, just like many other evil and bad things, is easy and often takes just one singular strike to commence, but to establish peace or achieve any positive and good thing, hard work is required and it always involves a process. In other words, it takes an event to commence war, but it takes a process to achieve peace. Arranging or organising things is difficult (nurture); not everyone can do it, but anyone, including infants, can untidy things (nature). No one has ever taught a 'normal' two-year-old how to untidy a room because nature offers every 'normal' child the ability to do that, as an avenue for learning. Whereas, making a room tidy comes with difficulty to a child, and can take a lifetime to master because teaching and learning are involved and tidying is not an inherent (natural) thing, but also a human-orchestrated activity. This is why children who could be doing something useful, like tidying up their rooms or picking up litter around their homes or streets, sometimes prefer to behave badly and then blame their behaviour on 'boredom.' Doing useful things requires nurturing, but nature is usually behind some instinctive drive to act without thinking. Though instincts can be good, human beings need to learn to question their instincts at times before acting in order to do what is right against what can be done. Given the offerings of nature, a child would instinctively prefer to jump over a neighbour's fence than knock on the neighbour's door to collect their football, which has inadvertently been kicked over the neighbour's fence. We know that anyone can decide to be locked up behind bars at any time because, to commit an offence or crime is very easy, but to regain freedom is not a decision the same individual or anyone can reach on their own, and it always involves a process. It takes only one step to jump into a deep hole, but it would require more than one step if, one would ever manage to come out of the hole. Anyone, including little babies, can take that one step into a deep hole, but even with the best will in the world, not everyone can do what it takes to climb out of the hole. This is how easy it is to do the wrong things, and how difficult it is to get things right.

To get rid of something bad which has taken hold requires not only patience but persistent and unrelenting, determined drive. Even with that, eradication will still, at times, prove impossible, and reduction becomes a more realistic prospect. This is why it is always better to nip in the bud anything bad that rears its head rather than wait for it to become deep-rooted. To change the culture and make girls' and women's education a priority will not be easy because it is the right thing to do.

The speed at which bad things spread is astonishing and needs to be fully understood in order to spring human beings into action when bad things happen. This is why there is no particular primary, secondary or university institution out there teaching people how to steal, carry a weapon, stand on the street corners doing nothing other than being mischievous, eat all day, destroy and scatter things, watch screens and play with gadgets loaded with inappropriate materials, cause trouble both in and outside the home, use drugs and alcohol, attend every party/disco and use bad language. These are so easy to do, and, because anyone can do these things by choice, they are not achievements and, as such, they attract no salary, award, or trophy. The only gain is linked to emotion, which is stimulating as one plays to whichever like-minded gallery is on hand to celebrate disastrous and unworthy causes that anyone by choice can perform. What would the children of this world observe and learn if every mother were aware and conscious of these facts and embedded these in their children during their formative years? These are the sorts of things an academically and morally-sound mother would arm herself with, but she would not be able to do this if there were no investment towards achieving them.

The fact that anyone can perform these activities that don't require teaching and learning means that they are, quite simply, worthless. This is because there is not much value attached to anything everyone can do. It is a simple economic principle that prices drop when a product is supplied in very large numbers. Even the price of Rolls Royces would drastically fall if every street were full of them. Only those lacking in self-esteem and insight feel they are achieving by indulging and making activities anyone can perform their primary or main occupation. The key to achievement in life rests with every child and/or adult reflecting on any activity they are involved in and moderating it if that activity is something anyone can do. Salaries, awards, and trophies are earned or won when one works hard and makes simple the activities others struggle to perform, or makes better the things others have to learn in order to do.

We know that the world is well resourced, and that the resources are located in different parts of the world. We also know that these resources are more than enough to make everyone in this world reasonably comfortable, and the resources do not need to be distributed equally in order to achieve this. We know that greed and selfishness are the main driving forces responsible for the suffering in our world. We also know that they are part and parcel of the human condition and that the only things that can moderate the greedy and selfish nature of human beings are sound moral values coupled with basic academic education.

We know that, with the exclusion of 'stories' and 'theories,' no one alive today can attest to having witnessed, as much as our memory can serve us, any change in the gestation period of human babies, which is approximately nine months. We also know that the gestation period is not likely to change, no matter the era, irrespective of the status or class of the bearer. We know that it must take a male and female to produce a baby but that only females can naturally carry the human foetus. All these things are unlikely to change, irrespective of one's status, creed, race, or culture. Nor are they likely to change no matter how human beings evolve through dietary intake, climate change, inter-cultural relationships, or science and technology. We know that no human baby has ever walked in three months or been able to differentiate between food and poison at six months of age. No human baby aged one month is capable of feeding themselves even if the food has been prepared for them by someone else; and no one-year-old-baby has ever been able to sprint away from danger or build a shelter. Human babies, aged one month old, cannot recognise danger. From this undoubted knowledge, it is inconceivable that any human baby would have survived without an adult looking after it. If this is logical, if this is the conclusion human beings reach based on what is known, not what is thought, based on assumption or someone else's 'story,' 'theory,' or 'persuasion', why then do human beings still query whether it was 'the chicken or the egg' that came first, when it comes to what type of shape human beings came into being on this planet earth?

From this knowledge, the chicken and egg debate may apply to other species that nature responds quicker to, as puppies walk within hours of birth and baby apes are independent at three years of age. But from what we know about the human baby, which has never changed and is unlikely to change, it is highly unlikely that any human baby would have survived without an adult care-taker. If this is certain based on what we know, then it is logical to believe that there were two adults (man and woman) that laid the egg (the baby). The debate can then proceed to how the two adults came about; was it the 'big bang' or were human beings created? Understanding and appreciating this would eliminate confusion and have a great impact on our understanding of human origins, which is key to knowing where human beings are currently and where human beings may be heading. When human beings understand where they came from...when they can eliminate the persistent search that creates confusion, and when they stop wandering about for answers then, the 'seed can rest in one place, germinate, and bear fruit.' No wandering seed can settle down, germinate, and bear fruit. Never, in the history of mankind, have human beings ever been settled on this issue of our origin which is littered with misconceptions and shadow-chasing.

Forget about what happened or may have happened thousands of years ago because this will only lead to further confusion. Consider an event as recent as the death of Princess Diana, in relation to which there is photographic evidence. The only fact known today is that the accident which killed her happened in a tunnel in France. Now, if human beings are still struggling with numerous permutations surrounding how she died, who is responsible for her death, and so on and so forth, what madness are we thinking concerning things that happened hundreds and thousands of years ago, for which there is no photographic evidence? No wonder the conspiracy theorists are having a field day in our world. Though it is okay to have a variety of angles on an event, especially in a world with so many perspectives and differing interest groups, it is vital to pursue the truth as much as possible using what is known as a determinant factor because, amidst all the theories, possibilities, and permutations, the truth lies somewhere in between.

Perhaps the question should be amongst all the variables and possibilities, which one is most likely? How can what is known help human beings find answers to what is not known? From what we know about the gestation of human babies, the logical conclusion is that there were adults who gave birth to and nurtured the baby; otherwise the baby would not have survived. We have noted a few of the things nature offers every normal child once it has arrived in this world and have understood that what separates human beings from other primates and animals is not offered by nature, but is orchestrated by human activities.

We have also noted that the only thing that can moderate the excesses of nature is good and sound nurturing through academic education and sound moral values. These values and moderations needed to be instilled in every child from birth and none is better placed to begin this process than mothers. The knowledge and appreciation of these facts hold the key to the improvement in the second metaphoric building because no one can talk about babies without talking about mothers, who carry the babies and who play the pivotal role in the lives of children more than anyone else. The importance of the role mothers play from the day of conception, duration of pregnancy, delivery, and the formative years of a baby's life, cannot be overemphasised. This has often been negated, undervalued, and, to some extent, ignored due to ignorance and lack of insight. The evidence of the dire consequences of this is felt around our world today.

On the basis of the results of the survey discussed below,

one can be confident in the knowledge that mothers (or mother figures) spend more time with their babies during their formative years than fathers or anyone else. Everyone is encouraged to carry out the simple act of asking themselves and/or the person next to them the following questions: 1. Were your parents both present during your formative years? If the answer is yes, then ask question 2. Which of your parents did you spend more time with, from the time you can remember until you became about five or ten years of age? And then question 3. Which of your parents had more impact on your life during this period? The answers to these questions are likely to produce a similar outcome. This is critical because no baby would ever speak a language or know that any language exists without it being introduced to him. What happens during this significant period of a child's life does have a huge impact on the child later in his developmental process and in adult life. Many of the things children learn during their formative years (good or bad) they may enhance, discard, minimise, replicate, or moderate when cognition kicks in on the basis of their interactions with other people, gadgets, and different environments. However, cognition is unlikely to touch those aspects of their behaviour that form part of their belief systems. For example, if a child from an early age is indoctrinated with the idea that human blood is sacred and that idea turns into a belief system for that child, which will stick with the child. Also, if the child is led to believe that one cannot take what one alone cannot give (life) and this forms part of the child's belief system as well, then, no matter what other influences the child is exposed to in later life, that child is very likely to find it difficult to demean human blood or take someone else's life.

Remember, if the child hasn't heard, seen, or touched

it, it quite simply does not exist for the child. This is also applicable to adults; for example, adults who speak English will find that there are many words in the English dictionary that are unknown to them, and whenever they stumble upon such words, confusion sets in as the quest to understand what the word means erupts, especially if the word is critical and holds the key to the appreciation of the sentence. Therefore whatever human beings haven't heard, seen, felt, or touched does not exist for them.

Now, if we know all these as facts, then, human beings, mainly men, are negating the needs of those who are in prime positions in terms of shaping the lives of policy-makers and decision-makers in all institutions, community leaders, religious leaders and heads of governments (girls and women) who progress to become the mothers of children of this world. Bear in mind that all the kings, queens, princes, princesses, cleaners, presidents, prime ministers, religious gurus, drug dealers, military personnel, kidnappers, terrorists, governors, senators, members of houses of representatives and houses of parliament, chief executives, and directors of multinational companies, the small, the big, the powerful, the mighty and all the indispensable people; the good, the bad, and the ugly of this world were all babies when they entered this planet earth and followed a route from their families. None of them arrived from planet Jupiter. Within these families comes the immense role of mothers in relation to their babies as noted above. One does not need to be a rocket scientist to accept the assertion that: **no mother alive has ever missed or been absent at the birth of her baby, but there is always the possibility of the 'best' of fathers missing the birth of their babies.**

Human beings have sought to be reactive instead of taking the proactive measures which would help in progressing this second building. It cannot be overemphasised that no matter how massive the problems and crises of this world are, there is a route to them. In order to find that route, the 'first principle' of engineering, I repeat, needs to be applied.

Message To All Mankind

In this world of affliction, we have all fallen short. Is it sin? We are all guilty of sin. My sins may be ten times more than yours but as long as we sin in thought, word and deed, I am not too far off from you. Therefore, do not ask me what my sins are instead; concentrate more on yours and me, on mine. My sins may be more or different from yours but they are all equally sins, I would not have approached any place of worship if I were righteous, as my shyness would not let me stand out from the rest. The rest indeed! From top to bottom, none is sinless and they sin more when they claim righteousness or pretend to be.

Being that all, in all honesty have fallen short, instead of flogging ourselves for our shortcomings or seeking to hide under the wings of an exposed fellow sinner on a 'holier than thou' platform, let us all in humility acknowledge and channel our sins to 'He' or 'She' who alone can deal with sin. Let our ill-fated past not determine or define our future. Let us commit ourselves to doing things better and differently for the benefit of one and all. Therefore, let bitterness, anger and the quest for revenge cease and be replaced with forgiveness, reconciliation, peace and love as highlighted under 'the abiding legacy of the man' below. Let mob rule end and be replaced by due process orchestrated by unbiased judicial, cultural and traditional systems. **Anyone who is not a thief will not steal even though someone has stolen from them. Seeking to mask one's inadequacies with another person's**

woes is deceitful, unjust and immoral. Let's learn to see bits of ourselves in the other person irrespective of their age, gender, sexual orientation, creed or race and on that premise, seek to make the other person's life a bit easier whenever we are in the position or have the chance to do so, especially if it won't cost us anything.

Beware, mankind, that nothing you have invented came with you on arrival into this planet Earth. Nothing you have built is built on thin air without a foundation. The foundations upon which you invented and built were here before your arrival. You have drawn inspirations from the sky, sea, land, birds of the air and fish in the sea in order to sing, swim and fly. Many things you have built came from sources you cannot categorically prove but one thing is certain: the foundations upon which you built and will continue to build are not and will never be yours. Therefore you cannot guarantee anything and you will remain vulnerable to many things, because you haven't got absolute control over most things, if anything. However, what you have built is commendable and impressive but likely to destroy you if you fail to use them in moderation or understand their limitations.

You have in the first instance built on foundations unknown to you and now is the time to build on foundations known and unknown to you by studying and understanding the messages coming from exploring the following: football, tree, aeroplane, fingers and human body. When this is done, a beautiful house would appear. A house that has everything human beings need. In that house, men would be the pillars, children the doorway but without women there would be no entry into the house, because they are the key. Just remember and keep in mind that no mother alive, no matter how bad or good has ever missed the birth of her child; mothers or mother figures spend more time with their babies more than anyone else and babies learn through observation. Therefore, what do you think a child would observe from an academically and morally sound mother they see most of the time? What do you think would happen when such a mother who understands the importance of every part of the system functioning well, and with her motherly instinct to care and nurture gets into a position of leadership? Let the world as a body invest in our girls, our women and watch our world change for the better for the first time. Many would ask; what about influence from peers, the violent and highly sexualised video games and music many children watch? The truth remains that, those peers and manufacturers of video games all route from the womb as well and if their own mothers raised them with good morals, they will not be polluting children with dangerous material to watch. It is very obvious on proper scrutiny that men have been and remain the problem. Now, let's get our girls and women in the right positions to provide solutions to the world's crises.

It cannot be over-emphasised that families, communities and nations represent the human body and its various parts. If any part feels too 'important' and 'special' to solicit for all the food coming into the body, when the rest or any part of the body goes without and starves, malfunctions or dies, the special and important part would suffer too. The leaves cannot deprive the stem and branches. If the leaves succeed in doing so, the leaves would not be spared of the consequences that follow. Our world's problems originated and continue to be propelled by individuals, families, communities and nations who have failed to appreciate the afflictions of all but

deluded themselves to think, they are invincible and too special. Such people one sees, even in peer group situations react with extreme measure in situations applicable to all. In doing so, they create more crises to themselves and others as they seek to live up to their unrealistic and deluded acclaim to invincibility. In every conflict, only communication through negotiation and compromise can bring about lasting and peaceful resolution. The deployment of violence in any conflict only worsens the situation. Let us think right and do things better for the posterityof this and future generations. Have we become too academically sophisticated that we have lost our 'common sense?'

Our fears are unfounded!

The negative fears such as; 'if I help him, her or them, they will become better than me or I will lose their respect or something else... if that person, group, community or nation becomes educated, it will spell trouble for me or us; the terrible fear based on the things we assume others may do to us because, that is what we are doing or are going to do to them, that fear which lends itself to instill fear of 'folks that are different from us' into our children 'the people of that particular colour, race, creed are dangerous and/or useless' are all unfounded.

The irony is that, once that seed of fear which can translate itself into seed of hatred and fear is planted; it can grow and become part of one's belief system and when it does, often no amount of education and/or socialization can change it. The seeds of hatred one plants in their children for a particular reason can germinate and grow into anything including horrific things, never imagined by the farmers (parents and/or society) that planted it. Let it be known that, even if all the children of this world were to have access to quality education, health care, nutrition and basic human needs met; that will not make all 'fingers' equal rather, it will make every finger stronger, healthier and suitable to contribute to the overall efficiency of the hand (our world). There will still be the large, medium and small people. The rich, not so rich and the poor will still be amongst us and, the tall and short will remain present. However, everyone would have had to opportunity to maximize their potentials to the benefit of mankind.

A candle (they say) loses nothing by giving light another candle rather; it helps to spread more light and help those in darkness to see.

The 'finger theory' should hopefully come to humanity's aid. An individual can only carry their own DNA and a nation can only have its own peculiar resource to bring to the table. No matter how a finger helps or supports another finger, the finger helped can only do better in what it does best in aid of the overall effectiveness of the hand. Every finger has and must continue to have a role to play. No one can steal another person's 24 hours in a day because; no one can have more or less than 24 hours in a day.

Just like the hand functions at its best when each finger is healthy, strong and independent but works in a complimentary and collective fashion with the rest; each individual, community and nation needs to be strong, healthy, independent with integration in mind to work in complimentary fashion within the rest of the humanity for our world to be healthier, stronger and function at its best. Independence with disintegration is a recipe for disaster. How can a finger separate itself from the rest and survive? The separated finger will automatically force the remaining fingers to over compensate and the overall efficiency of the hand will surely be weakened?

Humanity needs to remember that, if every finger was equal, performed the same duty, located at the same spot or start fighting against the other; the hand cannot function properly. Our world has not functioned properly due to these symptoms within it. Human beings need to understand that, though all fingers are not equal, they are all unique and with distinct attributes to offer for the effectiveness of the hand. Humanity needs to stop wallowing in ignorance amidst academic excellence and human ingenuity. Humanity will continue to suffer if it continues to be ignorant of the real essence of life. We need to stop building on old blocks, faulty and shaky foundations laid by our ancestors. A sensible child will stop papering over the cracks and take a good look at the foundation of the house handed to them by their parents, with a view to rebuild if the foundation is shaky and faulty. As such, members of this human race or family need to take a serious look at the foundations laid by our ancestors with a view to rebuild it. We need to stop papering over many ceaseless cracks that are threatening our world and its inhabitants if, we are sensible.

It is and will remain a waste of time...indeed disaster awaits this world if 'business as usual' is all human beings can offer. No matter what government is in power or policies they offer...

no matter the religious doctrines or who is promulgating them if, the mind-sets of human beings who alone can bring these to fruition remain crafty, rotten and rooted on revenge geared towards destroying themselves nothing will save us.

Our world will change positively when each toe is taken care-of and not stepped upon by those closest to it. Family members, colleagues, friends, neighbours, relatives and associates of all kinds take note! Simply start with yourself and those around you and the ripple effect will manifest in a health, peaceful, united and better-coordinated world.

So long as there's life in all situations of injustice; fight on, on the premise of justice, truth and innocence in the belief that 'no seed can bear new fruit to feed the many without first decaying in the soil.' Even if human justice fails, natural justice will never fail you, so long as your conscience and that of those who accuse you know of your innocence (though they choose to persecute you) for whatever reason.

Those who are emotionally strong and determined to understand their purpose in life will suffer setbacks but those setbacks will act like fuel in a car. Your challenges will remain your opportunities.

Hope on The Horizon

Are you feeling low today? Is life not worth it any more? Have you become desperate because all avenues seem to have been shut to you? Does it feel as though your tomorrow will never come? Are the feelings of worthlessness, hopelessness and emptiness too much to bear? Do you feel that everything has passed you by, and that everyone has deserted you and that loneliness has become your only companion? Are you in fear? Are you troubled that you are about to be found out? Are they closing in on you? Has your past suddenly caught up with you? Have you lost hope and faith in mankind and does there seem to be nothing within or out there that can lift this cloud, this burden and this pain from you? Does it feel as though everyone is against you? Have you built your wall so high that it seems as if, at any moment from now, it will come crashing down on you? Are you angry and frustrated because of what you have done or what someone else has done? Have they said you are no longer good enough so that you have that horrible feeling of rejection? Is the life you once knew drifting from you and you cannot bear the change?

Whatever the situation, whether you believe this or not, today marks the beginning of a change for the better in your life. Bear in mind that, if it can change for the worse, it can also change for the better. All you need is time and commitment to locate, from within you, your purpose in life. That obstacle is only a challenge, a contest between you and the issue, offering you an opportunity to discover a different location and the opportunity to redesign and rebuild. Have you ever lost something and it took you a long time to find? If you have, you will know that the longer it took to find, the greater the joy you had when you found it. How many times do you take time out to search for your purpose in life? Are you too busy to spare yourself a moment of reflection to locate this purpose, which often involves a process and not an event? Every human being came into this world with the ability to reflect and project, but have they learnt to use and apply these abilities in their lives? Your presence in this life is not an accident, and therefore there is a profound purpose to your being part of this world. Nothing you are going through now has happened for the first time, and there is always someone, somewhere, in the same boat as you; and someone somewhere is going through a worse situation. The only difference is your attitude and response and your approach to the issues surrounding you. There will never be happiness without sadness, day without night or a high without a low, and every human being, irrespective of status, creed and race, has gone through these times at one point or another and will continue to go through them until they depart from this world. Therefore you are not alone.

However, challenge yourself today and replace fear with hope, weakness with strength and problems with solutions. Don't give up or give in easily. Life will never bring unto you what you cannot deal with or handle. Replace a victim-mentality with a victory-mentality, a failure-mentality with a success-mentality and a hopeless-mentality with a hopeful-mentality. Whenever you give up on yourself, whenever you stop believing in yourself, you have asked everyone to give up and stop believing in you. Look for firm ground, convince yourself first that this is a firm ground and stand on that firm ground firmly and insist on it as a firm ground. Never depart from that firm ground until others who are standing on shaky ground can see proof that you are standing on firm ground. Once they see you are truly on firm ground, they are likely to join you. Just as Mohammed Ali said, 'I figured that if I said it enough, I would convince the world that I really was the greatest.' The anus managed to identify its purpose and later proved its worth to the rest of the body parts! Say no to the easy option. However, whatever you care about or choose to do, remember that taking your own life or someone else's life should not feature as an option. Again, I say never take what you as an individual cannot give. Life, yours and other people's, is sacred. It takes two to give life, and therefore one must not take it.

Remember, life offers all human beings just two guarantees: death and change. **No one will break out of this life, alive.** No one and no situation will remain the same, for there is nothing as constant as change! This simply means that every human being alive must die one day and, no matter what one is going through (good or bad), the situation will never remain the same; change must occur, whether it is intended or not, so long as one remains alive. The only question one needs to ask is, is it change for the better or worse? However, this offers real hope to those at the bottom of the pile, those on the floor who cannot fall any further. So long as they remain alive, when change occurs the only way for them to go is likely to be up. In contrast, for those who are at the top, when change occurs their direction is likely to be downwards. It does not really matter at which end of the spectrum one finds oneself, everyone is afflicted. All that is required of one for change to occur is patience – the ability to wait. Below are a few illustrations that suggest that good things can only happen to those who are patient, remain alive and WAIT!

Remember, the world in general lacks understanding. Often, when one is misunderstood by many, it does not necessarily mean that one is wrong. It simply means that the many who are set in their wrong ways cannot comprehend, relate to or grasp the information, as it is not delivered in the 'twisted' and 'obscured' language they understand. Therefore do not lose hope or get frustrated because you are misunderstood. Do not give up or give in; one day, your message will shine through because change must occur.

Note: there is nothing to conquer from the top! The top is littered with hazards. The top is not without affliction and not devoid of sorrow. Rather, it can be very lonely at the top, as leaves fall off from the top of a tree. The top is where the beautiful flower resides, but it is only beautiful for a little while before it fades away. The top is a route to nowhere because there is nowhere else to go. Blessed are those at the bottom for they fear no fall and supply the food that feeds those at the top. Without those at the bottom, those at the top will not exist. No wonder those at the top do whatever it takes to keep the food from the bottom flowing, in fear of what lies before them, as the height is too high and falling off often results in disaster.

No one conquers from the top. In order to conquer, one must be down or need to go down. No one can jump higher without first, going backwards. No seed can bear new fruit without first decaying inside the ground. Therefore, rejoice when you are down because you are about to conquer. Rejoice in negativity because you are about to discover positivity from your negative situation. Without new challenges and necessities there will be no new inventions. Discoveries are often made, not only in the physical world but in the human psyche, when challenges come, as things that one never thought about emerge. Therefore, be patient and calculated when man- or nature-induced storms hit your shores, and gather the positive information you wouldn't otherwise have known or thought about. Everything that comes to one comes for a reason. If only positives come, how would one recognise them as positives without negatives? Don't let the precipitating factors that led to your negative situation weigh you too down and deprive you of the opportunity it offers. Just think positively, reflect, project and be patient; you are about to conquer and your victory is round the corner. Think and plan no evil against your fellow human being no matter what the circumstances are. Be deep-rooted in your upright thoughts, even if physical setbacks occur; victory awaits. A head without a load feels no weight. Challenges are opportunities; hence necessity is the mother of all inventions. Every cloud has a silver lining, just try and locate it.

A Mother Who Left Before Her Hope Arrived

A woman whose baby daughter was adopted committed suicide because the courts refused to grant her request to have her daughter's picture and send presents for Christmas. Having waited for so long for a positive outcome and having got so frustrated, she decided to commit suicide. She took her own life, but guess what? The following day, a letter came from court saying that her request to have picture of her baby and to be able to send presents had been granted by the baby's new parents.

This news brought further devastation to the woman's family as she had left the world 24 hours before her good news came. If only! If only! If only she had waited just another 24 hours. Have you waited for too long? Does it feel as though the whole world is against you and all barriers have been lifted up against you? Has it become so bad that death seems the only way out? Do you want to end it, because that is the only way you can revenge and make 'them' feel guilty or get 'them' into trouble? Does it feel as though no one cares and everyone has let you down? Whatever you do, do not collude with others in letting yourself down. Keep in mind that even if people feel guilty or get into trouble because you took your own life, the last person to know that, the last person to celebrate that, is the dead 'you'. Everyone is marching in the same direction whether they like it or not, as death will surely come. So why try to hasten it? Why take the route to a dead end when change is inevitable for all who are alive, patient and waiting. Even if one decides to do nothing, so long as one remains alive change will surely occur without requiring a contribution. **Never leave before your hope arrives! This is not only applicable to suicidal ideation; it is also applicable to most things in life. So long as there is life and you know you are fighting for a just cause not a selfish goal; never give up or give in, you may be closer to achieving your desired outcome than you think, keep on trying and never take an irreversible, damaging or action that worsens the situation due to impatience and/or frustration.**

Suicidal? Let's Talk!

Did you know that, depression and suicidal thoughts are mainly triggered by feelings of loneliness 'why me, everyone else is better than me. I have lost everything, I am in the worst place possible and therefore, life is no more worthwhile. I cannot cope with the shame, the loss and the pain. I am now a shadow of myself, a source of pain and shame to my family, friends and associates. I am totally worthless and the world is better without the worthless me?' The fact is that, there is always strength in number. Even collective death feels better than dying alone that is why 'group therapy' works.

One of the things certain about life is that, everyone is afflicted no matter which end of the spectrum they occupy. Begin today to subscribe to the metaphoric ideology of viewing life as 'travelling on a motorway'. On a motorway, one is likely to see other vehicles around them (people in similar situations) no matter what they are going through. There will always be vehicles behind them (people they are in better position than) and vehicles ahead of them (people in better position than them). Therefore, one is never alone no matter their position or situation. It all depends on one's attitude to their particular issue(s). However, one of the two guarantees of life is that; change is paramount and inevitable. As a result, one is likely to overtake and be overtaken whilst travelling on a motorway.

Remember, it is important to let what one knows, not what one thinks or feels, guide one at all times. Therefore, what do we, as human beings, really know about suicide?

We know that there are two primary theories surrounding what happens when one dies. Science offers human beings one and religion offers the other. Science concludes that once someone takes their own life, as a preferred mode of departure, they die, and that death is death no matter the means by which it occurs. Once dead, that's the end and nothing happens after that! Religion concludes that death, irrespective of the mode of departure, is only a route to another form of existence 'in the spiritual realm' and that death is only applicable to the flesh, whilst the spirit lives on. Some religious doctrines believe in heaven and hell. Some have cited the 'death' and 'resurrection' of Jesus Christ the Author of Christianity as an example of 'life after death'. Most people of faith who believe that heaven and hell exist also believe that entry into either heaven or hell is based on one's deeds whilst alive on earth. However, for those who take their own lives by committing suicide, it is a firmly held religious belief by many that such people are destined to go to hell, where they will face perpetual pain and suffering.

We know these are all theories because no scientist or person of faith alive has died and come back to tell us which is true. One would obviously look stupid if one tried to be categorical about what happens after death, because anyone alive is unqualified to state such facts. Therefore, all we know is that these theories are simply possibilities. However, what is without doubt is that once someone dies there is no way back; whether it ends there or continues in a different sphere is irrelevant as the name of the game changes to *eternity*. This means that if science is right, that's it: no more pain for eternity. But if religion is right, the fact that one has taken one's own life means spending eternity in hell and more pain and suffering. Why would anyone in their right mind take a chance on such a gamble which no one alive can guarantee what happens next? From what we know, not what we think, it is a huge risk to step into the unknown based on what we think or what we have seen or heard others have done because; they were sick and tired of life. It would equate to going 'from the frying pan into the fire'. What happens, then, if in running away from a bad place one runs into a worse place with no escape route? Considering that, whilst one is alive, change will occur, and the fact that life guarantees death anyway, suicide should and must be considered as a 'no-no!' It should and must not feature as an option in anyone's life! That is why it must be considered as a form of mental illness, because at the point of making a decision such as taking one's own life, the mind is usually irrational, confused and fed up. If you find yourself in this state please don't wait for things to get worse; talk and seek help immediately. No situation remains the same! If you think you have caused your loved ones much pain and you want to end it by taking your life, then think again, because you would cause them even more pain and psychological torture if you killed yourself.

In all one thinks, says or does, one must not consider suicide as an option. In my numerous years as a practitioner within the mental health arena, many have come through our doors who had attempted or were in the process of attempting suicide. Some of their common slogans are, 'I want to get rid of this pain. I can't bear it any more. Nothing can be worse than how I feel right now. The world would be a better place without me. I feel worthless. I have nothing to live for. My life is so empty. No one cares about me. I want to end it all.' And to some who have people they would leave behind, they normally and insightfully say, 'I know it is a selfish thing to do. I know I shouldn't be thinking this way but when I am in that state, I lose all sense of reasoning.'

It is a well-known and well-documented fact that when someone reaches the threshold of committing suicide, they struggle to retain any sense of reasoning (hence it is seen as a symptom of mental disorder). It is also the case that when someone is saying, 'I want to kill myself', it is very likely, they are saying, 'I have an unmet but desperate need' than to mean 'I want to actually die', because those who really want to kill themselves often do not get the chance to tell anyone about their intentions.

It is my take that no one alive is really qualified to objectively advise anyone who wants to die without assumptions creeping in. It is also my take that the act of suicide is based on assumptions as well. I have always acknowledged my shortcomings in this area, especially when it comes to what truly happens when someone dies, and I hope you would too, irrespective of your religious beliefs or scientific theories. Suicide is one of those things in life one should not do simply on the platform that others had done it. This is because the many who have done it may have carried out the act, but none had managed to come back to testify that they accomplished their aim.

The only thing everyone knows is that when someone dies, their body becomes motionless. Anything after that is based on assumptions. Having said that, some people have suggested that one taking their own life is a 'selfish' thing to do. I have doubts about this position because suicide cannot be objectively a 'selfish' act. The word 'selfish' is linked to personal gain. Nothing can be classified as 'selfish' without having personal gain attached to it. Even if the body only becomes motionless and nothing else happens after that, it is difficult to see how that benefits anyone. One must have a sense of personal satisfaction to feel that one's act is a selfish act. The absolute fact about suicide is that no one has ever committed it and come back to say that they did/did not achieve their aim.

This remains a possibility but there is nothing to suggest that anyone committing suicide is not getting into a worse situation, especially when many people have a strong belief that hell awaits those who take their own lives and/or other people's lives. It is also a possibility that all the pain would go away, but a guarantee is that death is a dead end with no opportunity to change anything. However, in life there is hope and a guarantee of change which must happen whether one likes it or not. Also there is the guarantee of death as well, whether it is sought after or not. Therefore if death will definitely come, why not concentrate on bringing about or waiting for change rather than hurrying to die, when you are going to die anyway?

A person never knows they are suicidal until they have thought about killing themselves. And if there are no protective factors such as children, friends, pets or pleasurable activities, or the urge to die overrides these protective factors, then please talk, before attempting anything. If there is no time to talk please simply pose these questions to yourself: 'Am I choosing this option because others have chosen it in the past; am I really certain that those who chose this option in the past achieved their desired outcome; am I able to meet any of those people in this land of the living who has died and come back to share their experience; and am I really, really certain, I am not going from the "frying pan", which I can come out of whilst still here on earth, into "everlasting fire" when I kill myself?' Furthermore, 'What have I to lose if I take the view that "hell fire" is real for those who killed themselves and believe that whilst I am alive, change is inevitable?'

Bear in mind at all times that, life is like travelling on a motorway. You are likely not to be the first, last or only person it is happening or has happened to. Never worry too much about what others think or say about you, never worry too much about the situation you find yourself, whether self-inflicted or otherwise. The most important thing is what you do, think and say about yourself. Irrespective of how bad, the situation you find yourself; you will not appreciate the reason(s) if you choose to drown yourself in sorrow, become depressed or commit suicide. No one has ever learnt to jump or jumped higher without an obstacle in their way. As such, your challenges are your real opportunities. Do not waste them by unnecessary fear, panic and frustration which can lead to the act of suicide.

Whatever is going on in your life, no matter how traumatic and troubling; never despair or ask, why me? Rather think! There is a reason you are carrying that burden no matter, how unjust or horrible it might seem. Remain strong in search of the reasons and lessons. The answers will surely come. Dark cloud will surely disappear, ushering in a bright new dawn. It could well be that through your ordeal; many would learn something that would help that succeed in life. It is not happening to you in vain and the bigger the pain, the greater the gain. It doesn't matter how unfair, for the end will justify the means. Even if one is made to suffer for an act they did not commit, remember; out of adversity comes prosperity and no yam will ever bear new fruit without decaying in the soil. Success is only for those who carried on and refused to give up or give in.

Remember! Success is out there waiting for you. It only requires your will. If you will your heart to succeed and you are willing to try and try again and not willing to give up or give in, you quite simply will succeed. Be patient and work hard; your dawn will come. It is all about WILL.

The Man Without Shoes

In a town called Mbieri, a neighbouring Ogwa, a town located in Imo State, Nigeria, where I made my entry into this world without request, contribution or knowledge, there was a man named Iwem who had no shoes. In this town, people generally are very particular about the way they dress, especially on Sundays when they attend the church service. It is always the case that everyone turns up in their best attire and, if it were not for the prayers, songs and sermons, one would think Sundays are days for fashion parades in this town. However, Iwem was very poor and he could not afford a pair of shoes. He continuously braved the embarrassment and shame of this and went to church regularly in the hope that God would help him buy a pair of shoes. He continuously made this his singular supplication every Sunday.

Iwem heard many sermons of hope about being patient and remaining prayerful. He also heard the preacher speak about God not always delivering answers to prayers in the exact format people expect. But all he wanted was to have a pair of shoes, and he continuously requested this and expected it to happen. However, Iwem became so frustrated, and so tired of waiting and being patient, that he gave God an ultimatum. He said, 'Dear God, you know how many times I have come to church. You know the shame and embarrassment I have suffered but I continued to attend. I have not asked you for any other thing except to help me buy a pair of shoes. Either you are deaf or you don't care about me. I feel ashamed hearing some people in the church talking about me and at times laughing because I am the only person here walking bare-footed. It hurts me so much, I cannot take it anymore and I cannot get used to this. What have I done? Is my sin more than the rest of those who are here? God, I have heard that you do not do things sometimes the way people would wish, but with this, I cannot see any other way of doing it. I simply need a pair of shoes, and my patience has run out. I cannot wait any longer! Dear God, by next Sunday, being our harvest when people will notice me more, as they show off, if I must come here without shoes, I would rather come straight to you and do my worship in your presence instead of coming to this church in embarrassment.'

On the following Saturday, Iwem came out of his little hut at night and looked upwards and said to God, 'Dear God, I have waited till now and there is still no sign of the shoes I have been asking for. I can see why they say you can answer prayer in your own way. I assume the way you have chosen to answer this one is to have me join you up there. Because there is no way I am going to embarrass and humiliate myself anymore.'

In the early hours of Sunday, Iwem took a rope and set off to join his God. He was very angry and continued to mutter to himself, 'How can anyone live like this? What sin did I commit that is worse than the rest of the congregation? I will end this today.' As Iwem was muttering all these things to himself he arrived at a crossroads. He looked around the surrounding bushes, trying to make up his mind about the particular location where he would prefer to 'end it'. He decided to turn right at the crossroads. As soon as he turned, he saw a man who was a double ampu-tee singing and clapping his hands that early morning, full of joy. Iwem could not believe what he was seeing. He said to the man, 'Hello! What is your name and who are you?' The man stopped singing and clapping and paused for a while, then said, 'I don't like people interrupting my praise and worship. I have many days to interact with people; today I only use it to give thanks and praise. Anyway, my name is Anuri.' The man went back to his singing and clapping and ignored Iwem. In shock, Iwem threw down the rope and ran without looking back, straight to church.

He got to the church as the sermon was going on and screamed with joy, 'Prai... prai... prai...'

'Shh!...' said the Church Warden, 'Keep quiet! The sermon is going on. No one speaks when the sermon is going on!''Oh no!' said Iwem, 'I have a better sermon, a testimony... no sermon is better than my testimony. I cannot believe what I saw this morning. I am full of joy.' The preacher, shocked by what was going on, stopped preaching and all eyes were on Iwem who began to dance as he made his way to the front of the church bare-footed. People were looking at him in shock, thinking he had sud-denly become mentally disturbed because they had never seen him in such a happy mood. He was given an audi-ence and asked to give his 'better sermon and testimony'. Iwem looked up and was full of emotion as he said, 'I feel ashamed, happy and overjoyed that it took someone with-out legs to make me understand how lucky I am to have two good legs. If someone without legs can be happy and full of appreciations, how much more those with legs? I wasn't meant to be here this morning. I was on my way to God because all the time I have been worshipping here I have been coming bare-footed. I have been requesting one thing and one thing alone. I have been asking for God to help me buy a pair of shoes. I have suffered the embarrassment of coming here every Sunday without shoes. I became fed up with people talking about me and laughing whenever I passed by them. I was on my way this morning to kill myself, although I could not do it, when I saw someone without legs singing and clapping hands and seeming to be full of happiness. Then I realised how stupid and ungrateful I'd become. I feel so stupid now, but full of thanksgiving that I did not take an irreversible step. I wouldn't have been here with you again and I don't know what I would have said to God. Please, my brethren, help me to praise God for preserving my life this morning. I am humbled by the experience.'

The preacher got up and led the congregation through to a series of songs and then said, 'From what we have heard from Iwem this morning, he was right! There is no better sermon. The lesson is quite simple! The lesson is, in any situation in which a person finds themselves, they need to remain grateful and wait patiently. Now, I am moved in my spirit to direct that we are going to do something with this sermon today. The spirit directs me to request a special offering specifically for Iwem so that he has enough money to purchase a pair of shoes.' The congregation there and then raised enough money to buy more than a dozen pairs of shoes for Iwem. The preacher presented all the funds raised to Iwem. He was so overwhelmed and moved that he said, 'I cannot thank you and my brethren enough for this kind and generous gift. I give praise to Almighty God who has preserved my life and made all these things possible. I am speechless to the extent that all I can say is thank you! But I cannot forget how I got here this morning. Therefore I feel it would be wrong of me to take all the money you have given me without sharing it with the man without legs. Therefore, I would like it if someone would help me to go and bring Anuri here so he can share in this blessing.'

As soon as Iwem said that, many people volunteered and went with him to find Anuri. However, when they got to the spot where Iwem had found Anuri, there was no one there. Iwem was so disappointed that he said, 'I will not spend a penny until I have found Anuri.' The congregation dispersed and Iwem went on his own, in search of Anuri whom no one had heard of or seen before in the town.

Yet Another Baby

A parent was a bit concerned about being pregnant in 'old age'; there was more than a decade between this pregnancy and the previous child. The worry was multifaceted because of complications linked to pregnancy at an older age, a high cost of living as a result of having many other children to look after, having sleepless nights, nursery and school runs again and many more things. The healthy baby arrived via a caesarean section. Mother, father and baby were moved to the recovery room following a successful operation. Though mother and baby were doing as well as could be expected, parents were still going through a mixed reaction of 'joy and worry'.

However, in the recovery room were a husband and wife who had gone through a caesarean section a few hours before them, but their baby was not there with them. The husband was clearly showing signs of distress. Initially the newly arrived parents did not realise there was a problem until they heard the husband of the first C-section woman crying. Then, within minutes, clinicians arrived to inform them that oxygen was not circulating well around the baby. They stated that the heart of the baby was not functioning well, but reassured them that they were working hard to find out what was causing the problem. Hearing this, the newly arrived parents began to put life into perspective. All their worries then were to do with the other family, as it never crossed their minds when they were worrying what other parents could be going through. As a way of giving thanks and in recognition to what many parents were going through, the newly arrived parents made a commitment to support children born with a deformity.

Abiding Legacy
Of the Man

Nelson Rolihlahla (Madiba) Mandela was a leader of a particular kind. He was a leader who understood that leaders must serve both those who vote for and those who vote against them and those who love them and hate them, and that they must ensure representation for all and sundry. He was not going to be a leader for some parts and not other parts of the country. It was a calling; he was chosen and did not call or send himself. He was a leader whose pain and suffering as a result of oppression by others did not define him, but rather reconciliation, forgiveness, peace, and love for unity of all were his watchwords. He went against the normal and usual human instinct, which is to seek revenge. He was a leader who did everything within his power to strike the best deals for South Africa, but at no time did he pursue his quest for the best deals for South Africa to the detriment of other nations. He knew that exploiting other nations and putting their children in danger is not only unethical but immoral. He knew that if something was not good for the children of South Africa, then that thing was not likely to be good for the children of Uganda, or other places in the world. He understood that if one only looks after one's own biological children and ignores other children's welfare, those other children will surely present a risk to everyone in some way, shape or form. Therefore no one can be safe when others are unsafe. He worked tirelessly to ensure that South Africa played its part as a piece of the human jigsaw with the understanding that, for the leg to be useful and effective, it must be linked to the body and provide a service to the body.

He was not a leader whose policies were driven by the need for a second term; rather, he was a leader who believed in doing what was right for the many, not the few, in his country and for humanity in general. As a leader he was not intoxicated by power, and as a result he only served one term when he could have walked into a second term without going on a campaign trail. He recognised that other people could serve too and, just like Pope Benedict, he understood the huge responsibility and accountability placed on the office he occupied; and because of that sense of responsibility, he placed the needs of the masses above personal and selfish needs and gains. He considered his age and many other factors and made way for a progressive agenda. He recognised that the needs of the many must at all times take precedence over the needs of an individual, that the community is more important than an individual and that the tree is more important than the branches. Therefore he focused on the bigger picture and from there made smaller sketches.

He concentrated on providing an enabling environment for all citizens of South Africa to maximise their potential. He even had to learn another dialect, another language, in order to reach out and enhance communication with his people. He started a building which no man can complete on his own. The completion of this building he assigned to others and no one should miss this opportunity, lest the building turns into in ruins.

Nelson Mandela was a leader who as a shepherd, gateman and parent ate from the same plate, drank from the same cup and never left the gate unmanned and never abandoned his sheep for green pastures in another shepherd's field. He never served his children with poison and ran to another parent's kitchen to obtain food using the resources meant for feeding his own children. As a gateman and parent, he never left the gate unmanned for unscrupulous elements to come in and hurt his children. He was well aware that no sane person presents themselves as a gateman and leaves the gate unattended. He understood that those charged with providing health care and education must subscribe to them in order to properly regulate and monitor these most essential services that are pivotal to every child's growth and welfare. All through his life he received medical care in South Africa and all his children obtained their education in South Africa.

The biggest aspect of all is his sacrifice: Nelson Mandela was willing to pay the ultimate price so that people could live as human beings, not just exist like living things. In the end, he sacrificed 27 years of his life fighting for the dignity of humanity, during which time some high and mighty 'statesmen' described him as a 'terrorist'. In spite of his suffering, when he was released and whilst the world rejoiced and panicked at the same time, not knowing which way he would turn, he chose reconciliation instead of further conflict, love instead of hate, peace instead of war and forgiveness instead of revenge. In all he did, Mr Mandela left a legacy which shows that one achieves less when in pursuit of revenge and achieves more when in pursuit of healing, forgiveness, unity and peace. After all, isn't it obvious that when one wound opens up in the body, either by a deliberate act or by accident, what is required is for the body's system to do whatever it takes to ensure healing and not to open up more wounds which are likely to destroy the body? However, in spite of all that he did, he was still being human, and perfection was not part of our makeup. What he sought to achieve was excellence by pursuing the things that matter with zest and humility. That was why, when people sought to know what his thoughts were about being made a saint, he replied, 'I am a sinner who kept on trying.'

He also made it clear that all he wanted was for people to say, as he lay in the grave, 'Here lies a man who has done his duty on earth.' Many people may have been disappointed because they do not believe much has changed in South Africa, let alone in the world. The reality is that good things are hard to come by but are easily dismantled. It takes many hands to build but one hand to destroy. Good structures can be dismantled overnight but bad structures are often quick and easy to establish and spread very fast. However, bad structures are very difficult and slow to dismantle; years spent maintaining bad structures can take decades to dismantle and decades of maintaining bad structures can take centuries to dismantle. And in order to dismantle bad structures, complacency must never come into play. The watchwords are the 'double P' words (persistence and patience). These are the key words when it comes to fighting for freedom, justice, equality and independence and the dignity of human beings. Mr Mandela knew that if the agenda was to reverse a bad situation with another bad situation, and if justice, freedom or independence was sought with an agenda of instituting hatred and war against one another, then the aim would be defeated and the human race would continue in its misery. Mr Mandela drew a road map not only for South Africans but for the entire continent of Africa and the world. Therefore, if Scotland seeking independence from Westminster means moving to hatred against and war with Westminster when independence is achieved, and if the indigenous people of Biafra seeking independence from Nigeria means that there will be hatred towards and conflict with Nigeria, then people must think again! It would only amount to replacing a 'bad' situation with another 'bad' situation. It is okay for the hand to self-identify, but if self-identification means going into conflict with the leg, both the hand and leg will surely suffer and the entire body will feel the pain. Therefore, independence is not a bad thing so long as INTERDEPENDENCE remains the watchword! The aim of equality is defeated once it is geared towards holding the oppressor on a rebound and victory is not complete if revenge is part of it.

We are all different, just as the various parts of the body are, but we must bring our differences together in service to one another and the entire human race. Let us all do ourselves, our families, our communities and our nations proud by seeing ourselves in others and others in us.

Though Nelson Mandela prompts humanity to appreciate that the oppressor always dictates and determines the response of the oppressed, humanity was called on by Mahatma Gandhi to remember that 'an eye for an eye makes the world go blind', making both the oppressor and the oppressed culpable. And if the aim is to achieve equality, fairness and justice, whether for gender, race or creed, and the pursuit turns into an agenda that seeks the 'oppressed' to assume the position of the 'oppressor', then the whole aim is defeated and no purpose is served. Nelson Mandela was mindful of this, and clearly showed humanity how to go the other way and do the right thing, even though revenge seems a natural route to mortal beings.

The legacy of Madiba calls all mankind to review all conflicts. No one can be in conflict with someone or a group of people they don't know. That is why there are so many conflicts within families, because of raw emotions nature offers to all mankind. In most cases, these relationships begin well before they turn sour. Seeking to eliminate another person or group of people and send them to a place you are destined to go to yourself is a no-brainer. It is a place that no human being has been to and come back from, a place none can say with total certainty and conviction what is obtainable there. It is unknown to the living and known only to those who have nothing to do with the living. Why have human beings allowed this little bird to do so much damage to humanity? In reviewing these conflicts, it is clear that no one, no group and no nation must adopt a hardened position of insisting that nothing would work because, even with the best intentions, in this world everyone can only be as good or as the bad as the weakest link. Because the power to destroy is greater than the power to build; if the leg insists on not moving, the best intentions of the brain to get things moving will not work. If Madiba could reach out for forgiveness, reconciliation, peace and love to those who despised him, then why is it you and I cannot be reconciled with, forgive and mend fences with those whom we have offended and vice versa? Seeking to score points, manufacture propaganda and form cliques as ammunition against some person, group, community or other nation can only be destructive to the peace we all want and need. Any agenda of destruction against one is an agenda of destruction against all. The world weakens and malfunctions when any part of it is faulty, just like the entire body suffers when one part malfunctions. There is always another way... the way of peace, harmony and tranquillity. The hand of history is upon us all this day to work and walk towards peace and harmony to make this world a better place for this and future generations.

The Cost of Inaction

Human beings may remain in doubt as to how they came into being with many unresolved and 'irresolvable' things. But what is undoubted is the presence of forces beyond human beings' control as witnessed in the Philippines Typhoon Haiyan in 2013, the tsunami in Japan in 2011, Hurricane Katrina in United States in 2005 and Indonesian tsunami of 2004 to mention but a few. Human beings may never understand it, but relative peace would never be experienced on this earth until human existence is linked to how people treat one another, especially the children of this world and our most vulnerable. In a metaphorical sense, until we learn to leave the toilet seat the way we would like to find it, treat the other person, irrespective of their gender, race or creed, the way we would like to be treated; and until human beings discover 'heaven' by 'using the long spoon to feed one another and each other', humanity would continue to suffer. Human beings learning to do these will not be easy as nature does not, and will never offer these; rather nature offers every human being, from childhood, the ability to leave the toilet seat the way we all hate to find it. The job is not for someone else but for you and me to do. 'Yes we can' and we have to do it because, 'we are all in this (world) together'; echoes of

President Obama and Prime Minister Cameron respectively. At the end of every analysis, winners and losers will remain an illusion because human beings will win and lose together. If the hand damages the leg, it would have nothing to take it to the kitchen or shop in order to provide food for the mouth through which it feeds. Therefore, the hand that caused the damage will suffer the consequences of damaging the leg, in the long run.

The life and death of Madiba presents mankind with the footprint and yardstick, and serves as a catalyst that informs human social interactions. His legacy offers each individual and mankind in general, the singular opportunity to evaluate their lives and relationship with others. This opportunity needs to be grasped because inaction and/or business-as-usual can only ignite, in psychiatric terms, a major deterioration in the psyche of human beings, leading to major relapse in an already crises/evil-infested world. This would commence crises and confusion of unimaginable magnitude in our world yet unknown to mankind. The kind of crises human defences, resources, ingenuity, power and control has not seen and cannot handle. Our world would not only witness crises of immense and unimaginable proportions generated as a result of the interplay between the immature second metaphoric building and agents of destruction contained in the first metaphorical building (skyscraper), but would also witness the intensity, in terms of severity and frequency of natural disasters, of things beyond the reach and realm of humanity. No one irrespective of status, gender and creed would be able to safeguard their safety or exempt themselves from their effects and impact. If human beings fail to review and redress the current status quo with a view to making things better for all; our world would witness such devastation that no nation, and/or the 'disunited' United Nations, can manage let alone, deal with. One may be able to control inside temperature but would never control outside temperature of our world. Human beings need to learn to stop 'eating from their own flesh and stealing from their own pockets'.

This world has not seen anything yet, if human beings continue to wallow in ignorance amidst their ingenuity and intellectual ability. If human beings continue in the same vein our world naturally would react because action produces reaction; and if human beings are determined to continue eating from their own flesh and stealing from their own pockets, having been led to witness how to heal themselves through Madiba's life and lessons from his departure, then the immense power of nature over inferior human capabilities would be unleashed and the foundations of our world would be shaken. Rebellious human beings, who have eyes but cannot see, ears but cannot hear, may say 'let's wait until then' but then it may be too late! The likelihood is that if the brain fails to act properly and the ears fail to hear; the eyes would not disappoint because, it would see.

Though not a prophet or seer, rather a failed seminarian who did not get the calling; though not a preacher, rabbi, priest, imam or pastor, everyone needs to appreciate that there is more to this life that meets the eye, hence my enrolment into the university of life. There are also lines, in-between lines and the small print.

Already, between March and May 2014, the world has started to witness extreme and frightening occurrences that suggest that more will come and no one is safe if human beings fail to redesign the way they relation to one another: person to person, family to family, community to community and nation to nation. If human beings negate 'the abiding legacy of the man', in preference to the hype and in pursuit of business as usual. Within this period we have heard an army general describing the flooding and winds of over 100 miles per hour in parts of Britain as an 'unparalleled natural crises'. In the same year, the worst-ever disaster on Mount Everest was recorded when an avalanche left 12 dead and 4 missing in April 2014. Records of heat waves and cold temperatures are being recorded across the globe. In little over the space of one calendar month, a Malaysian plane with 239 passengers disappeared and a South Korean ferry capsized with nearly 300 passengers still missing towards the end of April 2014. Many families have been devastated and the world in shock with anger and pain by the news that hundreds of schoolchildren are presumed dead beneath the waters. Many people across the world felt as though their hearts were bleeding with sorrow as a deputy principal could not bear the 'guilt' of survival after his students had drowned, and as a result, committed suicide.

Power struggles and hatred that induce killings, accidents and wars are continually before us, resulting in many distraught and devastated families. We witnessed the kidnap of up to 200 girls who were sleeping in their dormitories by Boko Haram terrorists in Nigeria, the landslide in Afghanistan that wiped off an entire village with more than 2000 people dead which was considered as amongst the deadliest landslides to hit the country, the Turkish mine disaster which claimed the life of 301 people in May 2014, an incident described as the worst in the country's history, the slaughter of more than 118 people following a twin bomb blast in Jos, Nigeria and the 'time bomb' waiting to explode in Ukraine respectively. These incidents have placed crises in Syria, Egypt, Libya, Iraq, and many others hotspots, inside the middle pages of our broadsheets. A world, at war with itself. There seems to be nothing constructive in sight to stem the level of blood flow on our streets. Yet human beings term all of these as a 'mere' coincidence. But is it?

We live in a world where human beings, who are meant to be working together in partnership to benefit our world, have divided themselves along the lines of 'owners and renters, superiors and inferiors, important and less important'. This is as good or as bad as the various parts of our human body fighting amongst themselves; what hope for the body's survival and what hope for our world's survival? If things are going to improve, human beings need to learn for the first time the language of owning, renting and sharing in the world that everyone inhabits, which can be likened to different body parts inhabiting the same body. They also need to learn to be kind to themselves, otherwise who is safe in a world in which a neutral 'yes' can be misrepresented to mean 'yes!' with an exclamation mark, which changes the entire complexion and context of the word depending on the motive of the individual in question? In a world where most disagreements and conflicts start without third parties, it is usually 'their word against yours' and issues to do with who is likely to be believed often have age, gender, race or creed connotations, and with raw emotions people pander to who convinces them the most, not necessarily who is giving the facts. At times, the outcome will be decided 'on a balance of probability'. This is even scarier considering the fact that here, the subject matter is a singular and positive word 'yes': I am not talking about when one says 'no' or makes a full sentence which could be open to all manner of interpretations.

We need to learn to be kind to one another, otherwise we will be found wanting in dealing with human-generated crises, let alone natural crises, if we continue in this self-mutilating and self-destructive way of life. If only we can learn to be kind to ourselves, nature in turn will be kind to us. If we can learn to stop the deliberate killing, revenge, cheating and plotting against one another and ourselves, we would suddenly discover, for the first time in our human history, that we have all been craving peace and harmony.

When the Labour government in 1997 suggested pursuing an 'ethical foreign policy', it was hinting at 'something', and the jury is still out on whether they achieved it or not. Having said that the word 'ethical' is the word we, as individuals, families, communities and nations need to adopt when dealing with one another in this world we all share and inhabit together.

Human beings have always and can only build on foundations already laid. Whatever human beings build may be theirs but the foundations upon which they build might not have been theirs. Human beings have never and will never be able to build on thin air. Nor would they have invented anything without something on which to base those inventions; there would be no supersonic aeroplanes without gliders and there would be no gliders without the bats and birds of the air, which human beings did not bring with them on arrival. Even if human beings develop the ability to build on thin air, the thin air will still not be theirs. The basis for every invention, past, present and future, was already in existence prior to human beings' arrival on this planet. All human beings have done and are doing is making discoveries through the power of cognition that is secondary to natural behaviour, which is influenced by environmental factors.

Therefore human beings can only have limited control over anything they build, and everything they build will have the capacity to serve and/or destroy them. Everything human beings build to fortify and protect themselves has the capacity to destroy those it is meant to protect and fortify, because the true owner of the gun is not the person that bought it but the person in possession of it. So long as human beings do not own the foundations, they cannot claim total ownership of anything because they cannot assume full control. No one brought the foundation when they arrived on this planet earth; no nation, no community and no individual manufactured the ground and hence none of these can prevent natural disasters from occurring irrespective of how much human beings study, 'understand' and seek to protect themselves from them.

Science has done a lot of good in providing answers and giving hope to humanity; however, as long as human beings cannot physically examine or explore the sun, nurture will continue to play second fiddle to its superior 'nature'. It serves as a reminder to recall that, as recently as in 2011, the Japanese tsunami turned the surroundings of the Fukushima nuclear power station into a desolate land for a period of time. This is because although the power station may belong to Japan, the foundations upon which it is built and all that lies beneath it have nothing to do with Japan or any human being on this planet. Therefore, human 'defences' and 'sources of life' powered by nurture and human intelligence can easily become human 'offences' and 'sources of death' instigated by natural factors beyond human control. Human beings are not even equal to the storms that hit them, let alone the huge umbrella required to protect them from the storm. Everyone has a job to do here, and no one should allow their past to prevent them from changing for the better. These are manmade crises and man can solve the crises he created (see solutions below).

Madiba informed and reminded mankind that no one is born to hate but that if we can learn to hate then we can learn to love as well. To all believers, God is known to hate sin but love the sinner (you and I). Everyone, believer or unbeliever, and whether one does not 'do God' or does 'do God', is a sinner! However, even in our sinful ways, we must all challenge one another and ourselves because anyone linked to any act of evil through their knowledge of it who fails to do or say something to stop it, has inadvertently taken part in the evil act.

We, as human beings need to learn to condemn what is wrong irrespective of who is responsible for it. Remember that Adam colluded instead of condemning what Eve did, and then tried to blame her for his own failings. We need to condemn the act but not condemn or punish the person who committed the act because everyone has fallen and continues to (at one point or another) fall short. Hence acts deemed as 'sinful' in nature can only be condemnable, not punishable, by sinful human beings, and acts that break the law have to be punishable by a 'fair and just' law and not by an individual or illegitimate means, for example mob rule.

It is abundantly clear that no individual, no group, no community and no nation made this world; nor did anyone place themselves where they found themselves. Hence no one can claim sole ownership of the world. However, whoever or whatever put people where they find themselves has a purpose, and that purpose is not for anyone who is part of the furniture to 'manipulate' things to suit themselves alone, at the expense of others.

Rather, each person's aim (just like in a football team) must be to be the best they can be in their various positions and assist those in weaker positions, in the knowledge that the strongest position is as good as its weakest link. We are all players in different positions in this world, and no matter how good we are in our individual positions our role is not to dismiss other players, no matter how badly they have played. Their role is not to dismiss us, either, no matter how badly we have played, but all of us must self-identify and, if need be, support the rest who are not performing at their optimum levels in order to bring the best out of the team and ensure that everyone wins.

As players who are not responsible for choosing the players, we must give our best and assist others while on the playing field. We must also leave the manager, who is responsible for putting every player on the field of play, to choose who comes off or who goes onto the field of play.

If any of us tries to do the job of the manager who has put us in various positions, we create crises on the pitch, and surely everyone in the team would then be destined to lose. Therefore if anyone thinks that they have the physical strength or military might to wipe out another human being or group of human beings for their own 'convenience' they must think again, as they bring unseen wrath upon themselves and all of humanity. No matter how strong the brain is, it will certainly suffer too if it seeks to wipe out any part of the body for its deluded 'convenience'. The brain needs the anus as much as the anus needs the brain; neither chose their locations, none chose their role, but they both have to be different in order for the body to function!

If human beings sanitise all the parts of our world and harness the resources within them for the benefit of our world, just as if the various parts of the body were performing at their optimum levels, the body, as well as our world, will become a healthy place for all its inhabitants. There is so much waste of both human and nat-

ural resources due to mismanagement and conflicts. It was highlighted as the world converged in South Africa for the funeral of Madiba, and I did state that no one should lose sight of the abiding and enduring legacy of 'the MAN' amidst the hype. I therefore suggest a day of remembrance for Madiba (Madiba's Day) to be observed by everyone as a reminder of his legacy; and as a reminder of the duty we owe ourselves and one another.

Exit!

As we exit this book, I end with this brilliant extract from a friend on Facebook: 'Every king or queen was once a crying baby. Every great building was once a map. It is not important where you are today; the most important thing is where you will be tomorrow. Where you will be tomorrow takes precedence over where you are today and where you had been all along. Never be proud of the position you hold because after a game of chess, even the king and soldiers go into the same box.' Therefore be humane and ethical in whatever position you occupy or whatever job you do, because a doctor today will certainly become a patient tomorrow! Respect, love and peace to all humanity (shalom)!

About the Author

Prince Ezem Ihenacho is an Approved Mental Health Professional based in London, a Humanitarian, Broadcaster and the author of Hard Hitting! The real truth about men, marriage & infidelity published in 2010 as well as, Your Child, My Child, Whose Child which was published in 2012.

He is a father, an ex-seminarian who aborted priesthood because he did not get the calling. He was brought up in one of the world's largest families. In his family, there is always up to sixty children growing up at every given stage. The blend of his childhood experience in his rural village, Amaegbu, Ekwerazu, Ogwa, Imo State, Nigeria and his adopted 'first world' country, England has driven him to conclude that 'wisdom, knowledge and foolishness is not synonymous with any particular age, gender, status, nationality, creed or ethnicity.' Therefore the ordinary he states, can produce the extra-ordinary and vice versa when put in the right condition.'

www.ingramcontent.com/pod-product-compliance
Lightning Source LLC
Chambersburg PA
CBHW032102280326
41933CB00009B/737